Paris Bistros & Wine Bars

Paris Bistros & Wine Bars

A SELECT GUIDE

Revised Edition

Robert & Barbara
Hamburger

THE ECCO PRESS

THE ECCO PRESS
100 West Broad Street
Hopewell, New Jersey 08525
Published simultaneously in Canada by
Penguin Books Canada Ltd., Ontario
Printed in the United States of America

DESIGNED BY DEBBY JAY

FIRST EDITION

Library of Congress Cataloging-in-Publication Data

Hamburger, Robert, 1936–
Paris bistros & wine bars : a select guide /Robert & Barbara Hamburger.—[Rev. ed.]
p. cm.
Rev. ed. of: Paris bistros. 1st ed. 1991.
1. Restaurants—France—Paris—Guidebooks.
2. Paris (France)—Guidebooks.
I. Hamburger, Barbara.
II. Hamburger, Robert, 1936– Paris bistros.
III. Title.
IV. Title: Paris bistros and wine bars.
TX907.5.F72P3736 1994
647.95443'61—dc20 94-42171
ISBN 0-88001-417-2

The text of this book is set in Adobe Garamond

For Lewis and Arlene Wolberg,
Murray and Tilly Hamburger,
who fed us well and inspired us to seek out
and appreciate good food.

ACKNOWLEDGMENTS

We would like to thank Richard Abrams, Ellen and Joel Baumwoll, Sue and Jerry Fine, David Hamburger, Michael Hamburger, Evelyn and Bernie Kornfeld, Sofula Novikova, Nicolas Ranson, Jane Ross, Alison Salzinger, Meryl Salzinger, John Schriber, Al Sklar, Larry Saphire, Claudine and Allen Siegel and Liz Wolter.

Contents

III. Bistro Cuisine

IV. Ratings of the Best Bistro Dishes

APPENDICES

INTRODUCTION

Paris is a city of remarkable contrasts. A city of great tradition and great innovation, of consistency and radical change. But no matter how the city changes, its culinary traditions are still unsurpassed. Nowhere in the world are there restaurants of such richness and diversity: simple and humble, expensive and great. The famous three-star Michelin establishments lend glamour to the city but, when it comes to eating well, Parisians invariably return to their favorite bistros. The venerable bistros of Paris have managed to survive all the social, economic and gastronomic trends of the twentieth century and are still attracting stylish customers by serving the same memorable food that symbolizes the very soul of French cuisine.

Though the recession was certainly the impetus for restaurants lowering their prices, two simultaneous trends led to the emergence of a new generation of bistros throughout the city.

Celebrated chefs Michel Rostang and Guy Savoy were the first to realize public tastes were changing and had the insight to open modestly-priced annexes to their luxury restaurants. Extravagant dining was going out of fashion and Parisians, gripped with nostalgia for authentic old-fashioned tastes in a world of nouvelle cuisine, began demanding food evocative of the heartland. Exotic ingredients in bizarre combinations rekindled interests in what the French call *cuisine du terroir* or regional cooking, and diners were demanding down-to-earth, well-prepared food at reasonable prices.

Encouraged by the success of these distinguished chefs, others followed suit and, within the past few years, so many new places have opened most have yet to find their way into guidebooks.

What is a bistro? This frequently used word has become vague and is often misused in describing restaurants. The word *bistro* (or *bistrot*) was originally used to describe a public drinking place primarily serving wine and alcohol. It likely derives from *bistouille,* a derogatory term meaning *eau-de-vie* mixed with coffee. French licensing laws refer to them as *débits de boissons,* or places where liquids are sold. Bistros became popular shortly after the French Revolution, gradually evolving beyond simple *débits de boissons* into multi-service establishments where one could meet friends, buy postage stamps, cigarettes, lottery tickets, bet on horses and sometimes even enjoy a quick meal hastily prepared by the owner or his wife. By the turn of the 19th century some bistros had become full-fledged restaurants serving simple, earthy meals (*plats canailles*) that have, to this day, remained the foundation of bistro cuisine.

How does one distinguish a great bistro from a mediocre one? In France there is an old tradition of family and it is the involvement of family that gives the classic bistro its special identity. At first glance bistros may appear similar, but it is the "soul" of each that is unique, and the reflection of the devoted people behind it. An etiquette is built up through many generations. Younger family members are apprenticed to assume management with the same dedication to good food, its preparation, and service, as their parents and grandparents. The reputation and longevity of a great bistro is based on this consistency. While seasonal and special dishes may be presented, it is the classic specialties which have become synonymous with that restaurant which brings a highly critical and discerning clientele back year-in and year-out.

Defining the word "bistro" today is not so easy. Example after example contradicts the classic image of the cozy neighborhood spot with dark wood paneling, etched glass, mirrored walls, moleskin banquettes, a finely-crafted zinc bar and plenty of hearty food cooked and served by the owners in shirt-sleeves. Taking advantage of the incredible vogue for unpretentious restaurants, a myriad of places have opened possessing little to do with the original concept of bistro, yet considered by all but traditionalists to be true bistros. Obsessed gastronomes flock to the fashionable spots opened by renowned chefs and restaurateurs, but also among the current Parisian favorites are little places individually owned and run by talented young chefs who have struck out on their own, or with a spouse, to create contemporary versions of the neighborhood bistro rather than commercial enterprises.

These stylish new bistro-type establishments are not typical of other similar restaurants providing varied cuisine, pleasant atmosphere and service and reasonable prices. Here, the owner-chefs have been trained in the best traditions of haute cuisine and are constantly experimenting with new culinary concepts and various methods for adding distinction to basically bourgeois food. You will not find the usual range of simple menu choices. Instead, you will discover highly imaginative renditions of provincial favorites, each preparation made from the highest quality produce personally selected by the chef.

A further note—several of these places have sprung up in low-rent residential areas, decidedly off the beaten track, but you will find them well worth the trip for nowhere in the gastronomic mainstream will you find such extraordinary cuisine at such reasonable prices.

This guide is organized around the arrondissement plan of the city and divided into four parts. Part I begins with a list of the bistros grouped by their overall ratings according to our system of "stars." This is followed by a brief description of the 20 districts or *arrondissements* into which Paris is divided. Finally, the bulk of this section is devoted to a more complete review of each bistro, and is arranged by *arrondissement.* Price ranges are listed for each bistro in this section, and a clarification of the ranges follows: Inexpensive, $15.00 to $25.00; Moderate, $25.00 to $40.00; Fairly expensive, $40.00 to $75.00; Expensive, $75.00 to $130.00; Very expensive, $130.00 to $200.00. These rates are subject to changes in the currency rate of exchange. In late 1994 the rate was approximately five francs to the dollar. The above prices are estimated for a single meal, including gratuity and tax but without wine. Be warned that between the time this guide was written and your visit, a restaurant may change (closing dates are especially variable), so be sure to telephone to check whether the information in this guide is still valid. Part I also suggests places of interest in each *arrondissement.*

Part II is our wine bar section containing a brief description and critique of the wines and food found in our current fifty favorites.

Part III explains the dishes most commonly encountered on a bistro menu. We do not provide recipes, but describe the ingredients and preparation of each dish so you can have a general idea of what you would like to order. This listing includes some regional dishes as well as important menu terms and phrases. A short glossary at the end offers other useful terms.

Part IV contains a rating of what we consider to be the best bistro dishes and where to find them. We propose a list in descending order of where, in our estimation, the best or most interesting renditions of the dishes are presented. The overall rating of any establishment does not necessarily indicate the merits of every dish served there. A one- or two-"star" bistro may prepare a dish of four-star quality because it is a house specialty and connoisseurs will flock there seeking that particular item. Some of the most enjoyable dining experiences we have had are trying these wonderful foods in the lesser-known places. This section is followed by three appendices describing: bistros open on Sunday; other reliable bistros, aside from our top rated one hundred; and, a selection of further readings on the subject of bistros, wine bars, and wine. An alphabetical index follows of all the listed establishements.

There are many hundreds of bistros and wine bars scattered throughout Paris. Not every one of them is run with the same pride and respect for cuisine or customers. In many the food is delicious while in others it is only mediocre. We hope this guide will help in your selection and provide you some of the pleasure bistro dining has given us.

Paris Bistros & Wine Bars

PART I

The Bistros by Arrondissement

Paris is divided into twenty *arrondissements* (districts) spiraling clockwise around the first, which marks the center of the city. Each *arrondissement* has its own atmosphere and distinctive landmarks, so to know the number of the *arrondissement* is to know the style and character of the district.

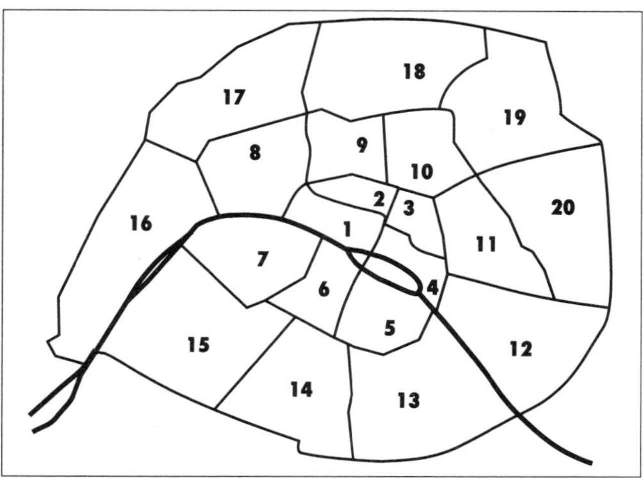

A Diagram of Paris Showing the Arrondissements

The 1er (meaning Premier) includes part of the Île de la Cité and the areas around the Louvre and Palais Royal. This is a tourist, shopping and business district with many hotels, restaurants, travel agencies, specialty shops, banks and government buildings. It is busy with commercial traffic during the day but quiet at night.

The 2e, 3e, and 4e (Deuxième, Troisième and Quatrième) include the areas of Les Halles (the old produce markets long-since demolished and moved to an area near Orly airport), Beaubourg and the Marais. These are among the oldest and most historic parts of the city but have undergone an astounding transformation during the last twenty years. The narrow, slummy streets and courtyards of Beaubourg and Les Halles have been turned into a large pedestrian area with a shopping mall, a large leisure center, and many new apartments, all dominated by the gigantic glass-and-steel Pompidou Center. The fine old *hôtels* (mansions) of the Marais, of which almost one hundred remain, are being cleaned and restored. Many are of great historic and architectural interest. Some are used to house museums, schools, libraries and cultural centers; others are being converted into luxury apartment houses. Trendy boutiques, antique shops, cafés and restaurants attract a yuppie crowd.

The 5e and 6e (Cinquième and Sixième) on the left bank comprise the areas of St.-Michel and St.-Germain-des-Prés. They are among the liveliest and most picturesque sections of the city but very different from one another. The 5e is student Paris, the Quartier Latin, "Boul' Mich'" and the Sorbonne. The 6e is intellectual and literary Paris; snobbish and avant-garde. The narrow mazes of streets are lined with book shops, publishing houses, antique stores, art galleries and boutiques of every description. Tourists, artists, writers, publishers, students, teachers, actors, models and others who simply live in the neighborhood crowd into the cafés morning, noon and night to talk, think, read, write, eat and drink.

The 7e (Septième) is on the left bank but has nothing in common with the 5e or 6e. It is mainly residential; an area of high rents and smart people; conservative and wealthy. There is little to attract the tourist except the historic monuments of the Tour Eiffel, the Invalides, Napoleon's Tomb, and the Musées d'Orsay and Rodin.

The most interesting spots are the sections around the Rue Cler and Rue St.-Dominique.

The 8e (Huitième) is the most diverse *arrondissement.* It is the district of the Étoile, Arc de Triomphe, and the Place de la Concorde. It encompasses the luxury areas around the Madeleine and Faubourg-St.-Honoré; the Avenues Montaigne and de Marigny with their expensive hotels, shops, restaurants and embassies; the champs-Élysées with its banks, airline offices, car showrooms, cinemas, nightclubs, cafés and fast-food joints; and the middle-class student and commercial areas around Gare St.-Lazare and Boulevard Haussmann.

The 9e (Neuvième) is the *arrondissement* of the Gaillion-Opéra, Pigalle and the Grands Boulevards (an area of about three miles leading from the Opéra to the Place de la République and Bastille). It is a shopping, theater and business district with banks, insurance companies and diamond merchants. The Grands Boulevards are solid with big department stores, boutiques, cafés, brasseries and movie houses. The smart end is near the Opéra; it gets seedier as you go east. The areas around Place Pigalle abound with sex shops, prostitutes, porn films and bookstores.

The 10e (Dixième) is largely unspoiled and dominated by two large train stations; the Gare du Nord and the Gare de l'Est. It doesn't have much to offer tourists, but the Rue de Paradis is worth a visit if you're interested in glass and china. Baccarat is at No. 30 bis.

The 11e, 12e, and 13e (Onzième, Douzième, and Treizième) are middle- and working-class areas, crowded with high-rise developments and small industries such as printers, mechanical enterprises, hide and leather shops and furniture manufacturers. A visit to the Bois de Vincennes is certainly worth a detour to the 12e. Some *quartiers* have large immigrant populations and each group maintains its characteristic shops, cafés and restaurants. The Asian restaurants in the 13e are the best in Paris.

The 14e and 15e (Quatorzième and Quinzième) are the old districts around Montparnasse and have in the last several years undergone much development. No longer the historic refuge of famous writers, poets and artists, the cafés, brasseries and movie houses continue to attract a lively and "hip" crowd. You can still get the flavor of the past at La Coupole or Closerie de Lilas. There are no great monuments to see among the quiet residential sections, but you can get glimpses of the way things once were.

The 16e (Seizième) contains the *quartiers* of Passy and Auteuil. Here the rich and super chic live on private, tree-lined streets, behind closed doors and ivy-covered walls. There are many parks, quiet gardens, embassies, museums, small villas and discrete hotels.

The 17e (Dix-Septième) is also a luxury area, although not as posh as the 16e. It is not a tourist area, but a visit to the Quartier Batignolles is interesting. In Rue Poncelet there is a lively market with an astounding choice of produce.

The 18e (Dix-Huitième) contains the slopes of Montmartre. The area is overshadowed by the great white basilica of Sacré-Cœur. There is still a country atmosphere here despite the hordes of tourists that crowd into the streets day and night. It is one of the most fascinating sections to visit and has largely survived reconstruction due to the steep and narrow streets of the Butte, which either come to an abrupt end or are connected by flights of steps. Small gardens, orchards and even a vineyard remain as reminders of what this charming old village once looked like. Another historic village of the 18e is la Goutte d'Or (The Drop of Gold). This is a commercial and working-class area of mixed nationalities mainly from North Africa, Morocco, the Ivory Coast and the French Antilles. The Arab groceries and the Afro-Antilles restaurants are among the best in the city.

The 19e and 20e (Dix-Neuvième and Vingtième) are the most remote *arrondissements.* They are the foreign *quartiers* of Paris. Waves of immigrants have settled here: Russian and Polish Jews, followed by Armenians, Greeks, Arabs, North Africans, Yugoslavs, Turks, Sephardic Jews and Orientals. There is an exotic mixture of food, shops, newspapers, cafés, etc. Among the new apartment blocks and large-scale developments can still be seen tiny houses, gardens and *impasses.* The main tourist attractions are the Parc des Buttes-Chaumont in the 19e and Père-Lachaise cemetery in the 20e.

Ratings

Of the thousand or so bistro-type restaurants in Paris we have personally selected the one hundred that currently best represent both the traditional old-fashioned and trendy modern-type establishments. The highest-ranking bistros (four stars) exhibit the most consistency, unstinting quality and generosity as well as a uniquely pleasurable ambience. The three-star places are generally on the same high plain but are perhaps a notch below in consistency. The bottom rankings (one and two stars) are representative of good, solid, quality bistros with some dishes of exceptional merit.

★ ★ ★ ★ THE BEST
★ ★ ★ EXCEPTIONAL
★ ★ VERY GOOD
★ ABOVE AVERAGE

★ ★ ★ ★

Chez Pauline 1er
Restaurant Pierre au Palais Royal 1er
Benoît 4e
Chez René 5e
L'Oeillade 7e
La Grille 10e
Auberge Pyrénées Cévennes 11e (Chez Philippe)
Le Villaret 11e
Le Petit Marguery 13e
La Régalade 14e
Chez Georges 17e

★ ★ ★

Le Cochon D'or Des Halles 1er (Chez Beñat)
Le Petit Bourbon 1er
Au Petit Tonneau 7e
Berrys 8e
Savy 8e
Anjou-Normandie 11e

La Tour de Monthléry 1er (Chez Denise)
Chez La Vielle 1er
Le Brin de Zinc . . . et Madame 2e
L'Ami Louis 3e
Baracane "Le Bistrot de L'Oulette" 4e
Le Grizzli 4e
Les Fontaines 5e
Chez Toutoune 5e
Allard 6e
Josephine 6e (Chez Dumonet)
Chez Maître Paul 6e
Le Petit Zinc 6e
L'Auberge Bressane 7e
Auberge "D'Chez Eux" 7e
La Fontaine de Mars 7e
Astier 11e
Le Chardenoux 11e
À Sousceyrac 11e
Chez Marcel 12e (Antoine)
Le Quincy 12e
L'Assiette 14e
La Cagouille 14e
Restaurant du Marché 15e
La Butte Chaillot 16e
Le Relais du Parc 16e
Les Gourmets des Ternes 17e
Marie-Louise 18e
À la Pomponnette 18e
Le Pouilly-Reuilly (Pré-St.-Gervais) 19e

★ ★

Lescure 1er
La Poule au Pot 1er
Chez Georges 2e
Aux Lyonnais 2e
À L'Impasse 4e (Chez Robert)
Le Vieux Bistro 4e
Campagne et Provence 5e
Moissonier 5e
Au Moulin à Vent 5e (Chez Henri)
La Rôtisserie du Beaujolais 5e
Le Caméléon 6e
Aux Charpentiers 6e
Chez Marie 6e
La Rôtisserie d'en Face 6e
Chez André 8e
Chez Edgard 8e
Au Petit Riche 9e
Au Gigot Fin 10e
Cartet 11e
Chez Fernand (Les Fernandises) 11e
L'Ebauchoir 12e
Les Zygomates 12e
Le Petit Plat 15e
Aristide 17e
Le Bistrot d'à Côté "Flaubert" 17e
Chez Fred 17e
Aux Becs Fins 20e

★

La Fermette du Sud-Ouest 1er
Le Brissemoret 2^{e}
Chez Janou 3^{e}
Au Gourmet D L'Isle 4^{e}
Le Trumilou 4^{e}
Le Langeudoc 5^{e}
Perraudin 5^{e}
Bistro de la Grille 6^{e}
Le Bistrot D'Henri 6^{e}
Marie et Fils 6^{e}
Polidor 6^{e}
Restaurant des Beaux-Arts 6^{e}
Chez L'Ami Jean 7^{e}
Chez Germaine 7^{e}
Au Pied de Fouet 7^{e}
Thoumieux 7^{e}
Le Roi du Pot-Au-Feu 9^{e}
À la Biche aux Bois 12^{e}
Le Bistrot du Dôme 14^{e}
Le Bourbonnais 14^{e}
Restaurant Bleu 14^{e}
La Gitane 15^{e}
Le Petit Mâchon 15^{e}
Le Scheffer 16^{e}
Le Petit Salé 17^{e}
Le Maquis 18^{e}
Boeuf Gros Sel 20^{e}

1er Arrondissement

Le Cochon D'Or Des Halles (Chez Beñat)

La Fermette du Sud-Ouest

Lescure

Chez Pauline

Le Petit Bourbon

La Poule au Pot

Restaurant Pierre au Palais Royal

La Tour de Monthléry (Chez Denise)

Chez La Vielle

Louvre—Les Halles—Palais-Royal

PLACES OF INTEREST

Centre National d'Art et de Culture Georges-Pompidou (Beaubourg)

L'Église Saint Germain l'Auxerrois

Fontaine des Innocents

Forum des Halles

Île de la Cité (*1er*, 4e)

Jardin des Tuileries (and *Arc de Triomphe du Carrousel*)

Le Louvre des Antiquaires

Musée des Arts Décortifs

Musée du Louvre & l'Orangerie

Opéra (*1er*, 2e, *9e*)

Pont-Neuf, Square du Vert Galant (*Bateaux Mouches* or *Vedettes*)

Quai de la Mégisserie (bird, flower and animal market)

Rue St. Honoré

Rue de Rivoli

LE COCHON D'OR DES HALLES (CHEZ BEÑAT) 

M. Beñat Errandonéa

Address: 31, rue du Jour, 75001 (across from L'Église St. Eustache)
Closed: Sat. lunch, Sun.
Price Range: Fairly expensive
Tel: 42-36-38-31
Metro: Les Halles
Credit: Visa, Amex
Remarks: Air-conditioning, non-smoking room

A legendary Les Halles bistro where the welcome is always friendly, the portions generous, and the setting steeped in the history of the ancient Les Halles market. Since 1989 Basque native Beñat Errandonéa has continued this tradition while introducing the hearty fare of his southwest region.

When *Le Cochon d'Or* opened it was surrounded by the central markets where, in the old days, it was customary to arrive between midnight and 3 A.M. and stay until dawn, sightseeing among the vast food stalls and eating crusty bread, onion soup and snails. Today it flanks a trendy shopping mall but the renovations have not erased the ambience of this fine old place. If you are a meat-eater, there are magnificent cuts of beef, lamb or pork prepared exactly as ordered. You might want to begin with a serving of bone marrow spread on crunchy toast and sprinkled with coarse salt and chives, or a crisp chicory-and-bacon salad served with a poached egg. Fish lovers won't be disappointed with classic sole Meunière. All the above was introduced by the former *patronne,* Madame Saunière, and continued by Beñat. This is a nice place to keep in mind if you're in the mood for superb renditions of southwest cuisine. Some count the *brandade de morue,* served with croutons and a mixed salad, as the best in Paris. Other outstanding Basque specialties include *cuisse de lapin confite* (preserved rabbit leg), *pipérade Basquaise* (Basque omelette) and prunes in Armagnac for dessert.

Recommended Dishes

Moelle Pochée à la Croque au Sel. Poached bone marrow with coarse salt and chives on toast.
Salade de Frisée aux Lardons. Chicory salad with bacon.
Pipérade Basquaise. Fluffy omelette with tomatoes, peppers, onions and sliced Bayonne ham.
Fricassée d'Escargots aux Girolles. Snails sauteed in butter and served with wild mushrooms.
Entrecôte Grillée Pommes Allumettes. Grilled rib steak with shoestring potatoes.
Andouillette de Troyes Moutard avec Frites. Grilled pork sausage, served hot, with mustard and superb french fries.
Onglet Poêlé aux Échalotes. Flank steak pan-fried with shallots.
Grillade de Porc à l'Ail. Grilled pork with garlic.
Rognon de Veau Grillé Entier Sauce Moutarde. Whole grilled veal kidney in mustard sauce.
Cuisse de Lapin Confite. Preserved rabbit leg with sliced garlic potatoes.
Navarin d'Agneau. Browned lamb stew with potatoes and onions.
Brandade de Morue avec Croûtons. Creamed salt cod garnished with croutons.
Sole au Four de Mme. Saunière. Baked filet of sole in butter sauce.
Raie aux Câpres. Skate in black butter and capers.
Tarte Fine aux Pommes. Thin apple tart.
Pruneaux à l'Armagnac. Prunes steeped in Armagnac.

Wine

Château Labégorce, Zedé (Margaux), Saint-Véran, Cahors, Brouilly.

La Fermette du Sud-Ouest ★

M. Jacky Meyer

Address: 31, rue Coquillière, 75001
Closed: Sun., holidays and August
Price Range: Fairly expensive
Tel: 42-36-73-55
Metro: Halles
Credit: Visa and MasterCard

Authentic regional specialties from the Gironde and Landes regions of Southwestern France are served in an authentic auberge *atmosphere.*

The decor is simple and pleasant but the ambience smart and intimate in this untouristy bistro near the Église Saint Eustache. The dining areas are located on two levels and decorated with regional memorabilia. Everything, from the foie gras to the *boudin,* not to mention the *cassoulet* and the *confit,* is cooked to perfection.

You can begin with a *pousse-rapière,* a lovely Southwestern apéritif made with Armagnac brandy and Champagne. It is especially good here.

Recommended Dishes

Cochonnailles. Assorted pork products.
Jambon de Campagne. Country ham.
Grattons de Canard. Salted duck fat "cracklings."
Palette de Cochon Confite. Preserved pork shoulder.
Confit de Canard aux Cèpes. Grilled preserved duck with large meaty wild mushrooms.
Andouillettes. Grilled pork sausages.
Gras-Double Fenouillard. Ox tripe with fennel.
Boudin Paysan. Grilled blood sausage served with onions and bacon.
Cassoulet à l'Ancienne. Bean-and-meat stew cooked in an earthenware pot.
Pintade au Chou. Guinea fowl with cabbage.
Cailles Farcies au Foie Gras à l'Armagnac. Stuffed quail with foie gras and Armagnac.

Magret de Canard aux Cèpes. Fattened duck breast with mushrooms.

Crème Caramel. Vanilla-flavored flan.

Île Flottante. Poached egg whites (meringue) floating in vanilla-custard sauce.

Wine

Côtes-de-Buzet, Madiran and Cahors.

Lescure ★★

M. Lascaud

Address: 7, rue de Mondovi, 75001
Closed: Sat. dinner, Sun., Christmas week and last two weeks in August
Price Range: Moderate
Tel: 42-60-18-91
Metro: Concorde
Credit: Visa
Remarks: Air-conditioning, Non-smoking room

A rustic atmosphere and generous helpings of simple French home-cooking are the attractions in this charming little bistro tucked away in a corner just off the Rue de Rivoli. The specialties vary from day to day and if you come early enough, you may find a seat among the tourists and faithful regulars who fill the place for lunch.

Customers have been sitting *coude à coude* (elbow to elbow), at tiny tables, under hanging garlands of garlic, onions, sausages and herbs since 1919 when Leon Lescure opened here. The place is still owned and operated by the second generation of his family, which continues the tradition of serving bourgeois plates at prices in the middle range. The service is a little harried but when the food arrives, it's always good. A fine *beouf bourguignon,* spareribs with red cabbage and a copious *poule-au-pot* (boiled, stuffed chicken) are among the choices. A few items from the Limousin region are also listed. If you want to wait for a place, there is a little zinc bar at the entrance, and during the summer, tables are set out onto the narrow sidewalk.

Recommended Dishes

Maquereau Frais à la Marinade. Mackerel fillets poached in white wine and served cold as a first course.

Pâté en Croute Chaude Salade. Pâté nestled in a hollowed-out slice of bread, served over salad.

Poule-au-Pot Farcie Henri IV. Stuffed chicken poached with vegetables.

Boeuf Bourguignon Garni. Beef cooked in red wine with bacon, small onions and mushrooms.

Confit de Canard "Comme en Limousin." Preserved duck grilled and accompanied by sautéed potatoes in oil.

Poularde au Riz Sauce Basquaise. Chicken served with rice and covered with tomato-and-green-pepper sauce.

Haddock Poché à l'Anglaise. Poached haddock English-style.

Filet de Canard Sauce au Poivre Vert. Fattened duck breast grilled with green peppercorns.

Vacherin aux Fraises ou Framboises. Meringue ring filled with cream and either strawberries or raspberries.

Tartes Maison. Fruit tarts (especially apricot).

Les Cabécous des Causses de Roc-Amadour. Special small round goat cheese from the Southwest.

Wine

Cahors or Macon Blanc.

Chez Pauline 

M. Andre Génin

Address: 5, rue Villedo, 75001

Closed: Sat. lunch (summer), Sat. evening, Sun., December 24–January 2. Usually last two weeks of July and first two weeks of August

Price Range: Expensive
Tel: 42-96-20-70
Metro: Pyramides
Credit: Visa, MasterCard, and Amex
Remarks: Air-conditioning, Non-smoking room

One of the finest bistros in Paris; everything is top quality. Its location is convenient, the decor lovely, the service friendly and professional and the cuisine incredible. It is a very comfortable place, polished and expensive.

Located just in back of the Palais-Royal not far from the Comédie Française, this upscale bistro is one of the most popular with chic Parisians and knowledgeable tourists. Chef Génin's mouth-watering cuisine is a mixture of Burgundian classics with some nouvelle touches. The menu, which changes several times a year, offers everything you might want: pâtés, foie gras, wonderful hot oysters, frogs' legs, grilled sole and *rouget* (red mullet), *langoustines* and fabulous Bresse chicken with truffles. During the autumn and winter fresh game is a specialty. Rabbit stews, wild ducks and succulent wild boar are exquisitely prepared. There are wonderful cheeses and desserts, including homemade sherbets, petit fours, a superb rice pudding and a *millefeuille* with strawberries which is something special. The wine list includes a number of outstanding bargains, but the house wines, usually a Brouilly or Chiroubles, are fruity and inexpensive. An extensive selection of imported coffees is also offered.

RECOMMENDED DISHES

Salade Tiéde de Tête de Veau Sauce Gribiche. Calf's-head salad served warm with a vinaigrette dressing.
Jambon Persillé Comme en Bourgogne. Cold pressed ham with parsley in a white wine aspic.
Terrine de Foie de Volaille. Chicken liver pâté.
Terrine de Lapereau en Gelée de Pouilly. Rabbit pâté in Pouilly wine aspic.
Foie Gras Frais de Canard. Fresh duck foie gras.
Chou Farci "Paysanne." "Peasant style" stuffed cabbage.
Raie au Chou Nouveau. **Skate with green cabbage.**
Ris de Veau en Croûte. Calf's sweetbreads served as a filling in a hollowed-out pastry.
Boeuf Bourguignon Garni de Pâtes Fraîches. Beef stewed in

burgundy wine with onions and mushrooms served with fresh pasta.

Côte de Boeuf Grillée et Son Gratin Dauphinois. Ribs of beef served with sliced potatoes baked with cream and browned on top.

Poularde de Bresse Rôtie (served for two). Roasted Bresse chicken.

Lièvre à la Royale (in season). Hare, boned and stuffed with foie gras and truffles, then braised in red wine and brandy.

Gâteau de Riz de Madame Ducottet. Rice pudding with fruit *confit* and vanilla custard sauce.

Crème Brulée à la Vanille. Custard, topped with brown sugar browned to a hard coating under a grill.

WINE

Beaujolais, Sancerre, Burgundy.

LE PETIT BOURBON

M. Patrick Lambert
M. Michel Derbane
M. Yves Jaffré

Address: 15, rue du Roule, 75001 (off rue de Rivoli)
Closed: Sun., Mon. and two weeks in August
Price Range: Moderate
Tel: 40-26-08-93
Metro: Pont-Neuf or Louvre
Credit: All major credit cards

A casually chic, intimate bistro newly established in the heart of Paris, featuring the refined cuisine of Michel Derbane whose restaurant, Chants de Piano, was one of the premier eateries in Montmartre.

In 1992, without fanfare or publicity, this attractive new restaurant sprang up between Saint Eustache and Samaritaine department store and became instantly successful. Skillfully created in a 1691 building, the dining room is highlighted by an exposed stone wall, discretely lit paintings of the Midi region created by the artist Jeaffroy, and the use of deep rich cream colors throughout. Two handsome chandeliers lend a special intimate touch.

The frequently changing menu is imaginative with great attention to detail. The classically-inspired cuisine features the finest quality ingredients that might include filet of beef, flamed sea bass with fennel, skewered scallops, rolled veal tongue or a salad of grilled giant shrimp. Great value is evident in the 140-franc (about twenty-five dollars) menu or the extraordinary 230-franc *menu dégustation.*

The soothing atmosphere of this upscale modern bistro in an otherwise funky commercial neighborhood with its exceptional cadre, refined cuisine and moderate price necessitates a visit, however the restaurant is very popular so reservations should be made well in advance.

Recommended Dishes

Salade de Gambas Roties au Vinaigre Balsamique. Salad of roasted giant shrimp in balsamic vinegar.

Tian de Légumes au Coulis de Tomate. Provençal vegetables baked and served in a shallow dish with a thick puree of tomatoes.

Foie Gras de Canard Cuit en Terrine. Cooked duck liver in an earthenware dish.

Ravioles d'Escargots de Bourgogne Persillés. Vineyard snails in raviolis and garlic butter.

Roulade de Tête et Langue de Veau Ravigote. Rolled head and tongue of veal in a cream sauce with shallots, herbs and spices.

Noisette d'Agneau en Tapenade et Caviar d'Aubergines. Fillet of lamb with crushed olives and eggplant puree.

Filet de Boeuf Béarnaise. Grilled filet of beef in a thickened sauce of egg yolks, butter, shallots, white wine and herbs.

Fricassée de Dinde aux Marrons. Turkey hen stew with chestnuts.

Rognons de Veau aux Grains de Café Grillés. Veal kidneys grilled with coffee beans.

Aile de Raie au Parfum de Muscade. Skate wing cooked with nutmeg flavoring.

Loup au Fenouil Flambé au Pastis. Sea bass with fennel flamed with anise-flavored aperitif.

Brochette de Saint-Jacques au Lard. Skewered scallops with bacon.

Clafoutis aux Cerises. Deep-dish cherry batter cake.

Marquise au Chocolat Crème Anglaise. Rich chocolate Bavarian cream cake covered with whipped cream and jellied syrup.

Tarte Tatin Crème Fraîche. Caramelized upside-down apple pie with lightly-soured cream on the side.

WINE

Chenonceau (red), Côte Chalonnaise (white), à la Découverte du Vignoble Francais (discoveries of little known country wines).

LA POULE AU POT 

M. Paul Racat

Address: 9, rue Vauvilliers, 75001 (Les Halles area, off rue Berger)
Closed: Lunch every day
Price Range: Fairly expensive
Tel: 42-36-32-96
Metro: Louvre or Les Halles
Credit: Visa
Remarks: Open until 6 A.M.

There are a few classic "bistros of the night" in Paris of which La Poule au Pot, along with La Tour de Monthléry are the most celebrated. From 7 P.M. to 6 in the morning, this animated art deco establishment serves the best chicken-in-the-pot and onion soup in the capital.

How could you not love this stylish 1930s all-night eatery complete with gleaming copper bar, black marble, and colorful lights reflected off strategically-placed glass mosaic columns. The bistro really comes alive after midnight and jumps 'til dawn seven days a week, except for Sundays when La Poule au Pot is open but uncommonly quiet.

The dish of choice is the quintessential *poule au pot garnie,* a brilliant melange of steaming broth, exquisite vegetables and the famous stewed chicken served together, with a slice of pâté, in an immense soup tureen. The other two house specialties, aside from the celebrated onion soup *(la soupe á l'oignon gratinée au vin blanc),* are the large vineyard snails served with a classic garlic butter *(escargots de Bourgogne)* and the huge serving of boiled beef, broth, and vegetables served in a pot *(pot-au-feu).*

Tasty bistro specialties, amiably served, in a jewel-like retro atmosphere insure a most memorable dinner or late night feast; truly an experience not to be passed up.

Recommended Dishes

Terrine de Campagne et sa Confiture d'Oignons. Country pâté on a bed of onion jam.

Soupe à l'Oignon Gratinée au Vin Blanc. Onion soup poured over a slice of bread with browned grated cheese on top.

Escargots de Bourgogne. A dozen vineyard snails with garlic butter.

Salade "Poule au Pot." Spinach salad garnished with sauteed chicken livers.

Crottin de Chavignol sur lit de Salade. Hot goat cheese salad on toast.

Oeufs Cocotte à la Crème. Lightly-cooked eggs in cream, prepared and served in a covered dish.

Andouillette de Troyes. Grilled sausage from Troyes.

Poule au Pot Garnie Maison. Chicken-in-the-pot.

Pot-au-Feu de Plat de Côte. Beef and vegetable broth served with platter of short ribs.

Confit de Canard "Maison." Preserved duck served with sautéed potatoes.

Rognon de Veau Henry IV. Veal kidneys garnished with artichoke heart filled with *Béarnaise* sauce.

Escalope de Truite de Mer au Champagne. Filet of salmon trout in Champagne sauce.

Soufflé Glacé au Grand Marnier (or ***Framboise).*** Frozen Grand Marnier soufflé.

Crème Brulée à l'Ancienne. Cream custard topped with caramelized brown sugar.

Tarte des Demoiselles Tatin à la Crème. Upside-down apple tart, whipped cream on the side.

Wine

Pinot Noir Bourgogne, Brouilly.

Restaurant Pierre au Palais Royal

Mme. Nicole & M. Daniel Dez
Chef: Roger Leplu

Address: 10, rue de Richelieu, 75001
Closed: Sat., Sun., August and most holidays
Price Range: Fairly expensive
Tel: 42-96-09-17
Metro: Palais-Royal
Credit: All major credit cards

This admirable establishment, once known as Pierre Traiteur, remains one of the most distinguished and best bistros in the city. The menu features finely executed classics and some flavorful, more modern, fish preparations.

The setting of this old house is calm and comfortable, consisting of brown-velvet banquettes, wood paneling, raw-silk-covered walls and pictures of the nearby Palais-Royal. There are two rooms, separated by a wooden bar, which are always packed, but the friendly service makes you feel immediately at home. The inspiration for the cuisine comes from the provinces, but you will find some of the most flavorful bourgeois cooking in Paris here. Fresh fish is flown in from Normandy each day, the Roquefort is superb and the desserts are ambrosia. There are two preparations that should not be missed: the *gratin dauphinois,* which may not appear on the menu but which can, nevertheless, be ordered, and the mackerel in cider, which is always on the menu.

Recommended Dishes

Saucisson Chaud Lyonnais Poché au Beaujolais. The Jésus de Morteau sausage poached in Beaujolais wine.

Terrine de Foie Gras de Canard. Pâté of duck foie gras.

Escalope de Foie Gras Chaud au Vinaigre de Xérès. Sliced *foie gras* in sherry vinegar, served warm.

Filets de Maquereaux Frais au Cidre. Mackerel fillets poached in cider and apples and served cold.

Jambon Persilée. Cold pressed ham with parsley in white wine aspic.

Andouillette en Fricassée à la Lyonnaise. Pork sausage sautéed with potatoes and onions.

Selle d'Agneau Rôtie à la Niçoise. Roast saddle of lamb with tomatoes, garlic, anchovies, and capers.

Pieds et Paquets. Marseillaise-style packets of mutton tripe cooked with sheep's trotters and tomatoes in white wine.

Gibiers en Saison. Numerous game dishes served in the fall and winter.

Lièvre à la Royal. Boned hare in a *foie gras,* wine, and truffle sauce, usually available October through December.

Estofinade Rouergate. Codfish stew.

Chou Farci à la Bourguignonne. Stuffed cabbage.

Raie au Beurre Noisette. Skate in black butter.

Coquilles Saint-Jacques. Scallops.

Filet de Bar Grillée au Beurre Blanc. Grilled fillet of sea bass in white-wine butter sauce.

Galette de Boudin aux Oignons. Blood sausage with onions.

Boeuf Ficelle à la Menagiere. Poached fillet of beef in its own broth served "housewife style" with vegetables and onions.

Rognon de Veau à l'Echalote Confite. Veal kidneys in a shallot *confit.*

Gratin Dauphinois. Sliced potatoes baked with cream, seasoned with garlic, sprinkled with Gruyère cheese and browned on top.

Râble de Lièvre (in season). Roast saddle of hare.

Lotte en Papillote. Monkfish baked in a pouch of oiled paper.

Daurade Grillée au Beurre Blanc. Grilled sea bream served in a white-wine butter sauce.

Tarte à la Pamplemousse. Grapefruit tart.

Tarte-Tatin. Upside-down apple pie.

Crème Renversée au Caramel. Caramel flan.

Mille-Feuille aux Fraises. Thin-layered puff pastry with strawberries.

WINE

Sancerre, Chinon, Bourgeuil, Beaujolais (all the important growths).

LA TOUR DE MONTHLÉRY (CHEZ DENISE)

Mme. Denise Benariac

Address: 5, rue des Prouvaires, 75001
Closed: Sat., Sun. and July 15–August 15
Price Range: Fairly expensive
Tel: 42-36-21-82
Metro: Louvre, Halles, or Châtelet-Les Halles
Credit: Visa

"Chez Denise" is an old all-night Les Halles institution which continues to maintain an atmosphere of conviviality and good cheer. Sour-dough bread from Poilâne, the famous Parisian baker, the Brouilly and the pot-au-feu *are as unchangeable as the place itself.*

An interesting mix of customers keeps this wonderful place busy day and night, so reservations are a must except possibly at 4 A.M. The decor is nicely warm. Celebrity portraits, lithographs, photographs and posters clutter the old stone walls. Overhead, wooden rafters are lined with hams and sausages undisturbed by little hanging lamps. A black-and-white tile floor, brass rails, a long bar at the entrance, old subway seats as banquettes, and red-and-white checkered cloths complete the scene. The hearty, straightforward cuisine includes sausages, stews, *ongelet* (steak) and delicious tripe served Normandy-style steaming hot in an enormous tureen. This is one of the most consistently popular bistros in Paris; a great early-morning "hangout."

RECOMMENDED DISHES

Cochonnailles (Assiette de Charcuterie). Assorted pork products.

Terrine de Foie de Volaille. Chicken liver pâté.
Tripes au Calvados. Tripes cooked in cider brandy.
Chou Farci. Stuffed cabbage.
Boeuf Gros Sel (Pot-au-Feu). Boiled beef with vegetables and beef broth.
Haricot de Mouton. Mutton stew with potatoes, turnips and onions.
Pied de Porc Grillé. Grilled pigs' feet.
Lapin à la Moutarde. Rabbit in mustard sauce.
Andouillette. Grilled pork sausage served hot with mustard and vegetables.
Onglet de Boeuf, Frites. Flank steak grilled with shallots and served with outstanding french fries.
Oeufs à la Neige. Egg whites poached in milk, served with vanilla custard.
Tarte aux Pommes. Apple tart.

WINE

Sancerre, Bordeaux, Brouilly, Provençal rosé and Muscat.

CHEZ LA VIELLE 

Mme. Adrienne Biasin

Address: 1, rue Bailleul or 37, rue de l'Arbre-Sec, 75001
Closed: Open for lunch only
Price Range: Fairly expensive
Tel: 42-60-15-78
Metro: Pont-Neuf or Louvre
Credit: Amex

Adrienne Biasin, distinguished chef, hostess and renowned bistro personality, prepares everything herself in a tiny kitchen across the hall from her delightful little six-table bistro. Simple home cooking is the specialty here and everything is of exceptional quality. Reservations should be made at least two weeks in advance.

Everything is *formidable* chez Adrienne. You'll begin with a choice of six or seven superb hors d'oeuvres, which arrive at your table on a cart. You are urged to help yourself from heaping bowls of stuffed tomatoes, sausage and potatoes, pâtés, *rillettes,* beets or celery root salad. The menu that day might include a lamb stew, beef with carrots, calf's liver, ratatouille or *boeuf à la mode.* It's all good and so are the desserts, especially the chocolate mousse and apricots or prunes. Located on the corner of Rue Bailleul and Rue de l'Arbre Sec, the cozy dining room with a timbered ceiling and lovely tile floor is homey and inviting. There is a bar behind which two motherly waitresses wait to serve the next course.

RECOMMENDED DISHES

Tomates Farcies. Stuffed tomatoes.
Terrines de Grand-Mère. Rustic country pâtés.
Céleri Rémoulade. Shredded celery root in spicy mayonnaise.
Rognon de Veau. Veal kidneys served minced.
Navarin d'Agneau. Lamb stew.
Boeuf Miroton. Slices of beef with a sweet onion sauce.
Boeuf à la Mode. Beef, pot roasted in red wine with vegetables.
Boeuf en Daube. Wine-flavored beef stew.
Sauté d'Agneau. Sautéed lamb.
Haricot de Mouton. Mutton stew with potatoes, turnips and onions.
Hachis Parmentier (order in advance). Minced-meat shepherd's pie.
Pot-au-Feu (order in advance). Boiled beef with vegetables and broth.
Ratatouille Parfumée. Eggplant stew with tomatoes, onions, peppers and garlic stirred in oil.
Gâteau au Chocolat. Chocolate cake.
Mousse au Chocolat. Chocolate mousse.
Gâteau de Riz. Rice pudding with fruit *confit* and whipped cream.

WINE

Country Wines, Saumur Champigny, Brouilly.

2^e^ Arrondissement

Le Brin de Zinc . . . et Madame

Le Brissemoret

Chez Georges

Aux Lyonnais

Bourse—Turbigo

PLACES OF INTEREST

La Bourse (Stock Exchange)

Cabinet de Médailles (Museum of coins, medals, artifacts, and royal treasures)

Covered passages (*Vivienne, du Grand-Cerf, du Bourg-l'Abbé de la Trinité, Basfour, Beauregard, des Panoramas, des Princes*)

Place du Caire

Quartier de la Presse

Rue des Petits-Carreaux and *rue Montorgueil*

Sentier (Garment District)

Tour de Jean-Sans-Peur

LE BRIN DE ZINC . . . ET MADAME 

M. Berdoulat

Address: 50, rue Montorgueil, 75002
Closed: Sun.
Price Range: Fairly expensive
Tel: 42-21-10-80
Metro: Étienne-Marcel, Halles or Sentier
Credit: All major credit cards

You'll immediately feel at home in this attractive bistro created on the premises of a famous old Les Halles bistro called La Grille. The menu is a mixture of traditional bourgeois dishes with some more modern inventions.

Many Parisians considered the opening of Le Brin de Zinc as the reopening of La Grille, a celebrated bistro when Les Halles was at its peak. La Grille originally opened as a wine shop in 1830 and continued in business as a bistro until about ten years ago. In 1990, the space was taken over and, without destroying the decor or greatly modifying the spirit of the cuisine, the old doors reopened. The pretty curved bar at the entrance dates from 1911. There are lovely mirrors, red banquettes and old fixtures and grilles that give one the feeling of going back in time as do dishes like onion soup, oxtails braised in red wine and stuffed pigs' feet. There is a cabaret next door, called "Et Madame," which opens around 10:30 P.M. and where you can hear French songs from the 50s until dawn.

RECOMMENDED DISHES

Poêlée d'Escargots en Ratatouille. Snails served over a stew of eggplant, zucchini and tomatoes.
Oeufs Pochés Toupinel. Poached eggs in baked potatoes.
Soupe à l'Oignon Gratinée. Onion soup served in its own pot with a thin crust of browned cheese.
Terrine de Gibier. Game pâté (in season).
Salade Montorgueil. Lentil bean salad with gizzards and preserved duck.
Queue de Boeuf Mitonée Braisée au Vin Rouge. Braised oxtail

simmered in red wine.

Canard Sauvage en Aîgre-Doux. Grilled wild duck in a sweet-and-sour sauce.

Boeuf Miroton. Slices of beef in broth with mustard and onions.

Entrecôte à la Moelle. Rib steak with bone marrow sauce.

Tête de Veau Avec Langue et Cervelle, Sauce Gribiche. Calf's head with tongue and brains in a cold vinaigrette of *cornichons* and capers.

Pieds de Porc Farcis. Grilled, stuffed pigs' feet.

Pavé de Cabillaud en Bourride. Fresh codfish stew served with *aïoli* (garlic mayonnaise).

Clafoutis aux Poires. Custard tart with pears.

Pot de Crème à la Vanille. Vanilla cream pot.

Marquise au Chocolat, Sauce Café. Chocolate mousse cake topped with coffee sauce.

Wine

St. Nicolas de Bourgueil/Chez Bruneau, Chinon Saint-Amour, Bandol, Bourgogne Aligoté.

Le Brissemoret 

M. Claude Brissemoret

Address: 5, rue Saint-Marc, 75002 (off rue de Richelieu)
Closed: Sat., Sun., and three weeks in August
Price Range: Moderate
Tel: 42-36-91-72
Metro: Bourse or Montmartre
Credit: All major credit cards

A strange, slightly decrepit but charming little "hole in the wall" with excellent food seasonally fresh and nicely prepared. There are some fabulous homemade desserts. Reservations must be booked well in advance, as this is an "in" Bourse restaurant.

Located directly behind Paris's stock exchange, across from the

Passage des Panoramas, the beautiful old facade of Brissemoret simply says *"VINS-RESTAURANT-A LA CARTE ET PLAT DU JOUR."* Inside, the small rectangular dining room has lace curtains, modern posters, a tile floor, old wine-colored velour banquettes, and a large central mirror. There is a stairway leading up to the w.c., but no longer an upstairs dining room. A small zinc bar at the entrance, simply set with a bouquet of fresh flowers, hides the antique kitchen beyond. Very white tablecloths and napkins of heavy linen cover the nine or ten marble-topped tables, each of which is set with a saltcellar and pepper mill. Homemade foie gras, mushrooms in cream sauce, hot goat cheese salad, marinated baby lamp chops served in a red wine sauce, *entrecôte* with marrow, guinea fowl with fruits and lamb kidneys in a fabulous mustard and onion sauce are served on handsome stoneware plates. Each main dish is carefully prepared and accompanied by an outstanding sauce. The house wine is a red Gamay de Touraine and there is a very fine and reasonably priced Calvados available.

Recommended Dishes

Filets de Maquereau Pochés au Vin Blanc. Poached fillets of mackerel in white wine.

Foie Gras Frais Maison. Fresh duck foie gras.

Salade de Foies de Volaille. Chicken liver salad.

Fonds d'Artichauds frais. Artichoke-bottoms salad in vinaigrette.

Côtes d'Agneau en Chevreuil. Lamb chops cooked like venison.

Dodine de Canard. Boned duck, stuffed and cooked over the coals.

Magret de Canard. Fattened duck breast in red-wine sauce.

Filet Mignon de Porc, Sauce Poivrade. Filet of pork in a brown black-pepper sauce.

Fricassée de Pintade aux Fruits. Light guinea fowl stew with fruits of the season.

Entrecôte Bordelaise et Moelle. Rib steak in bone marrow sauce.

Rognons d'Agneau Sauce Robert. Lamb kidneys in an onion-and-mustard sauce.

Saumon Frais Cru, aux Herbes. Fresh raw salmon with herbs.

Gâteau au Chocolat. Chocolate cake.

Tarte aux Pommes. Apple tart.

Wine

Crozes Hermitage/A. Graillot, Pouilly Fumé/Joseph Ballard, Gamay de Touraine.

Chez Georges 

M. Georges Constant
M. Brouillet

Address: 1, rue du Mail, 75002 (just off Place des Victoires)
Closed: Sun., holidays, and first three weeks of August
Price Range: Fairly expensive
Tel: 42-60-07-11
Metro: Sentier or Bourse
Credit: All major credit cards
Remarks: Air-conditioning, non-smoking room

Very popular, delightful old bistro with pushy waitresses, a fine wine cellar with many bargains and a menu offering all the bistro classics carefully and skillfully prepared. Reservations are advisable.

Chez Georges is a wonderful place with a simple hospitable look that typifies restaurants of the old style. The entrance is a kind of passageway and bar decorated by a wall painting of young couples and minstrels strolling through a medieval garden. Rows of mahogany-colored banquettes, closely spaced tables and giant arched beveled mirrors run along the walls on each side of the small alley-like dining room. A communal coat rack in the center breaks the monotony of the starkly simple tile floor. The long and varied handwritten menu rarely changes, to the delight of everyone who comes here. Among the nineteen appetizers available are eggs in a red-wine sauce with truffles. These can be followed by a choice of several classic fish or meat preparations, including such famous specialties as the *sole au pouilly,* the *pavé* (steak) *du mail* and the duck with *cèpes.* The house has an extraordinary cellar of fine old Burgundy and Bordeaux wines, but you can also order Beaujolais served by the pitcher.

Recommended Dishes

Salade de Museau de Boeuf. Beef headcheese salad.
Jambon Persillé. Parslied ham in white wine aspic.
Terrine de Foie de Volaille. Chicken liver pâté.
Oeufs en Meurette aux Truffes. Poached eggs in red-wine sauce with truffles.
Salade de Pissenlits aux Lardons. Dandelion greens salad, with bacon and new potatoes.
Steak de Canard aux Cèpes. Grilled duck fillet with sautéed wild mushrooms.
Cœur de Filet Grillé, Sauce Béarnaise. Grilled filet of beef with Béarnaise sauce.
Gigot d'Agneau Rôti, Gratin Dauphinois. Roast leg of lamb with sliced potatoes baked with cream and browned on top.
Pavé du Mail. Thick slice of beef served with a mustard sauce.
Rognon de Veau Grillée Henri IV. Grilled veal kidneys with artichoke hearts.
Raie au Beurre Noisette. Skate in black butter sauce.
Sole au Pouilly. Fillet of sole cooked in white Burgundy wine.
Tronçon de Turbot, Sauce Béarnaise. Thick grilled cut of turbot in a white-wine Béarnaise sauce.
Charlotte aux Poires. Baked custard pudding with buttered bread and sliced pears.
Baba au Rhum. Yeast cake steeped in rum syrup.
Profiteroles au Chocolat. Tiny cream puffs with melted chocolate sauce.

Wine

Beaujolais wines served by the pitcher, Côtes-de-Brouilly, Morgon.

Aux Lyonnais 

M. Pierre Vallée, Chef Bernard Jandot

Address: 32, rue Saint-Marc, 75002
Closed: Sun., holidays and August

Price Range: Moderate
Tel: 42-96-65-04
Metro: 4-Septembre, Bourse or Richelieu–Drouot
Credit: All major credit cards
Remarks: Non-smoking room

A lovely fin-de-siècle *bistro which commands a faithful following. The quality of the food, the cooking and the service are absolutely dependable. Its location in the Bourse area assures it is usually busy, so reservations are suggested.*

A few steps from Place Boïeldieu, just behind the Bourse is the lovely old red-and-cream facade of Aux Lyonnais. A picture of two provincial women welcomes you into the picturesque dining room. White and rose motif tile dados and arched mirrors adorn attractive turn-of-the-century walls molded with roses and garlands. Brass globe lights, lovely tile floors, etched glass windows, lace curtains and potted palms enhance the well-kept decor.

All the great wine villages of Beaujolais are to be found on what is described as the "Route de Beaujolais," and you will have no difficulty choosing a wine to accompany the basic bistro cuisine with some Lyonnais specialties. An 87F lunch menu includes *confit* and *cassoulet,* and a friendly all-female staff provides efficient and helpful service.

Recommended Dishes

Petits Pâtés Chauds, Enrobés d'Herbes Dans la Crépine. Pâtés served hot, enriched with herbs and wrapped in pig's membrane.

Saucisson Chaud Lyonnais, Pommes à l'Huille. Large slicing sausage with potatoes in oil.

Salade Frisée au Lard Avec Saucisson Chaud. Chicory salad served with bacon and slices of hot sausage.

Oeufs en Meurette. Poached eggs in red-wine sauce.

Pieds de Mouton à la Rémoulade. Sheep's feet in a mustard-mayonnaise sauce with chopped *cornichons,* egg and capers.

Poule Gros Sel avec Ses Légumes. Poached chicken with vegetables.

Gras-Double à la Lyonnaise. Ox tripe sliced and fried with onions, vinegar and parsley.

Pieds de Porc Grillés. Grilled pigs' feet.

Quenelles de Brochet au Beurre Blanc. Pike dumplings in a

white-wine butter sauce.

Raie au Beurre Brun. Skate cooked with brown butter, lemon and parsley.

Tarte-Tatin, Crème Fraîche. Upside-down apple pie served with slightly soured cream.

Oeufs à la Neige. Egg whites poached in milk and served with vanilla custard sauce.

WINE

"ROUTE DE BEAUJOLAIS" complete list of Beaujolais Crus served in full and half bottles.

3^e Arrondissement

L'Ami Louis

Chez Janou

Marais—Temple

PLACES OF INTEREST

Centre Culturel du Marais

Hôtel de Guenegaud
(*Musée de la Chasse et de la Nature*)

Hôtel de Libéral-Bruand
(*Musée de la Serrure*—locksmithing)

Hôtel Rohan

Hôtel Salé (*Musée Picasso*)

Le Marais (the northern half)

Musée Carnavalet

Musée du Conservatoire National des Arts et Métiers

Palais de Soubise
(*Archives Nationales—Musée de l'Histoire de France*)

Rue des Gravilliers

Rue des Rosiers (Old Jewish quarter)

St. Nicolas-des-Champs (Abbey)

L'AMI LOUIS ★★★

M. de la Brosse

Address: 32, rue de Vertbois, 75003
Closed: Mon., Tues., July and August
Price Range: Very expensive
Tel: 48-87-77-48
Metro: Temple or Arts-et-Métiers
Credit: All major credit cards

The most illustrious bistro in Paris, drawing a clientele from around the world. The dining room is dark and dingy, the waiters indifferent, but the food is sublime. Extravagant portions with prices to match.

This famous eating place with its little oval mirrors, its iron-legged marble-topped tables and its worn-out Art Deco trompe l'oeil ceramic tile floors was named after the restaurant's original maître d'hôtel, Louis Pedetos. It became the domain of the legendary Antoine Magnin during the 1930s. Magnin, a quiet man who always wore a red scarf tied under his thin white beard, was Paris's most renowned roasting chef, and as his reputation spread, L'Ami Louis became celebrated. When he died a few years ago, three members of the staff continued to manage the place. They have faithfully preserved its picturesqueness, its popularity and its prices. Everything here is superb, but people come for the outrageous slabs of Landes foie gras served with Bayonne ham, the best roast chicken in existence, the marvelous fresh snails, frogs' legs, Breton scallops and, in season, the game with mushrooms. An evening could cost you as much as at Le Taillevent, but here you will have the satisfaction of seeing mink coats tossed overhead to lay against the ancient walls' flaking paint.

RECOMMENDED DISHES

Foie Gras Frais de Landes. Fresh duck foie gras from the Landes region in Gascogne (four large slices).
Escargots de Bourgogne. Vineyard snails in garlic butter.
Confit de Canard Froid. Preserved duck *confit* served cold.
Cèpes Rôtis en Saison. Roasted wild mushrooms available from

fall to early spring.

Gibiers en Saison. Game available from fall through the middle of April.

Coquilles Saint-Jacques à la Provençale. Scallops sautéed with garlic and tomatoes (Oct. to May).

Côte de Veau Grillée à la Crème. Grilled veal chop served with a rich cream sauce.

Pigeon Rôti aux Petits Pois. Roast pigeons with tiny green peas.

Rognon de Veau Grillé à la Crème. Grilled veal kidneys in a rich cream sauce.

Côte de Boeuf Grillée Avec Pommes Allumettes. Grilled ribs of beef with shoestring potatoes (for two).

Poulet Rôti (for two). Roast free-range chicken.

Gigot d'Agneau de Lait Rôti. Roast leg and hindquarter of suckling lamb (Spring only).

Gâteau de Pommes de Terre à l'Ail. Potato cake with garlic and parsley.

Nougatine Glacée. Sweet walnut ice cream.

Wine

Fleurie (House red).
Extensive list of very expensive Burgundies and Bordeaux.

Chez Janou 

Mme. Janou Chauvelot
Mlle. Marie Odile Chauvelot

Address: 2, rue Roger-Verlomme, 75003 (Place des Vosges area)
Closed: Sat., Sun. and holidays
Price Range: Fairly expensive
Tel: 42-72-28-41
Metro: Bastille, Saint-Paul or Chemin-Vert
Credit: Visa

A delightful little oasis just behind the imposing Place des Vosges. Chef Janou and her charming daughter Marie-Odile have preserved the best parts of an authentic 1912 butcher shop-cum-neighborhood café and, with the addition of an outdoor wrap-around terrace, have transformed it into the most pleasant bistro in the Marais.

Since 1976, when Janou took over this space, she engendered in it all the attributes of a homey neighborhood bistro. Lots of green plants, lace café curtains, green-and-white-checked paper cloths mixed with white table linen, multi-colored tile floor, wooden bistro chairs, antique zinc coat racks, and distinctive globe lighting all add to the ambience of the place.

Chef Janou approaches each creation as if guests were visiting her in her home. She excels in uncomplicated, appetizing cold platters that usually consist of either foie gras, pork, rabbit or salmon accompanied by the freshest of garden vegetables or greens. Her signature dish, an open-face *tartine* of lightly-cooked foie gras, is served cold with a dash of fresh pepper. It should be noted that most of the vegetables and salad ingredients are grown in the family's extensive suburban garden. When available, the Jerusalem artichoke *(topinambour)* prepared with a hazelnut dressing is outstanding.

Many desserts are offered, but the rhubarb tart with crème fraîche is a special treat.

Probably because the oversize terrace lends itself to leisurely meals, an unusually large selection of aperitifs and wines are available, including many half-bottles.

RECOMMENDED DISHES

Salade de Pleurotes et Copeaux de Haddock. Salad of oyster mushrooms and shavings of smoked haddock.

Salade au Fromage de Chèvre. Warm goat cheese salad.

Topinambour. Jerusalem artichoke salad, served warm with hazelnut dressing.

Compote de Lapin en Gelée au Porto Blanc. Stewed rabbit, served cold in a jelly of juices and port wine.

Tartines de Foie Gras Cru au Poivre. Open-face *tartine* of slightly-cooked duck liver sprinkled with ground pepper.

Râble de Lapereau et sa Salade. Roast saddle of hare on a bed of greens.

Langue de Boeuf Vinaigrette. Ox tongue in a cold dressing of oil, vinegar, lemon juice, mustard, and seasoning.

Jarret de Veau aux 3 Légumes. Stewed veal shin with garden vegetables.

Saumon Mariné au Gros Sel. Fresh salmon marinated with sea salt.

Baba au Rhum à la Crème et au Coulis. Yeast cakes drenched with rum syrup, served with cream and a puree of berries.

Profiteroles au Miel et Chocolat Amer. Small pastries filled with cream and covered with bitter chocolate syrup and wild honey.

Tarte à la Rhubarbe. Rhubarb tart with lightly-soured cream.

Wine

Bourgueil, Saint-Véran, Brouilly, Morgon.

4e Arrondissement

Baracane "Le Bistrot de L'Oulette"

Benoît

Au Gourmet De L'Isle

Le Grizzli

À L'Impasse (Chez Robert)

Le Trumilou

Le Vieux Bistro

Hôtel-de-Ville

PLACES OF INTEREST

Bastille (July Column)

Cathédral de Notre-Dame (*Musée Notre-Dame*)

Église Saint-Paul—Saint-Louis

Hôtels de Sully, Sens, Beauvais, Lambert, Lauzin, Aumont

Hôtel-de-Ville

Île de la Cité

Île Saint Louis

Le Marais (Southern half)

Musée Victor Hugo

Notre-Dame-des-Blancs-Manteaux

Odéon (*Théâtre de France*)

Place du Marché Sainte-Catherine

Place des Vosges (3e, 4e)

Pont-Marie

Rue Saint-Antoine, Rue des Lions Saint Paul, Rue Pavée

Tour Saints Gervais et Protais

BARACANE "LE BISTROT DE L'OULETTE" 

M. Marcel Baudis
Chef: Frédéric Dupont

Address: 38, rue des Tournelles, 75004 (Place des Vosges area)
Closed: Sat. lunch, and Sun.
Price Range: Inexpensive
Tel: 42-71-43-33
Metro: Bastille or Chemin Vert
Credit: Visa and MasterCard
Remarks: Non-smoking room

L'Oulette *has departed from this location for its new home in the Bercy district and in the process has given up its bistro roots. Fortunately, chef/owner Marcel Baudis left behind the bistro* Baracane *which now must be considered one of the premier restaurants, offering regional cuisine of the Southwest.*

Although M. Baudis still oversees the running of his first understated, narrow little bistro, the actual cooking is in the capable hands of chef Frédéric Dupont who has wisely kept many of the tried-and-true dishes created by Baudis. The little restaurant, just steps from the magnificent Place des Vosges, specializes in the hearty regional specialties of Gascony where duck and fois gras reign supreme. Outstanding are the duck gizzard salad, the grilled duck breast and the famous *cassoulet* of beans loaded with generous chunks of preserved goose. Another perennial favorite is the lentil salad with slices of dried goose breast. The little *carte's* Southwest wines are the only thing to accompany this food and, fortunately, no bottle costs over twenty dollars. One reason for the immense popularity of Bistro Baracane is the ratio of quality to price. A complete dinner, excluding wine, can be had for about fifteen dollars and lunch even less.

RECOMMENDED DISHES

Salade de Foies de Volaille au Xérès. Chicken liver salad enriched with sherry wine.
Salade Quercynoise au Gésiers Confits. Regional salad with pre-

served duck gizzards.

Salade de Lentilles au Magret d'Oie Séché. Lentil salad with slices of dried goose breast.

Foie Gras de Canard Maison Cuit en Terrine. Duck liver, cooked and served in its own cooking dish.

Terrine de Pintade. Guinea hen pâté.

Cassoulet Maison au Confit. Toulousian-style stew with goose confit and beans from Tarbes in the Pyrénées. An outstanding specialty of this bistro.

Magret de Canard Grillé. Grilled duck breast.

Daube de Joue de Boeuf au Vieux Cahors. Beef-cheeks stew slow-cooked in Cahors wine.

Saucisse de Toulouse Faite Maison à l'Aligot. House sausage Toulouse-style served with a mixture of mashed potatoes and cantal cheese.

Filet de Mulet Poêlé à la Fondue de Tomate. Grey mullet pot-roasted with gently cooked tomatoes melted to a pulp.

Cabécou de Rocamadour. Goat's milk cheese.

Glace aux Pruneaux et à l'Armagnac. Prune ice cream drizzled with Armagnac brandy.

Clafoutis Maison. Fruit-filled batter tart.

WINE

Madiran, Tursan, Cahors, Gaillac, Pacherenc du Vic Bihl.

BENOÎT 

M. Michel Petit

Address: 20, rue Saint-Martin, 75004
Closed: Sat., Sun. and August
Price Range: Expensive
Tel: 42-72-25-76
Metro: Châtelet
Credit: None
Remarks: Air-conditioning

A beautiful old bistro opened in 1912 and run today by the grandson of its original owner. You will be charmed by the perfect old-world decor and the superb bourgeois Lyonnais cuisine. This is one of the finest bistros in the city and very popular with Americans. Reservations are essential.

Ignoring all fashions of the time, Benoît has preserved its French character and old-world charm for over three-quarters of a century. A five-minute walk from the Pompidou Center, located on a pedestrian street near the Tour St.-Jacques, the red-and-gold-trimmed awning and polished wooden facade contrast with lush potted evergreens. Inside, the light oak paneling is set off with mirrors, old photographs, brass globe lights, red banquettes and etched-glass wall dividers. A polished marble-topped bar near the entrance is crowded with glistening glasses and bottles. Fresh flowers and potted palms are scattered about. The menu, presented in an old leather frame, lists such famous specialties as salad of beef and brawn, mussel soup, beef with carrots *(boeuf mode),* grilled *boudin* (blood sausage) with apples, calf's tongue with herb sauce, roasted Bresse chicken and the *cassoulet maison.* There is an additional menu of daily specials. Desserts are delicious, with such delights as chocolate *marquise* with coffee-flavored *crème anglaise,* pear tart, apples in light puff pastry with *crème fraîche* and vanilla ice cream flavored with Grand Marnier and served with candied orange slices. The house Beaujolais is an excellent Brouilly.

Recommended Dishes

Saucisson Chaud de Lyon. Hot poached sausage.
Soupe de Moules. Large *terrine* of mussel soup.
Soupe d'étrilles. Cream of crab soup.
Compotiers de Boeuf en Salade à la Parisienne. Beef salad served with a large and varied choice of hors d'oeuvres.
Tartine de Rougets Barbets à la Tapenade. Thick anchovy paste with red mullet shavings served on a thick slice of bread.
Marmite Dieppoise du Pêcheur. Fish and shellfish stew with leeks, white wine and cream.
Boeuf à la Ficelle. Beef, first quickly roasted, then tied with a string and suspended in broth to poach.
Gras-Double. Sautéed ox tripe.
Selle d'Agneau en Rognonnade. Saddle of lamb with kidneys.
Boeuf Mode Braisé à l'Ancienne. Marinated beef braised in Beaujolais wine and served with carrots, mushrooms, turnips

and onions.

Tête de Veau Sauce Ravigote, Avec Langue et Cervelle. Calf's head, brains and tongue in vinaigrette.

Rognon de Veau Entier en Cocotte. Whole veal kidney, pot-roasted in a casserole.

Cassoulet Maison. White-bean-and-meat stew cooked and served in an earthenware pot.

Lièvre à la Royale. Whole boned hare stuffed with foie gras and truffles and braised in red wine and brandy.

Blanquette de Veau à l'Ancienne. Veal stew in a white cream sauce served with white rice.

Boudin Grillé aux Pommes. Large blood sausage served with apples and potatoes.

Feuilletée Chaude aux Pommes Avec Crème Fraîche. Hot puff pastry with apples and slightly soured cream.

Soufflé Glacé au Grand Marnier. Iced soufflé with Grand Marnier brandy.

Mousse au Chocolat. Chocolate mousse.

Marquise au Chocolat. Mousse-like chocolate sponge cake with butter cream filling.

WINE

Chiroubles, Morgon, Brouilly.

AU GOURMET DE L'ISLE ★

M. Jean-Michel Mestivier

Address: 42, rue Saint-Louis-en-l'Île, 75004
Closed: Mon., Tues. and August
Price Range: Moderate
Tel: 43-26-79-27
Metro: Pont-Marie
Credit: Amex and Visa

A very picturesque establishment with a rustic 16th-century dining room and an international clientele. The generous classic dishes are supplemented by a few Auvergnat and Limousin specialties. An in-

teresting selection of "little" country wines is offered at reasonable prices.

M. Jules Bourdeau, a young octogenarian, sold this famous old bistro a few years ago, but nothing has changed since his departure. Reservations are still indispensable; the incomparable *andouillettes "A.A.A.A.A."* are never greasy and still steeped in red wine with pork rinds and served with red beans. The fresh artichokes are accompanied by poached eggs in an herbal sauce, and the *charbonnée de l'Isle* (pork in red wine with bacon, baby onions, croutons and potatoes) is still the winning house specialty. There is now a *prix-fixe* tourist menu at 125F which includes an *entrée,* a main course, salad or cheese, and dessert or ice cream selected from the à la carte menu. The *crème limousine* is a caramel custard in warm chocolate sauce. You will be served by candlelight in a 300-year-old vaulted stone "cave" with hand-hewn beams and tapestries characteristic of the Île-St.-Louis cellars of old.

Recommended Dishes

Fond d'Artichaut Frais Saint-Louis. Fresh hearts of artichoke in vinaigrette.

Boudin de Campagne Pommes Fruits. Large slicing sausage, grilled and served with apple slices.

Moules Farcies Beurre Échalotes. Stuffed mussels in shallot butter.

Oeufs en Meurette. Eggs poached in red-wine sauce.

Tête de Veau Remoulade. Calf's head in a mustard-mayonnaise sauce with chopped *cornichons* and capers.

Faux Filet à l'Échalote. Broiled sirloin steak in shallot sauce.

Ris d'Agneau Braisés au Porto, Epinards. Lamb sweetbreads braised in Port wine, on a bed of spinach.

Cervelle Beurre Fondu et Pommes Vapeur. Brains in melted butter with steamed vegetables.

Charbonnée de l'Isle au Marcillac (Civet de Porc). Grilled pork stew with bacon and onions in a rich wine sauce. The outstanding specialty of the bistro.

Andouillette (A.A.A.A.A.) Rognons de Coq. Grilled pork sausage served with kidney beans in white sauce.

Pintadeau Grillé aux Lentilles Vertes du Puy. Grilled guinea fowl served with small green lentils.

Poires Cuites au Vin. Pears cooked in red wine.

Profiteroles. Ice-cream-filled pastries covered with melted chocolate.

WINE

Very inexpensive little country wines. Gaillac, Marcillac.

LE GRIZZLI

M. Bernard Arény
Chef: Jean-Claude Masson

Address: 7, rue Saint-Martin, 75004 (Les Halles area)
Closed: Sun., and Mon. lunch
Price Range: Fairly expensive
Tel: 48-87-77-56
Metro: Hôtel-de-Ville or Châtelet
Credit: All major credit cards

An authentic turn of the century bistro just a stone's throw from the luxury bistro Beñoit. Revitalized in 1990 by Pyrénées native Bernard Arény, it offers exceptional regional ham, country cheeses, and dishes of the Auvergne.

From the moment you enter this forty-seat restaurant located on a pedestrian mall in the rebuilt Les Halles district, you are exposed to the sights and smells of a genuine old-fashioned bistro. You are greeted by a skilled waiter, hand slicing generous slabs of smoked Auvergne ham at a long zinc service bar. One is keenly aware, by its pungent odor, of the presence of the magnificent overripe farm cheese Saint-Nectaire waiting to be served with chunks of crusty country rye bread.

The bistro operates on two levels with the working kitchen in the cellar. A narrow winding stair leads to the upstairs dining room and dishes are brought up from the basement by dumbwaiter. Basic bistro decor is evident in the cream-colored and mirrored walls, the lace curtains, and forest green moleskin banquettes.

The tempting bistro fare has a few outstanding specialties

demanded by most regulars: the cold ratatouille appetizer topped by a poached egg, the veal shoulder, the wild mushroom stew, the beef cooked *Ardoise*-style on a slate set directly over the flame, the milk-fed baby lamb from the Pyrénées and, for dessert, the hot savory *croustade* filled with prune and doused in Armagnac. A pitcher of wine from the Côtes-du-Marmandais is the perfect accompaniment for this fare.

Recommended Dishes

Jambon Au Couteau. Smoked Auvergne ham.

Ratatouille Froide à L'Oeuf Poché. Stewed provençale vegetables topped with a poached egg.

Salade de Mongettes au Confit. Green been salad with preserved meat.

Assiette de Cochonnailles. Cooked and cured pork specialties served with pickles and mustard.

Saucisson Chaud à la Pistache. Hot sausage flavored with pistachio nuts.

Blanquette D'Agneau à la Tomate. Lamb stew in white cream sauce with cooked tomatoes.

Lapin aux Raisins Secs. Rabbit cooked with prunes and dried raisins.

Confit de Canard, Pommes Sautées à l'Ail. Preserved duck served with sliced potatoes sautéed in oil and garlic.

Agneau de Lait des Pyrénées. Roast milk-fed baby lamb.

Fricot de Veau aux Cèpes Sèches. Veal shoulder stewed with white wine and dried wild mushrooms.

Pièce de Boeuf Cuite sur l'Ardoise. Thick beef steak cooked over the fire on a slate.

Calamars à l'Encre. Squid cooked in its own ink.

Crème Caramel. Vanilla-flavored custard encased in soft caramel.

Croustade Chaude aux Pruneaux à l'Armagnac. Hot pastry filled with prunes (or apples) and flamed with Armagnac brandy.

Flognarde. Thick, sweet jam pancake.

Wine

Côtes du Marmandias (served in a pitcher), Madiran (Chateau de Peyros), Cahors.

À L'IMPASSE (CHEZ ROBERT) 

M. André Collard

Address: 4, Impasse Guéménée, 75044 (off rue St. Antoine, near Place des Vosges)
Closed: Sat. lunch, Sun., Mon. eve. and August
Price Range: Moderate
Tel: 42-72-08-45
Metro: Saint-Paul or Bastille
Credit: Visa

A small, unostentatious family bistro with a most imaginative and refined menu reflecting the best of the market and the season. The clientele is a mix of chic Parisian regulars and American tourists. Reservations are advised in the evening.

Chez Robert is very much a family affair with all the Collards dividing their efforts. "Deedee" is in the kitchen, "Papa" is at the bar and Robert and his wife welcome and serve their guests with unfailing charm. The simple dining room has the look of a hospitable country inn with stone walls, tile floors, wrought-iron sconces, ladderback chairs with rush seats and wooden tables freshly set with white linen. In an adjacent room there are a few more tables and a wooden bar. Considering the remarkably high quality of the food, the prices are quite reasonable. *Blanquette de veau* (veal stew in cream sauce), *chou farci* (stuffed cabbage) and *civet de lapin* (rabbit stewed in wine) are marked as specialties, but everything is good. Among the dozen appetizers are a *terrine* of skate with mint, gazpacho and fresh salmon marinated in dill and lemon. Stuffed fillets of chicken and duck in a bilberry and vinegar sauce make an outstanding main course. The fish, always fresh, is simply prepared but flavorful. There are several desserts, but the *tarte-Tatin* (an upside-down caramelized apple tart, native to the Sologne region and reputedly named for the two sisters who invented it) is delicious.

RECOMMENDED DISHES

Terrine de Girolles. Mushroom mousse served cold.
Terrine de Lapin en Gelée aux Concombres. Rabbit pâté in a

wine-vinegar aspic with cucumbers.

Foie Gras Frais de Canard en Terrine, Maison. Fresh duck liver pâté served in a *terrine.*

Filet de Cabillaud Sur Compotée de Tomate à l'Huile d'Olive et au Basilic. Fresh cod fillet on a bed of stewed tomatoes in olive oil and basil.

Pavé de Volaille aux Myrtilles. Breast of duck and stuffed chicken breasts in a bilberry (similar to blueberry) sauce.

Civet de Lapin. Rich rabbit stew.

Blanquette de Veau à l'Ancienne. Veal stew in a white sauce of cream and egg yolks served with white rice.

Chou Farci. Stuffed cabbage.

Tournedos de Veau à la Crème de Ciboulette. Veal steaks, stuffed with baby vegetables and foie gras, served in a chive-seasoned cream sauce.

Île Flottante à la Fleur d'Oranger. Orange meringue floating in vanilla cream custard.

Tarte-Tatin. Very generous upside-down apple pie.

WINE

Château Bellevue-la-Foret, Côtes-de-Frontonnais.

LE TRUMILOU 

M. Jean-Claude Dumond
Chef: Raymond

Address: 84, Quai de l'Hôtel-de-Ville, 75004
Closed: Monday
Price Range: Moderate
Tel: 42-77-63-98
Metro: Pont-Marie or Hotel-de-Ville
Credit: Visa

There is an old-time Parisian atmosphere in this delightful quayside bistro offering generous helpings of very good home cooking at reasonable prices. Request a window table with a view of the Seine and

Notre-Dame. The sidewalk tables are not recommended because of the traffic.

Located on the *quai* between the Pont d'Arcole and the Pont Louis-Philippe, Trumilou is a pleasant spot for a homespun meal. It is a rather large place with three dining rooms. Two are rustic in decor. The larger of these, crowded with tables and decorated with bucolic scenes, is less cozy than the smaller of the two, which is simply outfitted with banquettes, a crystal chandelier and fresh flowers. The third is a no-frills bar with a pinball machine. No matter where you eat, opt for one of the *prix-fixe* menus. The most expensive one offers a good choice of *entrées,* including pâté, herring, sausages and a delicious *salade Niçoise.* Poultry is a specialty, so there are several excellent selections. A delicious *poulet Provençal* (chicken in tomato sauce) and roast guinea fowl with sautéed potatoes can be recommended. Sautéed lamb is another good choice. In addition to these, the à la carte menu lists three or four fish dishes. Desserts are typical, but the Cantal cheese and coffee ice cream are excellent.

Recommended Dishes

Filets de Hareng. Marinated herring fillets.

Assiette de Cochonnailles. Platter of assorted pork products *(saucisson, rillettes, pâté).*

Moules Marinière. Mussels cooked with wine wine, shallots and parsley.

Crudités. Lavish helpings of fresh raw vegetables.

Pot-au-Feu (Avec Os à Moelle et Légumes). Boiled beef with marrow bones, vegetables and broth.

Étouffade de Boeuf. Beef casserole with vegetables in a wine sauce.

Piperade. Scrambled egg omelette with tomatoes, peppers and onions.

Poulet Provençal. Roast chicken with onions, garlic and tomatoes.

Canard aux Pruneaux. Grilled duck with prunes.

Ris de Veau Grandmère. Sweetbreads cooked with onions, mushrooms and potatoes.

Sauté d'Agneau. Sautéed lamb.

Gigot d'Agneau, Haricots Blancs. Roast leg of lamb with white beans.

Gâteau de Riz Avec Un Sabayon. Rice pudding with fruit *confit,* in an egg-yolk-and-wine mixture.

Pêche Melba. Cold peaches served on ice cream with raspberry purée.

Wine

Saint-Pourcain, Saumur Champigny.

Le Vieux Bistro 

M. Jean Fleury
M. Fernand Fleury

Address: 14, rue du Cloître-Notre-Dame, 75004 (on the Île de la Cité)
Open: Daily
Price Range: Fairly expensive
Tel: 43-54-18-95
Metro: Cité
Credit: Visa
Remarks: Open Sunday

In the shadow of Notre-Dame Cathedral, M. Fleury has managed to maintain the high standards that have made his "old bistro" a popular spot with smart tourists who appreciate fine French food and service.

In an area full of tourist traps and fast-food joints, Le Vieux Bistro, across the street from the great cathedral, is a welcome relief, even if a bit expensive. The smaller front dining room masks the church's dark, imposing walls with delicate lace curtains. The refined atmosphere is carried into the larger back room decorated with mirrors, moleskin banquettes, draperies, provincial chairs and marble tables covered with white linen.

The cooking is basically bourgeois with a well-prepared repertoire of bistro classics like *boeuf bourguignon, blanquette* of veal, beef filet with marrow, veal kidneys in mustard sauce, pike *quenelles,* escargots, frog's legs *provençale* and an especially good duck stew *(civet de canard).* The *tarte-Tatin* flamed with Calvados is widely acclaimed. The impressive cellar favors the burgundies, which are served in oversized tulip-shaped glasses, but a good selection of humbler wines such as a Beaujolais and other *vins courants* are also available.

Recommended Dishes

Pâté de Tête à l'Ancienne. Headcheese served in an earthenware cooking dish.

Escargots. Twelve vineyard snails in garlic butter.

Saucisson Chaud à la Bourguignonne. Large hot slicing sausage accompanied by warm potato salad.

Salade de Magret de Canard Fumé. Smoked duck breast salad.

Onglet aux Échalotes. Flank of beef grilled with shallots.

Gratin Dauphinois. Sliced potatoes baked with cream, sprinkled with cheese and browned under the grill.

Andouillette Duval à la Ficelle, au Sancerre. Pork sausage from *Duval* roasted then steeped in Sancerre wine.

Boeuf Bourguignon. Beef stewed with red wine, onions and mushrooms.

Civet de Canard. Rich duck stew.

Carré d'Agneau à la Provençale. Roast rack of lamb with tomatoes, garlic and onions (for two).

Rognons de Boeuf Sauce Moutarde. Calf kidneys in mustard sauce.

Coeur de Filet à la Moelle en Papillote. Filet mignon baked in a pouch and served in a marrow sauce.

Mignon de Veau aux Champignons, à la Crème. Veal filet in a rich mushroom-cream sauce.

Coquilles St. Jacques, à la Provençale. Scallops sautéed with tomatoes, garlic and onions.

Crème Caramel "Maison." Vanilla-flavored flan.

Tarte-Tatin Flambée au Calvados avec la Crème Fraîche. Upside-down apple pie flamed with Calvados brandy and topped with slightly-sour cream. A specialty of the house.

Wine

Well composed wine list favoring burgundies. Côtes du Rhône, Brouilly, Fleurie, Givry.

5ᵉ Arrondissement

Campagne et Provence

Les Fontaines

Le Languedoc

Moissonnier

Au Moulin à Vent (Chez Henri)

Perraudin

Chez René

La Rôtisserie du Beaujolais

Chez Toutoune

Quartier Latin—Panthéon

PLACES OF INTEREST

Boulevard Saint-Michel (*Place St.-Michel*)

Églises de Saint-Séverin, Saint Étienne-du-Mont, St. Médard et St. Julien-le-Pauvre

Église du Val-de-Grâce

Hôtel le Brun

Institut du Monde Arabe

Le Jardin des Plantes et Muséum National d'Histoire Naturelle

La Mosquée de Paris (The Paris Mosque)

Musée de l'École Superieure des Beaux-Arts

Musée de Sculpture en Plein Air

Musée des Thermes et l'Hôtel de Cluny (The Cluny Museum)

Le Panthéon

Quai de la Tournelle

Rue Mouffetard and Place de la Contrescarpe

La Sorbonne

Campagne et Provence 

M. Gilles Epié
Chef: Alain Gérard

Address: 25, Quai de la Tournelle, 75005 (across the Seine facing the Île Saint-Louis)
Closed: Sat. lunch, and Sun.
Price Range: Fairly expensive
Tel: 43-54-05-17
Metro: Maubert-Mutualité
Credit: Visa and MasterCard
Remarks: Air-conditioning

This country/casual bistro just opposite Notre Dame on the left bank seems a good bet for a Provençal fix when you get the urge.

When famed young Chef Gilles Épie moved his elegant restaurant, Miravile, to a less confining location, he wisely retained this space and installed his talented second Alain Gérard as chef. Together they have created a moderately priced Provençale-inspired menu where one may encounter many of the most popular dishes one would find in Provence and the Riviera including ratatouille, stuffed salt cod *(brandade de morue),* grilled tuna steak, sardines, red mullet, slow-cooked beef stews *(daubes)* and *pieds et paquets* of tripe (tripe cooked in the style of Marseilles).

The decor chosen for this rather small space is intelligently conceived. Deep-hued cream-colored walls are offset by hand-painted sea-blue wooden chairs with straw seats and the room is filled with colorful fresh flowers. This country casualness seems just right as compliment to the cuisine.

Recommended Dishes

Mesclun aux Olives. Mixed salad of baby greens and olives.
Soupe de Moules au Pistou. Mussel soup with basil.
Salade Niçoise. Salad with olives, anchovies and tuna.
Farci de Ratatouille. Stewed eggplant, squash, tomatoes and garlic.
Tian de Daurade. Sea bream and vegetable mixture, cooked and served in an earthenware dish.

Pieds et Paquets à la Marseilles. Mutton tripe rolled into packets and cooked with sheep's trotters.

Brandade de Morue Pimentée. Vegetables stuffed with creamed, peppered salt cod.

Daube de Canard aux Olives. Slow-cooked duck stew.

Lapin à la Tapenade. Rabbit cooked in a thick anchovy paste with capers, olives and tuna.

Farcon de Thon au Parmesan. Grilled tuna steak served on a bed of semolina.

Raviolis de Boeuf en Daube. Slow-cooked stew of meat-filled ravioli.

Rouget à l'Huile d'Olive. Red mullet cooked with olive oil.

Pain Perdu Aux Prunes. French toast with prunes.

Tarte aux Myrtilles. Blueberry tart.

WINE

Côtes-d'Aix, Côtes-de-Provence.

LES FONTAINES

M. Roger Lacipière

Address: 9, rue Soufflot, 75005 (Panthéon area)
Closed: Sun. and August
Price Range: Moderate
Tel: 43-26-42-80
Metro: Luxembourg or Cardinal Lemoine
Credit: Visa
Remarks: Open until midnight.

Don't be deceived by appearances. The neon lights, formica bar, paper tablecloths have all the trappings of a nondescript corner café, but be assured the back-room restaurant serves some of the tastiest and best-prepared quality cuisine to be had in all Paris.

Self-taught Chef Roger Lacipière, a native of the Cantal region of central France, has wide experience in running a bistro. His beautifully-aged grilled steaks are superb, and in the fall and winter the finest game is available. The daily menu, two pages long and written entirely by hand, appeals to both the impoverished student or well-heeled gourmet. He likes to keep both kinds of patrons happy. Each morning, M. Lacipière personally shops in Rongis and has a positive genius for selecting the best quality meats, fish and vegetables. He handles all the cooking chores and his good-humored waiters turn this banal establishment into a culinary joy.

Located just down the street from the Panthéon, at lunchtime Les Fontaines is packed with Sorbonne students, left-bank types and tourists. It turns more sedate in the evening when a leisurely meal may be enjoyed.

Recommended Dishes

Chèvre Chaud sur Salade. Hot goat cheese salad.
Terrine de Foie Gras de Canard Maison. Duck liver pâté.
Terrine de Gibiers. Game pâté.
Céleri Rémoulade. Shredded celery root in spicy mayonnaise.
Pigeonneau Rôti, Sauce Foie Gras. Roasted Bresse pigeon in thickened foie gras sauce.
Civet de Biche Maison. Deer stew thickened with blood.
Belle Entrecôte Poêlée. Pan-fried beef rib steak.
Tête de Veau Gribiche. Pieces of calf's head and tongue, sliced, poached and served in a thick vinaigrette.
Ris de Veau Forestière. Sweetbreads garnished with wild mushrooms, bacon and potatoes.
Côte de Boeuf. Roast ribs of beef (served for two).
Spécialités de Chasse. Outstanding game dishes available seasonally.
Arrière de Lapin Rôti à la Moutard. Whole rabbit back roasted in mustard sauce.
Rognons de Veau Dijonnaise. Veal kidneys in a mustard sauce.
Pavé au Poivre avec Frites. Thick beef steak and peppercorns accompanied by perfect french fries.
Fricassée de Lotte au Curry. Curry-based monkfish stew.
Raie au Câpres. Skate cooked in black butter and capers.
Fricassée de Homard. Lobster stew in white wine and cream.
Filet de Colin aux Pleurotes. Filet of hake fish with oyster mushrooms.
Île Flottante. Spongecake, kirsch and maraschino cherries covered with custard sauce.
Charlotte aux Framboises. Molded ladyfinger dessert with raspberries and custard.

Crème Caramel. Vanilla-flavored custard encased in soft caramel.

Wine

Gamay-de-Touraine, Loire Valley wines.

Le Languedoc ★

M. Pierre Dubois

Address: 64, blvd. de Port-Royal, 75005 (at rue Berthollet)
Closed: Tues., Wed., August, and Dec. 21 through Jan. 5
Price Range: Moderate
Tel: 47-07-24-47
Metro: Gobelins or Port-Royal
Credit: Visa

The delightful country atmosphere and spaciousness of the dining room coupled with some of the most consistent cuisine de ménage (homecooking) *available in Paris makes for the tremendous popularity of this out-of-the-way bistro. It is in great demand from the editors and copy writers of the numerous publishing houses along the blvd. du Port Royal, making reservations imperative.*

Look for the impressive pot-shaped "Le Languedoc" sign out front leading into a large glass-enclosed terrace. Inside, the natural wood dining room is decorated with pretty peach-and-white-checkered café curtains and tablecloths. The roomy tables are surrounded by provençal wicker chairs, a fine wooden bar is alongside the entrance and old-fashioned Chardin prints grace the walls. The simple home-style food includes such entrees as country hams and sausages, herring filets brought to the table (and left there) in a large *terrine* and little *grillons* of preserved, cooked pork and goose bits. The famous *cassoulet* contains generous additions of preserved goose and provence-style frogs' legs are always on the menu.

Recommended Dishes

Jambon d'Auvergne. Cured Auvergne ham.
Filets d'Harengs, Pommes Tièdes. Marinated herring filets served in a large *terrine* with warm potato salad.
Haddock à l'Anglaise. Fried haddock in eggs and breadcrumbs.
Grillons Corréziens. Pork and duck *confit* bits.
Gigot d'Agneau Grillé, Haricots Verts. Grilled leg of lamb with string beans.
Cassoulet au Confit d'Oie. White-bean-and-meat stew with preserved goose, served in an earthenware pot.
Cuisses de Grenouilles à la Provençale. Frogs' legs in tomato sauce with garlic and basil.
Bavette d'Aloyau. Large joint and filet of beef grilled.
Médaillons de Lotte à l'Americaine. Thin round slices of monkfish cooked in a white wine sauce with garlic, shallots and tomatoes.
Pêche Dijonnaise. Peach with black currant sauce.
Mousse au Chocolate Maison. Chocolate mousse.
Clafoutis aux Fruits. Batter fruit tart.
Vacherin Maison. Meringue ring filled with whipped cream, ice cream and fresh berries.

Wine

Vin du Rouergue (house red), Vin Rouge du Tarn, Gaillac.

Moissonnier 

M. Louis Moissonnier

Address: 28, rue des Fossés-Saint-Bernard, 75005
Closed: Sun. eve, Mon. and August
Price Range: Fairly expensive
Tel: 43-29-87-65
Metro: Cardinal-Lemoine or Jussieu
Credit: Visa and MasterCard
Remarks: Non-smoking room

Widely known, very popular, family-run bistro with down-to-earth, substantial, old-fashioned food inspired by Lyonnaise cuisine.

Appearing in every guidebook and "best" list, Moissonnier is well known for its copious portions of partly Lyonnaise, partly traditional food. A large menu (the one in English is not as complete as the one in French) begins with *les saladiers Lyonnais* at 60F per person. The *saladier* is a rolling cart of hors d'oeuvres consisting of large bowls of lentils, kidney beans, pickled calf's feet, sausages, *museau* (beef brawn), red cabbage, herring, *rillettes, rosettes,* white sausages and cold beef in salad. Following this, a long list of choices includes such favorites as beef with a sweet onion sauce *(boeuf miroton),* grilled pigs' feet with red kidney beans, tripe, steak, salt pork with lentils, chicken in raspberry vinegar and several freshly made desserts. The atmosphere downstairs is gay with a typical bistro ambience and decor: a zinc bar at the entrance, elbow-to-elbow tables, little chairs, banquettes, fresh flowers and pleasant lighting. Upstairs is hot, noisy and smoky, decorated with tacky fake-white-brick walls, wine kegs, and bright lights. Don't expect fabulous food, but you will certainly eat well in picturesque surroundings.

Recommended Dishes

Saladiers Lyonnais. Choice of a dozen fish, meat and vegetable salads brought to the table in large bowls.

Rosette de Lyon. Large dry pork sausage, sliced and eaten cold.

Saucisson Chaud Pommes à l'Huile. Hot Lyon sausage with sliced potatoes in oil.

Oeufs en Meurette. Poached eggs in red-wine sauce.

Quenelles de Brochet. Pike dumplings in cream sauce.

Pieds de Porc Panés, Grillés aux Haricots Rouges. Grilled breaded pigs' feet with red kidney beans.

Civet de Lapin aux Pâtes Fraîches. Rabbit stew in a thickened wine sauce served with fresh noodles.

Petit Salé aux Lentilles. Pickled pork simmered in garlic, onions and herbs accompanied by lentils.

Boeuf Miroton. Slices of beef in broth with onions and mustard.

Gras-Double Sauté Lyonnaise. Ox tripe sliced and fried with onions, vinegar and parsley.

Tablier de Sapeur Sauce Gribiche. Breaded ox tripe served with spicy mayonnaise sauce.

Andouillette au Vin Blanc et Échalotes. Grilled pork sausage with white wine and shallots.
Boudin Noir. Large grilled blood sausage.
Mousse au Chocolat aux Zestes d'Oranges. Chocolate mousse with orange rind.
Gâteau de Riz. Rice pudding.

WINE

Wines available by the pitcher: Macon Villages Blanc, Arbois Blanc, Saint-Nicolas-de-Bourgueil, Brouilly, Morgon, Arbois Rouge.

AU MOULIN À VENT (CHEZ HENRI) ★ ★

M. Gerard & Mme. Josette Gelaude

Address: 20, rue des Fosses-Saint-Bernard, 75005
Closed: Sun., Mon. and August
Price Range: Fairly expensive
Tel: 43-54-99-37
Metro: Cardinal-Lemoine or Jussieu
Credit: Visa

An authentic old-time neighborhood wine bistro specializing in beef and Beaujolais. It is widely known and very popular, so reservations are suggested.

The mill which gives this restaurant its name stands on one of the rolling hills of the Beaujolais vineyards. Moulin-à-Vent, a deeply colored red wine, is the most prestigious of the crus from the region. At Chez Henri the wine-bar decor hasn't been changed in years and the original zinc counter still sports little half-barrel wine kegs to match the half-barrel overhead lights. The handwritten *carte,* with specials marked in red, begins with a few salads, Burgundy snails, foie gras, many sausages including a selection from the Ardèche and the famous house Provençal frogs' legs. Huge cuts of steak and a hefty *boeuf bourguignon* are the favored main courses, but there are also a few veal, duck and lamb selections. Desserts like *tarte-Tatin,* chocolate *charlotte* and *île flottante* are typical, but the prunes stewed in Armagnac are special and a fruity Berthillon sherbet is always refreshing.

Recommended Dishes

Foie Gras de Canard Maison. Fresh duck foie gras.

Andouillette Grillée au Vin Blanc. Pork sausage grilled with white wine.

Escargots de Bourgogne. Vineyard snails in garlic butter.

Jambonnette de l'Ardéche, Pommes à l'Huile. Dried salt pork sausage shaped like a ham, served with sliced potatoes in oil.

Cochonnailles au Poids. Assorted pork sausages, priced according to weight.

Salade aux Haricots Verts et Champignons Crus. String bean and raw-mushroom salad in vinaigrette.

Grenouilles Fraîches Sautées à la Provençale *(October to May).* Sautéed frogs' legs with tomatoes, garlic and onions.

Coquilles St.-Jacques Fraîches à la Provençale *(October to May).* Scallops sautéed with tomatoes, garlic and onions.

Boeuf Bourguignon. Beef stewed in red wine with onions and mushrooms.

Le Boeuf Saignant "Dit à la Ficelle." Beef lightly roasted, then tied with string and lowered into simmering broth. Served rare.

Côte de Boeuf Bourguignonne *(for two).* Roast ribs of beef.

Châteaubriand, Entrecôte, Faux-Filet. Several outstanding varieties of superb-quality beef cuts.

Sole Meunière. Filet of sole sautéed in butter with parsley and lemon juice.

Tarte-Tatin Chaude. Upside-down apple pie served hot.

Gâteau de Riz Crème à l'Anglaise. Rice pudding in vanilla custard sauce.

Glace Pruneaux à l'Armagnac. Prune ice cream drizzled with Armagnac.

Wine

Vast selection of top-quality Beaujolais. St.-Amour.

PERRAUDIN ★

M. Hubert Gloaguen
Mme. Marie-Christine Kvella

Address: 157, rue Saint-Jacques, 75005
Closed: Sun., Sat. and Mon. lunch, two weeks in August
Price Range: Inexpensive
Tel: 46-33-15-75
Metro: Luxembourg or Odéon
Credit: None

Simple good-quality food in an authentic bistro atmosphere frequented by a mixed clientele of regulars, tourists and yuppies. Sunday brunch is served, after which you may choose to walk up to the Panthéon where such notables as Victor Hugo, Louis Braille and Zola are laid to rest.

Herbert Gloaguen, the new *patron* (who also owns Bistrot d'André in the 15e), and his sister, Marie-Christine Kvella, continue to run this popular old Sorbonne haunt in the style of the past. An old barroom with bistro brownish-red-and-cream walls, dark wood and tile floor is brightened by mirrors, posters and lace doilies draped over hanging lights. The large zinc bar is adorned with fresh flowers and the tables set with red-and-white cloths covered with paper. *Entrées,* which include salads, eggs, ham, quiches and soup, range in the evening from 16F to 25F unless you choose a dozen very good Burgundy snails. The *plats* from 45F to 60F include simple meats, sausages, poultry and poached salmon. A salad, string beans or *frites* are extra, and *crème fraîche,* for a supplement of 5F, is a nice accompaniment to the typical desserts. A *dégustation* menu of wines keeps the bar busy and the 68F Sunday brunch menu includes fresh-squeezed juice, toast, bacon, pancakes and eggs.

Hubert Gloaguen operates two other recommendable bistros, Bistro d'André 232, rue Saint-Charles, 75015 tel: 45-57-89-14 and Le Keryado, a bistro specializing in Bouillabaise (32, rue Regnault, 75013 tel: 45-83-87-58).

Recommended Dishes

Escargots Vrais de Bourgogne. Vineyard snails in garlic butter.
Quiche Lorraine de Mamie. Custard tart with bacon, eggs and cream.
Rollmops et sa Crème Fouettée et Citronnée. Marinated, rolled herring fillets with thick cream.
Tarte à l'Oignon Maison. Onion tart as found in Alsace.
Oeufs Cocotte à la Crème et au Bacon. Eggs in custard cups with cream and bacon.
Gigot d'Agneau et Gratin Dauphinois. Roast leg of lamb with sliced potatoes, baked in cream and browned on top.
Navarin. Lamb stew.
Boeuf Bourguignon à l'Ancienne. Beef stewed in red wine with onions and mushrooms.
Petit Salé. Lightly salted cooked pork.
Andouillette de Vouvray, Sauce Moutarde et Pommes Frites. Grilled pork sausage with Vouvray wine served in a mustard sauce with french fries.
Brandade de Morue. Creamed salt cod.
Tranche de Saumon à l'Orseille. Thick slice of salmon in sorrel sauce.
Compote de Pommes du Jardin. Stewed apples.
Crème Caramel à l'Orange. Vanilla-and-orange-flavored flan.
Tarte-Tatin Maison. Caramelized upside-down apple pie.

Wine

Cahors de Domaine, Saint Amour, Sauvignon Blanc.

Chez René 

M. Jean-Paul & Mme. Jacqueline Cinquin

Address: 14, blvd. Saint-Germain, 75005
Closed: Sat., Sun., August and Christmas week
Price Range: Moderate
Tel: 43-54-30-23
Metro: Cardinal-Lemoine

Credit: Visa
Remarks: Non-smoking room

A steady clientele frequents this unpretentious old bistro which has been serving copious portions of straightforward Burgundian specialties and wine for decades.

On warm nights a few sidewalk tables are set under the light-blue awning of Chez René, which spans the corner at Blvd. Saint-Germain and Quai Saint-Bernard. The atmosphere is engaging as waiters in long aprons open bottles of the house Chénas and Juliénas to accompany hearty portions of parslied ham, burgundian snails, frogs' legs, pike dumplings, eggs in red-wine sauce, hot sausages, red meats, beef stews, *coq-au-vin* and an excellent steak in *Bercy* butter with *frites*. There are brass rails above the moleskin banquettes, simple wooden bistro chairs and tables, each set with a pepper mill and mustard jar, scattered about the linoleum floors of the unpretentious dining room. Prints, posters and paintings add a cheerful note to the darkening cream-colored walls. A small bar faces the entrance and the owners are always ready with a warm and friendly welcome.

RECOMMENDED DISHES

PLATS DU JOUR

Pot-au-Feu *(Mondays).* Boiled beef with vegetables and broth.

Haricot de Mouton *(Tuesdays).* Mutton stew with white beans.

Gras-Double *(Wednesdays).* Ox tripe, sliced and fried with onions, vinegar and parsley.

Boeuf à la Mode *(Thursdays).* Braised beef simmered in red wine with vegetables.

Blanquette de Veau *(Fridays).* Veal stew in white cream sauce, served with white rice.

Assiette de Cochonnailles. Assorted pork products.

Saucisson Chaud Pommes à l'Huile. Hot sausage with sliced potatoes in oil.

Gratin de Blettes. Swiss chard crusted with grated cheese and browned bread crumbs.

Quenelles de Brochet à la Crème. Pike dumplings in butter cream sauce.

Coq au Vin. Chicken stewed in red wine with onions and mushrooms.

Cuisses de Grenouilles à la Provençale. Sautéed frogs' legs with tomatoes, garlic and onions.

Boeuf Bourguignon. Beef stewed in red Burgundy wine with onions and mushrooms. The outstanding specialty of the bistro.
Entrecôte Bercy Pommes Sautées. Sautéed rib steak in a shallot-and-bone-marrow sauce served with sautéed potatoes.
Andouillette au Pouilly. Grilled pork sausage in white Burgundy wine.
Plateau de Fromages. Top-quality cheese platter.
Crème Caramel. Vanilla-flavored flan.
Gâteau de Riz Maison. Rice pudding with fruit *confit.*
Mousse au Chocolat. Chocolate mousse.

WINE

Extensive selection of first-rate Beaujolais. Chénas, Juliénas.

LA RÔTISSERIE DU BEAUJOLAIS 

M. Alain Robert

Address: 19, Quai de la Tournelle, 75005
Closed: Mon.
Price Range: Moderate
Tel: 43-54-17-47
Metro: Maubert-Mutualité or Cardinal-Lemoine
Credit: Visa
Remarks: Non-smoking room

Run by Alain Robert, but the brainchild of Claude Terrail, this stylish new bistro is located across the street from its most famous sister, La Tour d'Argent, and has developed a winning formula: a splendid list of Beaujolais wines, a small menu of well-prepared Lyonnais sausages and enticing rotisserie meats and poultry, all at very good prices.

Whether you choose a sidewalk table in the glass-enclosed terrace with a view of Notre-Dame, the barroom to the left of the entrance, or the dining room to the right, you will need to book ahead as this popular spot is usually filled with an upscale crowd.

Begin with the house *kir* made with Macon wine and select one of the daily specials listed on a large blackboard. You will find things like roast pigeon or quail, veal chops, saddle of lamb, grilled Lyonnais sausages or chicken stewed in Beaujolais wine. Fresh cheese and delicious fruit tarts are also enjoyable.

Recommended Dishes

Saucisson Chaud, Beurre. Little hot sausages served with sliced potatoes in oil and bread and butter.

Foie Gras de Canard. Fresh duck foie gras.

Filets de Hareng, Pommes à l'Huile. Marinated herring fillets accompanied by potatoes in oil.

Caille Rôti. Quail roasted on the spit.

Pigeonneau de la Bresse aux Petits Pois. Bresse squab roasted on the spit and served with tiny peas.

Piece d'Agneau Rôti. Lamb roasted on the spit.

Andouillette Grillée (A.A.A.A.A.) Sauce Moutarde. Grilled pork sausage with mustard sauce.

Sabodet Rôti au Beaujolais. Grilled pigs'-head sausage from the top-rated House of Bobosse, served hot in slices.

Coq-au-Vin du Beaujolais. Chicken stewed in Beaujolais wine with carrots and boiled potato.

Sandré Braisé à l'Oseille. Pike-perch cooked over the coals with sorrel.

Filet de Dorade en Bouillabaise. Fillet of red sea bream in a hearty Provençal fish soup.

Crème Caramel. Vanilla-flavored flan.

Mousse au Chocolat. Chocolate mousse.

Savarin aux Fruits. Cake ring drenched with brandy and filled with fruits.

Wine

Featuring all the Duboeuf Beaujolais crus.

CHEZ TOUTOUNE ★★★

Mme. Colette Dejean
Chef: Marc Baudry

Address: 5, rue de Pontoise, 75005 (midway between blvd. St. Germain and Quai de la Tournelle)
Closed: Sun., Mon. lunch
Price Range: Fairly expensive
Tel: 43-26-56-81
Metro: Maubert-Mutualité
Credit: Visa, MasterCard and Amex

A small, crowded, cheerful little bistro serving giant-sized portions of country-style cuisine with a light Provençal touch. Everything is freshly prepared, and based on market availability. The new chef has expanded the menu with many imaginative dishes.

Mme. Colette Dejean, better known as "Toutoune," has created a landmark in the 5e *arrondissement* with her popular country restaurant and home-style cooking. There are no reservations accepted, but regulars line up to claim one of the 50 or so places in the brightly lit dining room crowded with tables. Eclectic artwork and posters decorate the white-plaster walls along with café curtains, a blackboard menu, red-and-white cloths and napkins providing a young and gay ambience. The *prix-fixe* menu begins with a large *soupière* steaming with the soup of the day (all you can eat) followed by a large choice of *entrées,* including a superb duck *terrine.* Main courses of beef, lamb, veal, rabbit, tripe and duck are accompanied by freshly baked baguettes and fresh noodles. There is a takeout shop, Toutoune Gourmande, located at 7, Rue de Pontoise, carrying many of her best products.

RECOMMENDED DISHES

Soupière Chaude ou Froide. Warm or cold soup tureen.
Bulots à l'Aïoli. Sea snails with garlic mayonnaise.
Mille-Feuille de Tomates, Mozzarella au Basilic. Puff pastry with tomatoes, mozzarella cheese and basil.
Foie Gras Frais des Landes au Vin de Muscat. Fresh Landes *foie gras* served with a glass of sweet white wine.

Fricassée d'Escargots à la Catalane. Snail stew with tomatoes, garlic and onions.

Rôti de Roussette à la Coriandre. Roast rock salmon with coriander.

Pintadeau Fermier à la Citronnelle. Roast farm guinea fowl made with lemon liqueur.

Mille-Feuille de Veau de Lait et Aubergines. Roast suckling calf in puff pastry with eggplant.

Pieds de Veau aux Lentilles. Grilled stuffed calf's foot served on a *beignet* (fritter) with lentils.

Estouffade Provençale. Meat stewed in a sealed pot with tomatoes, garlic and *aubergines* (eggplant).

Agneau de Pré Salé au Gratin Dauphinois. Roast leg of lamb (pastured in salt fields) served with sliced potatoes cooked in cream and browned on top.

Tête de Veau aux Légumes Vinaigrette aux Herbs. Calf's head served hot with baby vegetables in vinaigrette.

Andouillette. Superb-quality grilled pork sausage.

Dos de Saumon au Sarrasin. Salmon cooked in buckwheat flour.

Feuilletée de Pommes Tièdes. Hot apple puff pastry.

Crêpes Fines au Pralin d'Amandes. Thin pancake with praline of toasted almonds.

Nougat Glacé aux Épices. Nougat ice cream with spices.

Wine

Minervois, Sancerre, Gamay Rouge de Touraine. Bordeaux "Reserve Toutoune."

6e Arrondissement

Allard
Bistro de la Grille
Le Bistrot D'Henri
Le Caméléon
Aux Charpentiers
Joséphine (Chez Dumonet)
Chez Maître Paul
Chez Marie
Marie et Fils
Le Petit Zinc
Polidor
Restaurant des Beaux-Arts
La Rôtisserie d'en Face

Saint-Germain—Luxembourg

PLACES OF INTEREST

Boulevard Saint-Germain, Place St.-Germain,
and the *Église Saint-Germain-des-Prés*
École des Beaux-Arts and *l'Hôtel de Conti*
Église Saint-Sulpice (*Delacroix* mural)
Fontaine des Medicis
Hôtel des Monnaies (the mint)
Institut de France
Jardin et Palais du Luxembourg (*Musée Luxembourg*)
Musée de la Poste
Musée Zadkine
Place Furstenberg (*Atelier Eugène Delacroix*)
Place de l'Odéon
Quais Malaquais-de-Conti and *Grands-Augustins*
Rue de Rennes
Rues de Seines, St.-Andres-des-Arts, Buci, Jacob

or to hang out in the evening with friends for conversation, people-watching and decent food.

Located in the heart of Saint-Germain-des-Prés, Bistro de la Grille is a few steps from all the major sights and some of the most interesting galleries, bookstores, and trendy boutiques in all of Paris. This neighborhood spot was once a *Jacobin* rendezvous and still lists as one of the most popular meeting places in the most action-filled part of the city. While the food is not elaborate, it neverthless is quite good and if you stick to the basic bistro classics, can even be exceptional. An added plus is the fresh seafood bar serving moderately-priced selections of oysters, clams, mussels, snails and crawfish. The *plats* most worth pursuing are the *pot-au-feu,* the *daube de boeuf,* the *tête de veau,* the *civet de canard,* the *Lyonnais saucisson* and the large Burgundy snails. The most striking feature of this place, aside from the walls covered with photos of early film stars, is the big, beautiful bar on the ground floor where a meal may be had. The restaurant however, is located upstairs on the *première étage.* Here it is more sedate, with tables covered in pretty plastic cloths printed with Provençal designs adding to the gaiety and liveliness of the place. One can have a three-course meal for 100F at lunch or 150F for dinner, but our advice is to choose one main course *à la carte* or a large platter of assorted shellfish.

Recommended Dishes

Escargots de Bourgogne. A dozen vineyard snails in garlic butter.

L'Os à Moelle sur Pain Campagnard. Bone marrow spread served with country bread.

L'Assiette des Saucissons Secs de Lyon. Platter of dry Lyonnais sausages.

Tête de Veau et sa Sauce Gribiche. Head of veal in a mustard-mayonnaise sauce with capers.

Plateau de Fruits de Mer "Maison." Large platter of assorted shellfish.

Daube au Vieux Vin Rouge. Slow-simmered beef stew with reduced red vintage wine.

Traditionnel Pot-au-Feu de Boeuf à la Moelle. Boiled beef with vegetables, bone marrow and broth.

Saucisson Chaud de Lyon, Pommes Vin Blanc. Lyonnais sausage served with hot potato salad.

Civet de Canard au Vieux Vin Rouge. Duck stewed in vintage red wine.

Hachis Parmentier et la Salade Paysanne. Meat and potato casserole (shepherd's pie) accompanied by a peasant-style salad.
Escalope de Saumon aux Champignons Sauvages. Thin slice of salmon with wild mushrooms.
Tarte-Tatin. Caramelized upside-down apple pie.
Gateau de Riz, Raisins de Corinthe. Rice pudding with raisins in custard.

WINE

Chateau Haut-Larose (Bordeaux), Sancerre Blanc, Beaujolais de Notre Vigneron, Chinon, Saumur Champigny, Gamay.

LE BISTROT D'HENRI ★

M. Henri Poulat

Address: 16, rue Princesse, 75006
Closed: Sun., Mon. lunch
Price Range: Moderate
Tel: 46-33-51-12
Metro: Mabillon
Credit: All major credit cards

A modest place with no sign on the white facade to indicate its presence. The atmosphere is relaxed and the cuisine skillfully prepared by owner-chef M. Henri Poulat.

This bright restaurant on pretty little Rue Princesse is very much a neighborhood favorite. Crowded tables fill the tiny dining room, gaily decorated with an amusing modern fresco. A long window in the rear opens onto the kitchen and a small bar serves as a waiter's station and cashier's desk. The *carte,* written on file cards, lists about a half-dozen *entrées* and eight main courses. The *entrées* include hot goat cheese salad, mozzarella with tomatoes, country ham, *terrine* and Corréze sausage. The next line on the *carte* reads *GRATIN DAUPHINOIS avec: romsteck* followed by calf's liver with onions, duck with peaches, free-range chicken in vinegar sauce and a lamb stew Moroccan-style. Desserts change each day, but there is always *patisserie* and a splendid fruit compote.

A delightful tiny annex, Le Mâchon d'Henri, is located just around the corner (8, rue Guisarde, tel. 43-29-08-70) serving quintessential Lyonnais bistro fare.

Recommended Dishes

Assiette de Jambon de Campagne. Platter of cured and smoked country ham.
Os à Moelle. Bone marrow spread, served with toasted slabs of country bread.
Saucisse Sèche de Corrèze. Poached country sausage.
Pavé de Coeur de Romsteck Avec Gratin Dauphinoise. Thick piece of grilled rumpsteak served with sliced potatoes baked in cream and browned on top.
Foie de Veau Confiture d'Oignons. Grilled calf's liver on a bed of onion preserves.
Gigot Rôti au Four. Roast leg of lamb.
Veritable Poulet Fermier au Vinaigre. Roast free-range chicken in a vinegar sauce.
Rognons de Veau de Lait Nature. Grilled lamb kidneys.
Crème Caramel. Vanilla-flavored flan.
Compote Grandmère. Stewed apples and pears.
Mousse au Chocolat. Chocolate mousse.

Wine

Saumur-Champigny, Beaujolais.

Le Caméléon 

M. Raymond Faucher
Mme. Jacqueline Faucher

Address: 6, rue de Chevreuse, 75006 (off blvd. du Montparnasse)
Closed: Sun., Mon. and August
Price Range: Moderate

Tel: 43-20-63-43
Metro: Vavin
Credit: None

The cuisine is basically bistro, but every item on the menu is prepared with originality and imagination. Listen to the owner's advice before ordering one of the Loire wines.

A bar, old-fashioned flowery wallpaper, multicolored tile floors, marble tables, high-backed wooden booths, brass wall lights, pastel drawings and dozens of photographs provide a vibrant setting for some interesting food. Both traditional and more inventive dishes are prepared by chef Thierry Thibault. Fresh pâté, poached oysters in a red-wine butter sauce with mushrooms and a superb shredded oxtail salad with chicory are some of the marvelous starters.

Salt cod is a specialty and served in several ways: cold in a vinaigrette, *à la Provençale* with a bold *aoïli,* or simply with a fresh-tomato-and-herb sauce. There is duck *confit* with roasted potatoes and sorrel sauce, veal in tomato sauce with noodles and breast of chicken with a sweet and sharp green-pepper sauce. Everything is done with a certain flair. Desserts are delicious and, if it's on the menu, you might like to try the tea soufflé in a cool mint sauce.

Recommended Dishes

Salade de Queue de Boeuf Tiède. Shredded oxtail salad. One of the specialties of the bistro.

Cochonnailles. Selection of first-quality pork products.

Pâté de Campagne. Coarse country pâté.

Frisée aux Lardons. Chicory salad with bacon.

Salade d'Haricots Verts, Foie Gras. Fresh string bean salad with foie gras.

Terrine de Courgettes aux Poivrons. Baby zucchini and sweet peppers presented in an earthenware dish.

Terrine de Langoustines aux Mousserons. Melange of crawfish and small white-and-yellow wild mushrooms.

Tendron de Veau aux Pâtes Fraîches. Stew made from the cartilage-filled rib meat of veal, accompanied by fresh pasta. The other outstanding specialty of the bistro.

Boeuf en Daube. Beef braised in red wine with vegetables, slow simmered and served in an earthenware pot.

Saucisse de Campagne Maison. Large country pork sausage.
Hachis Parmentier. Minced-meat Shepherd's pie.
Sauté d'Agneau à la Menthe Fraîche. Lamb sautéed with fresh mint.
Morue Provençale en Aïoli. Creamed salt cod with garlic mayonnaise.
Poêlée de Turbot aux Aubergines. Pot-roasted turbot on a bed of eggplant.
Foie de Canard Maison au Bonnezeaux. Duck livers cooked in a sweet white wine from Anjou.
Bavette du Boucher. Skirt steak served butcher's style with bone marrow.
Crème Caramel. Vanilla-flavored flan.
Mousse au Chocolat Blanc. White-chocolate mousse.
Tarte-Tatin. Upside-down apple pie.
Crème Brûlée au Citron Vert. Rich custard dessert topped with caramelized sugar and fresh lime.
Fondant au Poires. Pear cake from a recipe of M. Faucher's grandmother.

WINE

Saumur-Champigny, Sancerre, Chinon, Gamay d'Anjou, St. Nicolas de Bourgueil

AUX CHARPENTIERS 

M. Pierre Bardèche
Mme. Colette Bardèche

Address: 10, rue Mabillon, 75006 (close to the church of St. Sulpice)
Closed: Sun. and between Christmas and New Year's
Price Range: Moderate
Tel: 43-26-30-05
Metro: Mabillon, St.-Sulpice or St.-Germain-des-Prés
Credit: All major credit cards
Remarks: Non-smoking room

Historically a carpenters' canteen, today a b.c.b.g. *(*"bon chic, bon genre"*—i.e., Yuppie) hangout, but still serving solid plates of bourgeois cuisine with an emphasis on meat. Drinks are dispensed from behind the long old-fashioned zinc bar in authentic bistro style.*

Aux Charpentiers is one of the best-known and popular Saint-Germain-des-Prés bistros with a long and colorful history. The carpenters for which it is named formed an organization of "companions" dating back to the medieval guilds. The members—master carpenters and cabinetmakers—made the restaurant their rendezvous. Today there is no trace of them left in the area except in the two large dining rooms here, which are decorated with prints and photographs commemorating those days. Located steps away from the lovely Square and Church of St.-Sulpice, the bistro continues to thrive, serving the traditional *plats du jour* for which it is famous. With a few new salads, *ratatouille* and gazpacho added to the *entrées,* and only one or two fish specialties, the *carte* offers basic, uncomplicated food with good, but rather expensive, wine.

The Bardèche family operates a fish bistro/restaurant called L'Écaille de PCB located just across the street (5, rue Mabillon, tel. 43-26-73-70). It is highly recommended for oysters, lobsters and expertly-prepared fish dishes.

Recommended Dishes

PLATS DU JOUR

***Sauté de Veau** (Mondays).* Pan-fried veal.

***Boeuf Mode aux Carrottes** (Tuesdays).* Braised beef simmered in red wine with carrots.

***Petit Salé aux Lentilles** (Wednesdays).* Lightly salted cooked pork.

***Jarret de Veau et Ses Legumes** (Thursdays).* Veal knuckle served with a garnish of vegetables.

***Aïoli de Morue et Ses Legumes** (Fridays).* Creamed salt cod with garlic mayonnaise and vegetables.

***Chou Farci Campagnard** (Saturdays).* Stuffed cabbage.

Fromage de Tête aux Echalotes. Headcheese with shallot sauce.

Salade de Chèvre Chaud. Hot-goat-cheese salad.

Foie Gras de Canard Frais Maison et Son Verre de Sauternes. Fresh duck foie gras accompanied by a glass of Sauternes.

Boeuf à la Ficelle. Beef, slightly roasted, tied with a string and lowered to poach in broth with vegetables.

Boeuf en Daube. Braised beef with vegetables slow-simmered and served in an earthenware pot.
Pied de Porc Ste. Ménéhould. Pigs' feet grilled in bread crumbs.
***Côtes de Boeuf** (for two).* Roast ribs of beef.
Andouillette de Troyes à la Ficelle. Poached pork sausage.
Boudin. Large blood sausage.
Caneton Rôti, Sauce Olives et Porto. Roast duckling in a port-wine sauce with olives.
Mousse au Chocolat. Chocolate mousse.
Tarte Pralinée aux Poires. Pear tart with almonds.

WINE

Vins de Bordeaux, Côtes-du-Rhône, Vins de Loire.

JOSÉPHINE (CHEZ DUMONET) 

M. Jean-Dominic Dumonet
Chef: Jean-Christian Dumonet

Address: 117, rue du Cherche-Midi, 75006
Closed: Sat., Sun., July and Christmas week
Price Range: Expensive
Tel: 45-48-52-40
Metro: Falguière
Credit: Visa and MasterCard

A perfect neighborhood eatery featuring superb foie gras, fresh seafood that arrives daily from Normandy, extraordinary wines and an authentic Parisian bistro atmosphere. In season, the truffle adds its subtle flavor to many dishes: truffles in puff pastry with eggs, shredded over fresh foie gras or in a ragoût *with Champagne sauce.*

Otherwise known as Chez Dumonet after its proprietor, M. Jean Dumonet, this charming family restaurant is amazingly unspoiled by its popularity. The long, bright dining room is sectioned into three distinct areas by etched-glass-and-wood dividers. There is a long bar at the entrance, tastefully decorated with a huge floral arrangement echoed by fresh flowers set on each table. Old tile floors, blond-oak paneling, beveled mirrors and cream-colored walls covered with nautical prints, posters and paintings complete the simple decor. The meal begins with an *amuse-bouche,* followed by wonderful *terrines,* stuffed mushrooms, artichoke hearts with fresh vegetables, sliced duck breast with mustard sauce, flaky sole in a smoky butter sauce, or grilled foie gras. Desserts are also delicious, and a light *millefeuille* or a Grand Marnier soufflé may be enjoyed by two people if ordered before dinner.

A rotisserie-style bistro annex is just next door serving moderately-priced dishes (La Rôtisserie Chez Dumonet, 117, rue du Cherche-Midi, 75006, tel. 42-22-81-19). The spit-roasted leg of lamb is a stand-out.

Recommended Dishes

Jambon des Landes. Cured and mildly smoked Landes ham.

Foie Gras de Canard Frais. Fresh duck foie gras served in a variety of ways: "natural" with black truffles, "block" with raisins, garnished with sorrel or grilled with artichoke or celery.

Pied de Veau Vinaigrette. Slices of calf's foot in a spicy vinaigrette.

Compote de Lapin Champenoise. Hot rabbit *terrine.*

Boeuf Bourguignon aux Nouilles Fraîches. Beef stewed in red wine, onions and mushrooms served with fresh noodles.

Navarin d'Agneau. Lamb stew with potatoes and onions.

Gigot d'Agneau Duranton aux Haricots Blancs *(Wednesday lunch).* Roast leg of lamb with white beans.

Tournedos Rossini. Heart of the beef fillet grilled with truffles.

Andouillette Truffée Feuillitée. Grilled and truffled pork sausage in a puff pastry.

Cassoulet. Meat-and-white-bean casserole with sausages, pork, garlic and preserved goose.

Confit de Canard. Preserved duck seasoned with duck fat and served with sautéed potatoes.

Ris de Veau aux Morilles. Braised sweetbreads with wild mushrooms.

Gigot de Lotte à l'Ail en Chemise. Encased monkfish cooked in a garlicky white-wine-and-cream sauce.

Turbot Grillé Béarnaise. Grilled turbot with a hollandaise sauce of shallots, tarragon and white wine.

Tarte Fine Chaud aux Pommes. Hot, thin apple tart.

Suprème au Chocolat Albertine. Brioche hollowed-out and filled with chocolate sauce.

***Soufflé au Grand Marnier** (for two).* Light, puffy whipped egg dessert flavored with Grand Marnier brandy.

Millefeuille Jean-Louis. Thin layers of puff pastry sandwiched with cream and preserves (for two).

WINE

Beaujolais and a superb selection of Bordeaux wines—one of the richest in Paris.

CHEZ MAÎTRE PAUL 

M. Jean-François Debert

Address: 12, rue Monsieur-le-Prince, 75006
Closed: Sat. lunch, and Sun.
Price Range: Fairly expensive
Tel: 43-54-74-59
Metro: Odéon or Luxembourg
Credit: All major credit cards

After a recent change of ownership the bistro received a much needed enlargement and face lift but the delectable regional food and wine from the Jura and Françhe-Comté remained the same.

Jean-François welcomes a clientele of regulars and connoisseurs to his refined and comfortable newly-remodeled restaurant, a short walk from the Odéon. For thirty-five years the tiny kitchen has been turning out generous portions of specialties made with regional products and wines. You might like to try the *saucisse de Montbéliard,* a grilled cumin-flecked pork sausage served with potatoes and garnished with parsley and a dash of vinegar, followed by either the *ris de veau au vin de paille* (calf's liver in a straw wine) or *poulet au vin jaune* (chicken in a rich wine sauce with mushrooms and tomatoes). There is a marvelous fish stew *(marlotte d'anguilles au vin d'Arbois)* and *sandre* (pike-perch) in a heady wine sauce with garlic, shallots and cream. There are two dining rooms, but you will have to call in advance to reserve one of the well-spaced tables on the ground floor elegantly set with fresh linens, flowers and crystal ware. A special word about the wines of the *Jura* served at Chez Maître Paul: they are rarely found outside their region and all are distinctive and full of character, particularly Vin Jaune and Vin de Paille. One of the world's greatest wines, Château-Chalons can also be found here.

Recommended Dishes

Jambon Cuit du Jura. Cooked Jura ham.

Escargots au Vin d'Arbois. Snails in a Jura-wine sauce.

Saucisse de Montbéliard Chaud, Pommes à l'Huile. Grilled cumin-flavored sausage with sliced potatoes in oil.

Cochonnailles. Excellent-quality pork products (*rosettes, terrines, jambon, saucisses,* etc.).

Saumon Sauvage Beurre Blanc. Wild salmon cooked in a white-wine-butter sauce.

Filet de Sole au Château Chalon. Fillet of sole cooked in a white-wine sauce.

Filets de Sandre à la Comtoise. Fried pike-perch fillets.

Foie de Veau au Vin de Paille. Grilled calf's liver cooked in a Jura-wine sauce.

Poulet au Vin Jaune. Chicken cooked with mushrooms, tomatos and white Jura wine.

***Entrecôte à la Vigne Ronne** (for two).* Rib steak cooked with grapes and *marc* (brandy).

Plateau de Fromages. Outstanding selection of regional cheeses *(Cancoillote, Comté, Vacherin, Morbier).*

Gâteau aux Noix. Walnut cake.

Tarte aux Pommes. Apple tart.

Wine

Arbois/Pupillin, Château-Chalons, Vin Jaune, Vin de Paille (dessert wine).

CHEZ MARIE 

M. Bertrand Destreman
Mme. Marie Bouillé

Address: 25, rue Servandoni, 75006 (Palais du Luxembourg area)
Closed: Sat. lunch, Sun., and August
Price Range: Moderate
Tel: 46-33-12-06
Metro: Saint-Sulpice
Credit: Visa and MasterCard

An upscale clientele of publishers, film stars, politicians and other branché *types frequents this charming Left Bank bistro serving classic, old-fashioned food, seasonally fresh and delicious.*

On the corner of rue Vaugirard, facing the Luxembourg Palace, Marie Bouillé graciously welcomes fashionable guests to her little place, now one of the most popular spots in the area. The simple decor has a delightful turn-of-the-century elegance with a gleaming zinc bar, graying mirrors, spotless tile floors, old posters, and numerous souvenirs of the past. Small ceiling fixtures provide light during lunch and are replaced by candles in the evening. The menu changes each month, but favorite dishes such as pan-fried snails, scallops with endives or watercress, veal sweetbreads and kidneys, the *gâteau au chocolat* (chocolate cake), or frosted walnut cake can usually be found. An excellent menu at 160 francs (thirty dollars) includes a choice among three entrées, three main courses and three desserts. The wine list has a good selection of minor *crus* from Bordeaux.

RECOMMENDED DISHES

Rillettes de Saumon au Poivre Vert. Minced preserved salmon spread with green peppercorns.

Marinière de Moules et Purée de Poivrons. Mussels cooked with shallots, white wine and herbs on a bed of mashed peppers.

Oeufs Coque à la Purée de Morilles. Boiled eggs set in a puree of wild mushrooms.

Fricassée d'Escargots aux Pleurotes. Creamed stew of snails and oyster mushrooms.

Salade de Boudin au Noix. Walnut-studded sausage salad.
Navarin d'Agneau. Lamb stew with potatoes and onions.
Magret de Canard aux Figues Fraîches. Fattened duck breast with fresh figs.
Filet de Boeuf, Sauce aux Girolles. Filet of beef in a wine sauce with wild mushrooms.
Mignon de Veau à la Crème d'Estragon. Veal filets in cream sauce with tarragon.
Gigue de Chevreuil, Sauce Grand Veneur. Haunch of young deer in a highly-seasoned brown game sauce with currant jelly.
Poëlade de Ris de Veau aux Pleurotes. Pot-roasted sweetbreads with oyster mushrooms.
Raie au Beurre de Câpres. Skate in black butter sauce with capers.
Saint-Jacques au Beurre de Mandrine et Brocolis. Scallops cooked with orange butter accompanied by broccoli.
Crème Brûlée. Cream custard topped with caramelized brown sugar.
Gâteau au Noix. Walnut torte.
Mousse Noisette Sauce Caramel. Chilled hazelnut mousse with caramel sauce.

WINE

Sancerre, Ménétou-Salon, Brouilly, Chiroubles, Bordeaux wines.

MARIE ET FILS 

Mme. Marie Steinberg
M. Guillaume Barclay

Address: 34, rue Mazarine, 75006 (at blvd. Saint-Germain)
Closed: Sun., and Mon. lunch
Price Range: Moderate
Tel: 43-26-69-49
Metro: Odéon
Credit: All major credit cards

Soupe de Potiron à la Crème. Creamed pumpkin soup.
Pintade aux Lardons et aux Choux. Guinea fowl with bacon and braised cabbage.
Blanquette de Veau au Riz. Veal stew in white sauce with white rice.
Poule-au-Pot Sauce Supréme. Stuffed chicken with vegetables in a creamy sauce.
Boeuf Bourguignon. Beef stewed in red wine with tiny onions and mushrooms.
Ragoût de Porc Mijoté à l'Ancienne. Slow-simmered pork stew.
Sauté d'Agneau aux Flageolets *(Thursdays).* Pan-fried lamb with small green kidney beans.
Lapin à la Moutarde *(Saturdays).* Rabbit in mustard sauce.
Petit Salé aux Lentilles *(Tuesdays).* Lightly salted cooked pork with lentils.
Tripes à la Mode de Caen. Tripe with kidney fat, cider, calf's feet and Calvados simmered in a heavy casserole, served steaming hot with boiled potatoes.
Baba au Rhum Avec Crème Anglaise. Yeast cake drenched with rum syrup and served in vanilla custard sauce.
Gâteau de Riz aux Raisins de Smyrne. Rice pudding with raisins in egg custard.

WINE

Beaujolais Villages, Cahors, Sancerre, Côtes-du-Rhône, Château Magondeau.

RESTAURANT DES BEAUX-ARTS ★

M. Laurent Bargeau

Address: 11 rue Bonaparte, 75006 (at rue des Beaux Arts)
Open: Daily all year
Price Range: Inexpensive
Tel: 43-26-92-64
Metro: Saint-Germain-des-Prés
Credit: None
Remarks: Air-conditioning, non-smoking room

One of the best-known and least expensive bistros in Paris, this is a famous old Saint-Germain-des-Prés hangout across the street from the École des Beaux Arts. The enormous prix-fixe menu at 79F offers virtually every bistro dish in the book plus spaghetti bolognaise and a vegetarian plate. Cheese or dessert, a quart of red wine, and service are also included.

Talented *cuisinier* Laurent Bargeau directs this ancient art-student eatery which is almost in its original *fin de siècle* condition with a picturesque art nouveau entrance, a beautiful curved bar, and murky wall paintings executed by the Beaux-Arts professors and students. The two-level restaurant contains several cozy little dining rooms. Opt for the two on the main floor where the best view of the open kitchen, art work, and fascinating people watching can be had. Quick and friendly service is performed by waitresses in black garb who dish out immense portions of classic *bourgeois* dishes set out on white tablecloths. Of particular note is the legendary *pot-au-feu os à moelle,* the authentic *confit de canard aux cèpes, pommes sarladaises* and one of the most generous *tarte-Tatins* with *crème fraîche* to be had in town. One must not forget the perfectly grilled meats accompanied by mountains of *frites.*

Recommended Dishes

Assortiment de Charcuteries. Assorted pork products platter.
Douzaine d'Escargots. A dozen snails in garlic butter.
Omelette aux Cèpes. Three-egg omelette with wild mushrooms.
Soupe de Poisson Maison. Shellfish and fish soup.
Sardines Grillées. Grilled sardines.
Cuisses de Grenouilles à la Provençale. Frogs' legs in a rich tomato sauce with garlic and basil.
Confit de Canard aux Cèpes, Pommes Sarladaises. Preserved duck leg with sautéed wild mushrooms and baked, sliced potatoes with truffles.
Hachis Parmentier. Minced meat and potato hash (shepherd's pie).
Navarin d'Agneau. Brown lamb stew with potatoes and onions.
Pot-au-Feu avec Os à Moelle. Boiled beef with vegetables, marrow bones, and broth.
Coq-au-Vin. Chicken stewed in wine.
Filet de Boeuf Grillé avec Frites. Grilled beef fillet served with french fries.
Boeuf Bourguignon. Beef stewed in red wine with tiny onions and mushrooms.

Saumon Grillée ou Poché Sauce Béarnaise. Piece of salmon either grilled or poached and served with a hollandaise.
Filet de Lotte au Poivre Vert. Monkfish fillet in a green pepper sauce.
Tarte-Tatin à la Crème Fraîche. Caramelized upside-down apple pie.
Mont-Blanc. Puree of sweetened chestnuts and whipped cream, served with white cheese.

WINE

Muscadet Sur Lie, Cahors, Côtes de Blaye, Beaujolais Villages, Saint-Nicolas-de-Bourgueil.

LA RÔTISSERIE D'EN FACE 

M. Jacques Cagna

Address: 2, rue Christine, 75006
Closed: Sat. lunch, Sun.
Price Range: Moderate
Tel: 43-26-40-98
Metro: Odéon or Saint-Michel
Credit: Visa or MasterCard
Remarks: Air-conditioning

Just across the street from Jacques Cagna's famous two-starred restaurant, this first of two rôtisserie-style bistros was opened in January 1992 and has become immensely popular, attracting a young, knowledgeable, Left Bank following.

A variety of meats and poultry grilled on an open rôtisserie are what draws the crowds for the daily 7:30 P.M. or 9:30 P.M. seating to this uncluttered, modern-style bistro. The dish of choice is the spit-roasted free-range chicken served with mashed potatoes, but lamb, pork, duck, beef and sausages are also tastefully roasted on the spit. For those who prefer a more traditional meal, three fish dishes and several meat and poultry plates are nicely done in or on the stove, each accompanied by all the usual garnishes. The price of the three-course fixed-price menu is about thirty dollars without wine. The bottled wines tend to be pricey, but there is an unusually varied selection of well-priced half bottles.

A large but narrow dining room with peach-colored walls adorned by attractive animal prints, flowered window curtains, brick-tile floors, plush-bottomed chairs, indirect lighting, and a long bar where meals may be served, lend a distinctly homey yet modern-looking ambience to the restaurant.

A second bistro, "La Rôtisserie d'Armaille (6, rue d'Armaille, 75017, Tel: 42-27-19-20), was opened by Chef Cagna in November 1992 featuring a similar, but slightly more expensive, fixed-price menu.

Recommended Dishes

Pâté en Croûte de Canard au Foie Gras. Duck pâté in a pastry case.

La Petite Friture d'Éperlans, Sauce Tartare. Fried smelts with tartar sauce.

Raviolis de Petits Escargots et Champignons en Bouillon d'Herbes. Little pasta packets filled with snails and mushrooms.

Coquelet Grillé, Sauce Diable. Grilled cockerel in a "hot" wine and vinegar sauce.

Joues de Cochon aux Carottes et Pommes Fondantes. Pigs' cheek stew, a recipe of Jacques Cagna's mother.

Selle d'Agneau au Thym, Gratin Dauphinois. Spit-roasted saddle of lamb and scalloped potatoes.

Poulet Fermier de Challans, Purée de Pommes de Terre. Spit-roasted farm chicken, mashed potatoes, served for two.

Maquereau Grillé. Grilled mackerel.

Saumon d'Écosse Grillé. Grilled Scotch salmon.

Clafoutis de Banane et Noix de Coco. Banana and coconut batter-tart.

Vacherin Glacé au Caramel et Noix. Ice cream meringue with caramel sauce and nuts.

Tarte Alsacienne Tiède aux Pommes. Hot apple and custard tart.

Wine

Varied wine list includes seven whites and fifteen reds. We suggest the "Vins du Mois" as the most interesting.

7e Arrondissement

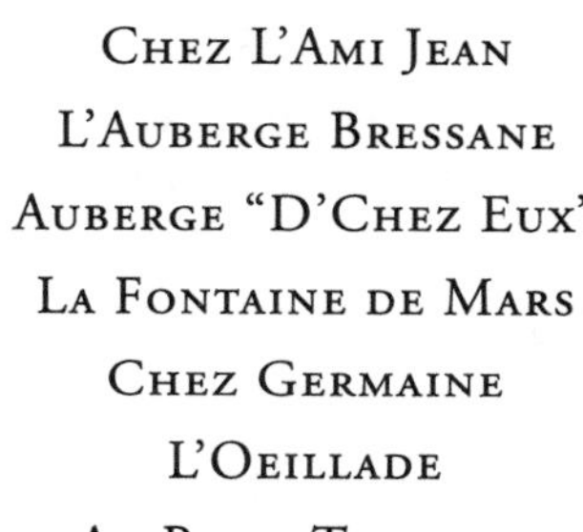

Chez L'Ami Jean

L'Auberge Bressane

Auberge "D'Chez Eux"

La Fontaine de Mars

Chez Germaine

L'Oeillade

Au Petit Tonneau

Au Pied de Fouet

Thoumieux

Tour-Eiffel

PLACES OF INTEREST

Égouts de Paris (Paris sewer tours leave from the *Place de la Résistance*)

Hotel Biron (*Musée Rodin*)

Invalides, Tombeau de Napoléan and the *Musée de l'Armée*

Musée d'Orsay

Palais Bourbon

Pont Alexandre III (7e, 8e)

Pont d'Iena

Rue du Bac

Tour Eiffel, Champs-de-Mars and the *École Militaire*

Chez l'Ami Jean ★

M. Pierre Paqueguy

Address: 27, rue Malar, 75007 (off rue Saint Dominique)
Closed: Sun. and August
Price Range: Inexpensive
Tel: 47-05-86-89
Metro: La Tour—Maubourg or Invalides
Credit: Visa

Opened in 1931 as a Basque restaurant, this popular neighborhood spot continues to provide a good selection of regional specialties and wines. The cooking is still basically Basque, but not exclusively, so many traditional bistro plats *are included on the menu.*

This rustic little bistro is filled with Basque sports memorabilia, in particular from the world of rugby. The walls are covered with team pictures, trophies, banners and all manner of mementos. The sports theme is carried over into the bar area, where central casting has skillfully placed wonderful old characters noisily extolling the virtues of this or that rugby team. The cuisine is unpretentious but l'Ami Jean does serve some truly Basque dishes, practically impossible to find outside the region. Most outstanding is the spicy Béarn vegetable soup *garbure,* the paella, the tiny squid with tomatoes *(chipirons)* and of course the Basque scrambled eggs, *piperade,* which comes with cured Bayonne ham. The perfect wine to go with this hearty fare is red Irouléguy. With an alcohol level of 14%, this wine is full of fruit and has that spicy *goût du terroir* which complements the food, including the egg dishes. Save room for either the *crème caramel* or the *gâteau Basque,* a marvelously rich cream-filled cake. After the meal stroll down to the nearby Seine and across the lovely Pont de l'Alma.

Recommended Dishes

Jambon de Bayonne. Cured Bayonne ham.
Anchois Frais Marinés. Marinated anchovies, served cold.
***Garbure** (dinner only).* Béarn vegetable soup served in an earthenware *toupin.*
Bloc de Foie Gras de Canard. Fresh duck foie gras.

Terrine de Lapin au Foie de Canard. Rabbit and duck liver pâté.

Piperade. Basque omelette with tomatoes, peppers and onions. Served with sliced Bayonne ham.

Poulet Basquaise. Chicken cooked with tomatoes, peppers, *chorizo* (sausage), mushrooms and red wine.

Confit de Canard des Landes, Pommes Sarladaises. Grilled preserved duck served with sliced sautéed potatoes and truffles.

Paëlla Valenciana *(dinner only).* Chicken, seafood and sausage mélange cooked with rice and saffron.

Chipirons à la Basquaise. Tiny stuffed squid (calamaries) stewed in their own ink with tomatoes.

Coq-au-Vin du Chef. Chicken stewed in red wine with onions and mushrooms.

Escalope de Veau "Ami Jean." Veal chop in cream sauce *gratinée* (browned on top).

Pot-au-Feu. Boiled beef with vegetables and broth.

Crème Caramel. Vanilla-flavored flan. Reputed to be the best in Paris.

Mousse au Chocolat. Chocolate mousse.

Mystère Flambé à l'Izarra. Ice cream dessert flamed with Izarra, a Chartreuse-like liqueur made in Bayonne.

WINE

Muscadet, Madiran, Cahors, Irouléguy.

L'AUBERGE BRESSANE

M. Jérôme Dumant
M. Stéphane Dumant

Address: 16, avenue de la Motte-Picquet, 75007 (Les Invalides area)
Closed: Sat. lunch, Sun., and first 3 weeks of August
Price Range: Fairly expensive
Tel: 47-05-98-37
Metro: Tour-Maubourg
Credit: Visa and MasterCard

Remarks: Air-conditioning

Presided over by Mme. Chollet for more than forty years, this charming Burgundian inn, plucked from the hills of Beaujolais, was taken over in 1993 by two brothers in their early thirties. Within a year they were awarded the prestigious honor "Bistro of the Month" by Gault-Millau.

Forget nouvelle cuisine, forget *chichi* precious atmosphere, forget expensive meals with tiny portions, forget stuffy overbearing waiters. The two young brothers who, fortunately for us, retrieved this country inn do absolute wonders with the rich regional food of Burgundy. The charcuterie arrives straight from Lyon, the snails from the vineyards of Burgundy, the cheeses from the premier house of Martie Cantin and the wines, of course, from Burgundy and Beaujolais where they are selected first-hand by Jerome and Stephane. Three remarkable dishes can be singled out among many: the *poulet fermier aux morilles,* the Bresse chicken in cream sauce brimming with flavorful *morille* mushrooms; the *quenelles de brochet gratinées comme à nantua,* a classic execution of pike dumplings garnished with a rich puree of crayfish tails and truffles, and the incomparable rendition of *coq au vin* made here with the finest Juliénas wine. Top off your meal with a Cognac Moyet and coffee and we guarantee perfect contentment.

Recommended Dishes

Fonds d'Artichaut en Salad. Salad of artichoke bottoms.

Terrine de Campagne à la Mode de l'Auberge. Garlicky country terrine.

Escalopes de Foie Gras Chaud. Thin slices of foie gras served hot.

Pissenlits aux Lardons, Oeuf Poché. Dandelion salad with bacon and a poached egg.

Le Plat des Cochonailles du Beaujolais. Assorted sausages, pâtés and pork products.

Beignets d'Escargots de Bourgogne. Burgundy snails in fritters.

Filet de Boeuf des Vignerons à la Moelle. Large cut of beef filet with bone marrow sauce.

Cuisses de Grenouilles Sautées en Persillade. Frog legs sautéed and garnished with chopped parsley and shallots.

Andouillette au Vin Blanc de Macon. Grilled pork sausage in white burgundy.

Rognons de Veau à la Moutarde. Veal kidneys in mustard sauce.

Poulet Fermier à la Crème aux Morilles et Pommes Pont-Neuf. Free-range chicken in a creamy sauce with morel mushrooms and classic fries.

Coq au Vin Comme à Julienas. Chicken stewed in Beaujolais wine.

Quenelles de Brochet Gratinées Comme à Nantua. Pike dumplings with a sauce of crayfish tails and truffles.

Saumon Grillé, Sauce Béarnaise. Grilled salmon in a sauce made of egg yolks, shallots, butter and white wine.

Clafoutis aux Cerises. Deep-dish batter cake with cherries.

Fromage Blanc au Coulis. Fruit puree in cream cheese.

Plateau de Fromages. Selection of cheeses from the house of Martie Cantin.

WINE

Coteaux du Lyonnais (Duboeuf), Beaujolais. Extensive list of Bordeaux and Burgundy wines. High quality and expensive.

AUBERGE "D'CHEZ EUX" 

M. Jean Pierre Court

Address: 2, Avenue de Lowendal, 75007 (behind Les Invalides)
Closed: Sun. and August
Price Range: Expensive
Tel: 47-05-52-55
Metro: École-Militaire
Credit: All major credit cards
Remarks: Air-conditioning, non-smoking section

An unpretentious family-style restaurant/bistro in the wealthy residential École Militaire quarter serving solid middle-class dishes and specialties of the Southwest.

It is imperative that this restaurant be approached with an empty stomach since the old-fashioned servings are famous for their richness and generosity. It is not uncommon for customers to make an entire meal out of the abundant and varied *mélangerie de cochonailles* featuring assorted hams, sausages, rillettes, terrines and pâtés, or the *chariot des salads* containing at least twenty mouthwatering combinations. Other house favorites include the goose foie gras accompanied by an excellent sweet Bordeaux wine, the cassoulet with its *confit,* the roasted free-range chicken with morel mushrooms, the grilled ribs of beef served for two, or the molded *timbale* of monkfish and salmon flavored with saffron.

The auberge-styled bistro is entered through a large covered terrace with charming little booths. Inside, the two spacious dining rooms are filled with well-spaced tables set out with red-checked tableclothes and a few burgundy-colored velour banquettes.

This impressive family-run establishment is an ideal place to visit with a few hungry and lively friends.

Recommended Dishes

Mélangerie de Cochonnailles d'Chez Eux. Abundant selection of pork products.

Chariot des Salades. Vast assortment of meat, seafood and vegetable salads.

Jambon de Bayonne. Authentic Béarn smoked ham from the Basque country.

Bisque de Crustaces. Thick cream soup of crabs, lobsters and shrimp served from an iron kettle.

Foie Gras d'Oie à l'Ancienne. Goose liver served cold accompanied by a glass of Château Loubens, a sweet wine of Bordeaux.

Cuisses de Grenouilles Provençales. Frogs' legs prepared with garlic, tomatoes and olive oil.

Poulet au Pot et Ses Legumes. Classically prepared chicken in a pot with carrots, leeks and consommé.

Poulet Fermier aux Morilles. Roasted free-range chicken with wild morel mushrooms.

Cassoulet au Confit d'Oie. White bean casserole with preserved goose.

Carré d'Agneau de Lait Rôti avec le Farcon Savoyard. Roast rack of milk-fed lamb accompanied by a baked potato cake.

Côte de Boeuf Grillée. Roast ribs of beef, served for two.

Boudin Noir, Pommes Fruits. Grilled blood sausage with apple.

Timbale de Lotte et de Saumon Safranée. Round mold of salmon and monkfish flavored with saffron.
Notre Bonne Glace à la Vanille. Homemade vanilla ice cream.
Farandole de Desserts. Assorted desserts wheeled out on the chariot.

WINE

Chinon (d'Olga Raffaut), Sancerre Blanc and Rosé (Archambault), Chiroubles (d'André Meziat), Cahors (Château La Gineste).

LA FONTAINE DE MARS

M. Jacques Boudon
Mme. Christiane Boudon

Address: 129 rue Saint-Dominique, 75007 (off Avenue Bosquet)
Closed: Sun.
Price Range: Inexpensive
Tel: 47-05-46-44
Metro: École-Militaire
Credit: Visa and MasterCard
Remarks: Non-smoking room

An old neighborhood eatery, convenient to the Eiffel Tower, with checkered tablecloths, zinc bar, lace café curtains, beveled mirrors and long banquettes, serving well-prepared southwestern cuisine at very reasonable prices. Honored by Claude Lebey in 1994 as "Best Bistrot of the Year."

After sixty years Paul and Andrée Launay sold their picture-perfect little bistro to a young couple from the Pyrénées who refurbished the dining rooms leaving all the wonderful kitchen bric-a-brac. The revamped menu includes an array of tempting regional specialties. Try to eat at one of the windows or on the little terrace facing a fountain constructed by Beauvallet between 1806 and 1809. The bas-relief represents the goddess Hygeia giving drink to the god Mars. This is still an ideal place for early dinner, as service begins at 7:30 P.M. and continues until 11 P.M. Most knowing customers drink the full-bodied Cahors from the Domaine de la Bergerie as accompaniment to the genuine Ardoise cassoulet filled with duck *confit* or a perfectly grilled thick steak. Upon request, delicious sliced potatoes sautéed in duck fat *(pommes rissolées à la graisse de canard)* make a wonderful side dish. The holdover finisher, *mystère au chocolat chaud,* is still the dessert of choice.

RECOMMENDED DISHES

Escargots de Bourgogne. Vineyard snails with garlic butter.

Assiette de Cochonnailles de Laguiole. Assorted pork products from Aveyron.

Filets de Maquereaux au Vin Blanc. Marinated mackerel fillets served cold.

Oeufs en Meurette. Poached eggs in red wine sauce.

Foie Gras de Canard au Sauternes. Duck liver accompanied by a glass of sauternes.

Tête de Veau Gribiche. Boiled calf's head in a mustard-mayonnaise sauce with capers, herbs and finely-chopped hard-boiled eggs.

Cassoulet au Confit du Canard. Languedoc stew with white beans, pork, sausage and preserved duck.

Pavé du Boucher Grillé. Thick slice of grilled beef steak.

Boudin aux Pommes Fruits. Large blood sausage served with warm sliced apples.

Poulet Fermier aux Morilles. Roast free-range chicken with morel mushrooms.

Gigot d'Agneau, Flageolets. Roast leg of lamb with baby lima beans.

Confit de Canard, Pommes Sarladaises. Grilled preserved duck leg and thigh accompanied by baked, sliced potatoes with truffles.

Filets de Rouget au Beurre d'Épices. Fillets of red mullet in herb butter.

Mystère au Chocolat Chaud. Vanilla ice cream in meringue topped with hot chocolate sauce and nuts.

Tarte aux Pommes. Puree of apple tart topped with thin glazed apple slices.

Wine

Cahors (Domaine de la Bergerie), Madiran (Château Bouscassé), Vin du Pays d'Oc (l'Enclos d'Ormessor), blanc et rosé.

Chez Germaine ★

Mme. Ingrid Blakeley

Address: 30, rue de Pierre-Leroux, 75007 (off rue de Sèvres)
Closed: Sat. dinner, Sun. and August
Price Range: Inexpensive
Tel: 42-73-28-34
Metro: Vaneau or Duroc
Credit: None
Remarks: No smoking

A tiny, very inexpensive and unpretentious place in an upscale neighborhood close to the Bon Marché department store. Freshly-made desserts, two or three daily specials, items from the grill, plus a dozen-or-so entrees are served in a cozy kitchen atmosphere.

The new owner Ingrid Blakeley took over this totally plain bistro from Germaine Babkine in 1993, and to the delight of everyone has not missed a beat. She still offers a 60F (twelve dollar) three-course meal, including a small carafe of wine, consisting of a small choice of simple, well-prepared bistro dishes such as ground pike dumplings, grilled calf's liver or stuffed tomatoes. The line starts to form for lunch around 11:45 A.M. and by 6:30 P.M. for dinner. Once the clients have squeezed into any available seat at the seven oilcloth-covered tables the doors are shut. If you are one of the lucky ones, prepare for a fine home-style meal at some of the lowest restaurant prices in Paris. No smoking is allowed in the dining room and, to discourage lingering, coffee is not served, but you will be treated to generous portions of steaming hot food, always well prepared. Enjoy sautéed wild rabbit with cornmeal porridge (polenta), creamed veal stew over white rice *(blanquette)* or roasted minced pork *(palette)* accompanied by french fries, to name a few. The dessert selection has expanded since Germaine's departure but her signature dish, warm apple *clafoutis* with thick cream, is still the most sought after.

Recommended Dishes

Terrine du Chef aux Champignons. Country pâté with wild mushrooms.
Tomate Monégasque. Tomato stuffed with tuna and hard-boiled eggs.
Blancs de Poireaux Vinaigrette. Stewed leaks in a vinaigrette dressing.
Potage. Thick hearty soup, served at dinner only.
Bourguignon de Boeuf. Beef stewed with red wine, onions and mushrooms.
Palette de Porc Rôti, Pommes Frites. Roast "palette" of pork with french fries.
Blanquette de Veau à l'Ancienne. Veal stewed in a white sauce with onions and mushrooms.
Pot-au-Feu Garni. Boiled beef with vegetables and broth.
Chateaubriand Grillé, Purée. Choicest fillet of beef served with whipped potatoes.
Lapin Sauté Chasseur Polenta. Sautéed wild rabbit over polenta.
Brandade de Morue. Creamed salt cod.
Quenelles de Brochet, Riz. Pike dumplings with rice.
Clafoutis aux Pommes Maison avec Crème. Custard batter-tart with apples and whipped cream.
Crème Caramel Maison. Caramel custard flan.
Gâteau de Riz aux Écorces d'Orange, Crème Anglaise. Rice pudding cake with orange peels.

Wine

Cuvée du Patron rouge, Côtes du Rhône rouge, Cahors, Rosé du Pays d'Oc.

L'OEILLADE ★★★★

Chef/Owner Jean-Louis Huclin
M. Pascal Molto

Address: 10, rue de Saint-Simon, 75007
Closed: Sat. lunch, Sun., and last two weeks in August
Price Range: Moderate
Tel: 42-22-01-60
Metro: Rue du Bac or Solférino
Credit: Visa and MasterCard
Remarks: Air-conditioning

A cramped and noisy Left Bank bistro guided by skilled and good-humored owners and offering a quality-for-price ratio unsurpassed in Paris.

This simple little bistro, situated on a quiet street in the vicinity of the tumultuous intersection where rue du Bac and boulevards St. Germain and Raspail converge, has become, in very short order, one of the most popular in Paris and is always under great pressure from foreign visitors for reservations.

The great draw here is an extraordinary three-course, 155F (about $25) fixed-price menu (slightly higher for the extra cheese course). There is an unparalleled selection of more than thirty choices prepared by a master chef and served in enormous portions. These beautifully presented classics of the bistro repertoire include shoulder of roast lamb, veal shank, thick steaks, roast chicken, *coq au vin*, fillet of sole, *brandade de morue,* and many more. In addition, there are many extras such as the hefty *terrine* passed from table to table, the excellent bread supplied by boutique baker Beauvallat and the dark, slightly tart chocolates served with coffee.

This delightful bistro should be on everyone's list. Our only advice is to go early and often.

RECOMMENDED DISHES

Caillettes de l'Ardèche. Tiny quail from Ardèche, stuffed with foie gras and baked like a pâté.

Fromage de Tête. Chopped pigs' head in jelly.

Aubergine en Rougail au Citron. Eggplant cooked with a spicy seasoning as used in Creole dishes.

Tian de Courgettes à la Provençale. Zucchini baked and served in a shallow earthenware dish.

Foie Gras Fait Maison. Exemplary fresh duck foie gras.

Civet de Lapereau aux Olives et Basilic. Rabbit stew with olives and sweet basil.

Foie de Veau au Vinaigre de Miel. Grilled calf's liver in honey vinegar.

Épaule d'Agneau Farcie. Boned and stuffed shoulder of lamb.

Jarret de Veau. Grilled veal shank.

Faux Filet Grille, Maître d'Hôtel. Grilled sirloin steak topped with a sauce of butter, lemon juice, parsley, salt, and pepper.

Poulet Rôti Fermier. Roasted free-range chicken.

Coq-au-Vin. Chicken stewed in wine sauce.

Filet of Sole Belle Meuniere. Fillet of Dover sole fried in butter and served with brown butter, lemon juice and parsley.

Brandade de Morue. Creamed salt cod.

Crème Brulée à la Cassonade. Rich custard dessert topped with caramelized brown sugar.

Mousse au Chocolat. Chocolate, egg yolks and sugar beat to mousse consistency.

Oeufs à la Neige, Crème Anglaise. Poached egg whites served with a vanilla custard sauce.

WINE

Bordeaux (Réserve de l'Oeillade), Vins de Pays de l'Ardèche, Bergerac.

AU PETIT TONNEAU 

Mme. Ginette Boyer

Address: 20, rue Surcouf, 75007 (off rue Saint Dominique)
Closed: Sunday
Price Range: Fairly expensive
Tel: 47-05-09-01
Metro: Invalides or Latour-Maubourg

Credit: All major credit cards.

One of the best-kept secrets of Paris is this extraordinary old-fashioned bistro offering one of the best examples of cuisine de femme.

In 1979 Owner/Chef Ginette Boyer took over this circa-1910 bistro and was shortly thereafter awarded the "Table de Maigret" —rarely, if ever, given to a woman. This award symbolizes excellence in the preparation of hearty, abundant bistro cuisine. Her authentic restaurant is entered through a dark lacquered wood-and-glass exterior revealing two intimate dining rooms with a dozen small linen-covered tables, bent-wood bistro chairs, a lovely little wooden bar, contrasting blue-and-brown floor tiles, and profuse fresh flower displays.

All of Chef Boyer's dishes are famous for flavor and she is unexcelled in the use of mushrooms. Her signature dish, *fricassée de champignons sauvages,* a creamed mushroom stew combining *pleurotes, trompettes des morts girolles, cèpes* and *cornes d'abondance* mushrooms, is truly extraordinary. Equally celebrated is her execution of the simple peasant dish, *terrine de volaille,* as flavorful as you will ever encounter. Ginette lists three other dishes as her specialties, the rack of lamb *(carré d'agneau)* served with her celebrated scalloped potatoes *(gratin dauphinois),* her duck breast *(magret de canard)* in a green pepper sauce and her veal kidneys *(rognons de veau)* prepared in a rich Madeira wine sauce. Turbot is accompanied by a stunning *beurre blanc* sauce. All these sumptuous dishes and more, made from the finest ingredients, are prepared in a miniscule kitchen by this master chef.

Recommended Dishes

La Salade Paysanne. Country salad with poached egg and bacon.

Terrine de Volaille Maison. Chicken and chicken liver pâté cooked and served in an earthenware dish.

Rillettes de Saumon et Toast. Preserved, seasoned salmon-spread with toast.

Rosette de Lyon. Large pork sausage served in slices.

Côte de Veau à la Normande. Veal chop cooked in a rich cream and Calvados sauce.

Rognons de Veau Sauce Madère. Veal kidneys cooked in a richly-flavored brown sauce made from Madeira wine.

Andouillette de Troyes Dijonnaise. Grilled pork sausages from the Champagne region, in mustard sauce.

Fricassée de Champignons Sauvages. Wild mushroom stew.

Boeuf Bourguignon. Beef stewed with red wine, onions and mushrooms.

Châteaubriand au Poivre. Thickest part of filet of beef grilled and sauced with peppercorns.

Carré d'Agneau, Gratin Dauphinois. Grilled rack of lamb served with scalloped potatoes.

Escalope de Saumon Frais. Slice of fresh salmon accompanied by a cream sauce and home-style noodles.

Turbot au Beurre Blanc. Whole turbot served with a butter cream sauce with white wine and shallots.

Tarte-Tatin, Crème Fraîche. Caramelized upside-down apple pie with lightly-soured cream.

Profiteroles. Pastries filled with vanilla ice cream and covered with chocolate sauce.

Clafoutis aux Fruits de Saison. Batter tart filled with seasonal fruit.

WINE

Bordeaux (Chez Boyer).

AU PIED DE FOUET 

M. Chich

Address: 45, rue de Babylone, 75007 (off rue Vaneau)
Closed: Sat. evening, Sun., August, Christmas week and Easter
Price Range: Inexpensive
Tel: 47-05-12-27
Metro: Vaneau or St. François-Xavier
Credit: None

Once the best-kept secret in Paris, this minuscule bistro with only four or five tables is now listed in virtually every guidebook. First-rate home-style cooking and fine, unpretentious wine are offered at bargain prices. This is an amiable little spot that oozes charm.

No reservations are taken and even if you get here early you will probably have to wait at the tiny museum-quality zinc bar where the personable new proprietor, M. Chich, will pour you a coffee or an aperitif. Formerly a coaching inn, the little dining room is cluttered with wagon wheels, harnesses and other memorabilia. Red-and-white curtains and tablecloths, a moleskin banquette along the wall, and tiny bistro chairs pushed as close together as possible, fill the room. Make sure to ask for *pommes purées,* the meltingly-creamy mashed potatoes served with the *entrecôte* (rib steak), but which may also be ordered *à la carte.* Other daily favorites are the *blanquette de veau* (veal stew), *rognons d'agneau* (lamb kidneys) and *confit de canard* (roast preserved duck). In addition to the traditional desserts, there is an array of tarts and a particularly tempting chocolate *charlotte.* You cannot miss the bright yellow-orange façade on the ancient Rue Babylone, a block or so away from the Swedish embassy.

Recommended Dishes

Maquereaux au Vin Blanc Maison. Mackerel fillets poached in white wine, served with potato salad.
Salade de Lentilles. Lentil salad.
Salade de Museau de Boeuf. Sliced prepared muzzle of ox in a vinaigrette.
Foies de Volailles Sautées. Sautéed chicken livers.
Blanquette de Veau. Poached veal in white cream sauce, garnished with tiny onions and mushrooms, served on rice.
Petit Salé aux Lentilles. Lightly-salted pickled pork with lentils.
Steak Tartare. Raw minced steak mixed with egg yolk, onions and capers.
Entrecôte, Pommes Purées. Beef rib steak with extra creamy mashed potatoes.
Rognons d'Agneau, Sauce Madère. Lamb kidneys in a rich, brown Madeira wine sauce.
Confit de Canard Maison. Preserved duck roasted and served with garlic potatoes.
Lotte au Poivre Vert. Monkfish in a green peppercorn sauce.
Filet de Saumon aux Pourpiers. Poached salmon fillet on a bed of salad greens.
Clafoutis aux Cerises. Deep-dish cherry batter tart.
Charlotte au Chocolat. Hot fruit pudding with chocolate cream.
Diplomate, Crème Anglaise. Custard dessert with candied fruit and lady fingers.

WINE

Chinon (Les Gravieres), Bourgueil (Domain des Ouches), St. Pourcain, Gamay Touraine, Rosé de Provence (Paquet).

THOUMIEUX 

M. & Mme. Bassalert

Address: 79, rue Saint-Dominique, 75007 (at rue Jean Nicot)
Closed: Monday
Price Range: Moderate
Tel: 47-05-49-75
Metro: La Tour-Maubourg
Credit: Visa
Remarks: Air-conditioning

A large and very popular bistro with the ambience and interior of a 1930s-style brasserie. Bright lights, bustling waiters and crowded elbow-to-elbow seating. The menu is extensive, the cooking above average in quality and below average in price. The portions are old-fashioned in their generosity.

A pleasant ten-minute walk from the Invalides brings you to this very popular neighborhood bistro which has an old-time atmosphere and cast of local characters that are hard to beat. The spacious dining room is always packed, so arrive early. Identical tables set in long rows and covered with white linens, bright wall sconces and overhead globe lights are reflected in the mirrored walls. Long banquettes, brass railings, potted palms and communal coatracks are spread throughout the room. Efficient waiters dressed in the traditional bistro uniform of long white apron and black trousers politely take your order.

Unpretentious dishes with a strong Southwestern accent are carefully prepared and tastefully presented. The *cassoulet,* for example, comes to the table in a handsome sealed earthenware casserole pot. There is a long and varied à la carte menu, but if you stick to the *prix-fixe* meals, a luncheon for two may be had for under thirty dollars.

This is a great place to sample the duck specialties from the Southwest and Limousin regions of France: *confit de canard* (preserved duck), *rillettes de canard* (duck pâté), *filet de canard maison* (garlic-enhanced steak of duck breast), *cuisse de canard aux pruneaux et filet d'oie fumé* (duck legs and smoked goose with prunes) and of course the *cassoulet.* The Cahors wine is a good choice to complement these rich dishes. There is additionally a considerably less expensive house *rouge* that is the next best thing. To keep the spirit of the Southwest, finish up with the *clafoutis,* the traditional custard-and-cake dessert from Limousin, made with black cherries and served with vanilla cream.

After your evening meal, work off the calories strolling over to the spectacular illuminated Tour Eiffel.

RECOMMENDED DISHES

Rillettes de Canard Maison. Tiny pieces of duck cooked in its own fat and served as a spread.

Pâté de Campagne. Coarse country pâté.

Charcuteries d'Auvergne. Assorted pork products.

Salade d'Epinards aux Lardons. Spinach salad with bacon.

Raie au Beurre Noir. Skate in black butter.

Cassoulet au Confit de Canard "Maison." Languedoc stew with white beans, pork, sausage and preserved duck served in an earthenware casserole. The outstanding specialty of the bistro.

Boudin Noir aux Châtaignes. Large grilled blood sausage with chestnuts.

Ris d'Agneau Sautés à la Provençal. Sautéed lamb sweetbreads in a rich tomato sauce with garlic and basil.

Côte de Boeuf Grillée, Sauce à la Moelle. Grilled rib of beef in bone marrow sauce (for two).

Tripes à la Mode de Caen. Tripe cooked with cider and Calvados brandy.

Filet de Canard "Maison." Duck breast seasoned with garlic and served with sautéed potatoes.

Gigot d'Agneau aux Flageolets. Roast leg of lamb with small green kidney beans.

Pieds de Porc, Sauce au Vin. Pigs' feet in wine sauce.

Médaillons de Lotte au Coulis de Poivrons Rouges. Round fillets of monkfish served with a red pepper puree.

Selle d'Agneau. Roast rack of lamb.

Flognarde aux Poires. Sweet flan with pears.

Profiteroles au Chocolat. Ice-cream-filled pastry covered with melted chocolate.

WINE

Cahors/Carte Noir.

8e Arrondissement

Chez André

Berrys

Chez Edgard

Savy

Étoile—Champs-Élysées

PLACES OF INTEREST

Arc de Triomphe

Avenue Marigny (the stamp market)

Avenues Montaigne and *Matignon*

Champs-Élysées

Église de la Madeleine

Église St.-Augustin

Gare St.-Lazare

Grand Palais

Musée Cernuschi

Musée de la Découverte (*Grand Palais*)

Musée Instrumental du Conservatoire National de Musique

Musée Jacquemart-André

Musée Nissim de Camondo

Musée de l'Orangerie

Parc de Monceau

Petit Palais

Place de la Concorde

Pont de l'Alma (*Bateaux Mouches* and *Vedettes*)

Rond-Point des Champs-Élysées (*Théatre du Rond-Point*)

Rue du Faubourg—St.-Honoré

Rue Royal

CHEZ ANDRÉ ★★

M. Alain Fourés for Groupe Gérard Joulie

Address: 12, rue Marbeuf (at rue Clément-Marot)
Open: Every day, all year
Price Range: Moderate
Tel: 47-20-59-57
Metro: Franklin Roosevelt or Alma-Marceau
Credit: All major credit cards
Remarks: Air-conditioning, continuous service from 11 A.M. to 1 A.M.

Expect solid bistro fare, served in traditional style, and surroundings frequented by many regulars and tourists. Located in the bustling Avenue Montaigne area, near the Champs-Élysées, lunch is always busy but not a madhouse like other restaurants in the district.

Soft lights, flowers and middle-aged waitresses dressed in black lend a sedate atmosphere to this comfortable, unpretentious old dining room, an institution on Rue Marbeuf since 1937. In 1991 when Gérard Joulie bought Chez André from the original owner's son it was agreed that the ambience and cuisine would remain unaltered and until now the promise has been scrupulously kept. Gérard Joulie also operates a chain of sixteen bistros throughout Paris under the name Batifol (14, rue Mondétour, 1er, Tel: 42-36-85-50) so a fear of change was not unfounded. The food is not elaborate but it is good and you will find many of the bistro classics from eggs in mayonnaise and Bismark herring to leg of lamb, calf's liver, ribs of beef, and a fine table of desserts. The *plat du jour* changes from lunch to dinner. A warm beef-and-potato salad makes an excellent appetizer or you might choose the soup *(potage du jour)* including a warming cream puree of vegetables. Bouillabaisse, grilled veal kidneys, and roast rack of lamb are some of the most favored specialties. Many patrons return for perfectly executed three-egg omelettes of ham, cheese, tomato or chicken livers. A splendid wine list is well endowed with some excellent *crus,* but the house Brouilly and Mâcon Viré, by the glass or carafe, are perfectly acceptable and reasonably priced.

Recommended Dishes

Terrine Grand Mère. Old-fashioned duck liver pâté.

Filets d'Harengs, Pommes à l'Huile. Marinated herring filets with sliced potatoes in oil.

Oeuf en Gelée ou dur Mayonnaise. Boiled egg in jelly or mayonnaise.

Salade de Boeuf aux Pommes Tièdes. Warm beef-and-potato salad.

Omelettes. Three-egg omelettes filled with ham, cheese, tomato or chicken livers.

Sauté d'Agneau aux Pommes Vapeur. Pan-fried lamb served with steamed potatoes.

Gigot d'Agneau Rôti, Pommes Mousseline. Roast leg of lamb with mashed potatoes.

Rognon de Veau Grillé, Beurre Bercy et Pommes Allumettes. Grilled veal kidneys with bone marrow and shallot-butter sauce, served with matchstick potatoes.

Côte de Boeuf Grillée "Fine Fourchette." Grilled rib of beef for the hearty eater (½ kilo).

Carré d'Agneau Six Côtes, Rôti à l'Ancienne. Roast rack of lamb (six chops).

Coquilles Saint-Jacques Fraîches à la Provençale. Grilled scallops with tomatoes, garlic and onions.

Bouillabaisse. Mediterranean fish soup.

Baba au Rhum. Yeast cake drenched in rum syrup and served with cream.

Mille-Feuille "Spécialité." Cream-filled puff pastry.

Crème Brûlée "Spécialité." Rich custard dessert topped with caramelized sugar.

Wine

Generous selection of diverse growths at very reasonable prices, especially Bordeaux *crus.* House wines: Brouilly *(rouge)* and Mâcon Viré *(blanc).*

BERRYS ★ ★ ★

M. Patrick Cirotte
Mme. Mireille Cirotte

Address: 46, rue de Naples, 75008 (Parc Monceau area)
Closed: Sunday
Price Range: Moderate
Tel: 40-75-01-56
Metro: Villiers
Credit: All major credit cards
Remarks: Open till 1 A.M.

Patrick Cirotte, one of the most talented young chefs of Paris and owner of the successful restaurant Le Grenadin, took the space next door in 1992 and opened a tiny bistro annex serving the specialties of his native region, Berry.

Modern, lean and clean, the tiny bistro is decorated with white stucco walls and an aquamarine bar. Berrys has about a dozen tables surrounded by black chairs, some of which are situated on a small overhanging balcony. The only ornamentation is a striking fresco in the style of Kandinsky executed by his jazz musician friend, Daniel Humair.

Regionally-inspired dishes prepared with the master touches of a superb chef are served by his charming wife, Mireille, at bargain basement prices. A complete meal without wine will cost about $25. The food is all prepared in the shared kitchen of his expensive restaurant, Le Grenadin. The chalkboard menu lists such dishes as thinly-sliced raw pike and cabbage, braised rack of pork, veal simmered in red wine, leek-and-goat-cheese tart, and the superb smoked ham of Sancerre. For dessert, a *poirat berrichon,* the chocolate-covered pear tart of Berry or the *chanciau aux pommes,* a savory thick apple fritter covered in a light egg custard.

Berrys exhibits an important variation in contrast with other important-chef spinoffs. Here there is no pretense or snob appeal—only good quality food at reasonable prices.

RECOMMENDED DISHES

Jambon de Sancerre. Smoked regional ham.

Salade de Brochet aux Deux Choux. Raw pike and cabbage salad.

Tarte aux Poireaux et Chavignol. Leek-and-goat-cheese tart.

Pâté aux Patates. Small hot patty filled with sweet potato.

Gâteau de Pommes de Terre et Andouille Fumée. Potato cake and large chitterling sausage served cold.

Andouillette et son Gratin de Macaroni. Small chitterling sausages served with crusted macaroni and cheese.

Carre de Porc Braise aux Épinards. Braised rack of pork with spinach.

Veau au Vin Rouge. Veal cooked in red wine.

Fricassée de Volaille au Sancerre. Creamed chicken stew sauteed with Sancerre wine.

Brandade de Cabillaud à l'Huile d'Olive. Creamed freshwater cod with olive oil.

Poirat Berrichon. Chocolate-covered pear tart.

Chanciau aux Pommes. Apple fritter covered in egg custard.

Clafoutis aux Figues. Thick batter cake with figs or apricot.

Wine

Loire Valley Wines. Sancerre (Chez Morin), Quincy (Jerome de la Chaise), Menetou Salon.

Chez Edgard

M. Paul Benmussa
Chef: Moulinier

Address: 4, rue Marbeuf, 75008 (off av. George V)
Closed: Sun., holidays, and first three weeks of August
Price Range: Fairly expensive
Tel: 47-20-51-15
Metro: Franklin Roosevelt or Alma-Marceau
Credit: All major credit cards

A fashionable, long-established house favored by a select clientele of government officials, media people, "society" and others who make the wheels turn. Newcomers, however, are not neglected and are greeted with equal enthusiasm by "Monsieur Paul," the famous Tunisian-born proprietor who manages to maintain the highest standards in both food and service, running a restaurant of really extraordinary merit.

The bright-red awning with "Chez Edgard" lettered in gold marks a festive corner spot on an otherwise drab street, a short walk from Avenue Georges V and the Champs-Élysées. Sidewalk chairs and tables surrounded by boxes of flowers create a garden setting while inside, red-and-black walls and glass-enclosed booths impart an air of sophistication and intrigue. There are some Southwestern departures from the traditional bistro versions of fish, shellfish and steak in the form of dishes like *salade Niçoise,* a *gratin* of calamaries, a fish-fry of little smelts, grilled red mullet or grouper in a basil-and-tomato sauce and a Provençal beef stew. Delicious ice cream desserts include a banana split, and the house specialty, a *coup du chef:* vanilla ice cream and fruit drizzled with Cointreau.

Recommended Dishes

Huitres et Coquillages. Fresh oysters and shellfish.
Terrine de Lièvre. Rabbit pâté.
Oeufs Cocotte à la Crème. Lightly baked eggs cooked and served in a *cocotte* dish.
Cuisse de Canard Grillé au Muscadet. Grilled duck leg in white wine.
Cervelle de Veau aux Câpres. Calf's brains with capers.
Onglet Poêlé à l'Étuvée d'Échalotes. Flank of beef pan-fried with shallots.
Rognon de Veau Grillé Vert-Pré. Grilled veal kidneys garnished with straw potatoes, watercress and parsley butter.
Daube de Boeuf à la Provençale. Beef braised in red wine with vegetables and herbs, Provence-style, with tomatoes, garlic and onions, served in an earthenware pot.
Palette de Porc aux Haricots Rouges. Roast pork shoulder with red kidney beans.
Navarin d'Agneau aux Fèves Fraîches. Lamb stew with potatoes and onions garnished with fresh broad beans.
Filet de Loup aux Cinq Poivres. Fillet of sea bass with five types of pepper.
Thon Frais Grillé, Coulis de Tomates au Basilic. Fresh grilled tuna with a puree of tomatoes and basil.

Crème Caramel. Vanilla-flavored flan.
Profiteroles Sauce Chocolat. Ice-cream-filled pastry covered with melted chocolate.
Feuilleté aux Fraises. Puff pastry filled with a strawberry *mélange.*

WINE

Saint-Pourcain, Côteaux d'Aix, Brouilly.

SAVY ★ ★ ★

M. Gabriel Savy

Address: 23, rue Bayard, 75008
Closed: Sat., Sun., and August
Price Range: Fairly expensive
Tel: 47-23-46-98
Metro: Champs-Élysées or Franklin Roosevelt
Credit: Visa and MasterCard

A classic regional bistro reflecting the cuisine of the Massif Central. For thirty years chef-owner Gabriel Savy has served his generous Aveyronnais daily specials with the house Cahors, regional cheeses and fine old Armagnacs. Lunchtime is crowded with Parisians who appreciate well-chosen ingredients and flavorful sauces.

This delightful bistro with its comic waiters has long fed the executives from the nearby studios of Radio Luxembourg as well as the models and staff of the famous haute couture houses on Ave. Montaigne and diplomats from the surrounding embassies of Norway, Germany and Brazil.

The front room, which is more like a corridor, has been dubbed *"Le Wagon"* (the Dining Car). The decor, in 1930s bistro style, is set off by marvelous art deco windows. You can eat here or in the paneled, less-congested room in the rear. The "Dining Car" has the atmosphere, though, and it's fun to watch the waiters climb over the tightly packed tables negotiating the narrow room while balancing their platters full of food. Aside from the ever-present daily specials, Savy offers a *petit farçou* (vegetable pancake), ham from the Auvergne and the *épaule d'agneau rôtie* (roast shoulder of lamb), which must be ordered for two. One of the few available seafood dishes is *Saint-Jacques grillées au beurre blanc* (grilled scallops in white-wine butter sauce). The cellar is stocked with good little growers' wines in case the house Cahors doesn't suit you. Finish the meal with the Cantal cheese or with a prune tart and a glass of old Armagnac.

RECOMMENDED DISHES

PLATS DU JOUR

***Navarin Agneau** (Mondays).* Lamb stew with potatoes and onions.

***Chou Farci** (Tuesdays).* Stuffed cabbage.

***Jambonneau Lentilles** (Wednesdays).* Prepared ham with lentils.

***Blanquette de Veau** (Thursdays).* Veal stew in a white sauce of cream and egg yolks.

***Pot-au-Feu** (Fridays).* Boiled beef with vegetables and broth.

Jambon d'Auvergne. Cured, smoked Auvergne ham.

Petit Farcou Aveyronnais. Vegetables-and-herb pancake.

Feuilleté au Roquefort. Puff pastry filled with Roquefort cheese.

Foie de Veau à l'Auvergnate. Grilled calf's liver with mashed peas.

***Épaule d'Agneau Rotie** (for two).* Roast shoulder of lamb.

Poule Farcie Aveyronnaise (Poule-au-Pot). Stuffed chicken poached with vegetables.

Coquilles Saint-Jacques Grillées au Beurre Blanc. Grilled scallops in a white-wine butter sauce.

Tarte au Prunes. Prune tart.

Glace Noix et Miel. Walnut ice cream with honey.

Charlotte au Chocolat. Baked custard pudding in molded ladyfingers, filled with chocolate.

WINE

Cahors, Morgon.

9e *Arrondissement*

Au Petit Riche

Le Roi du Pot-au-Feu

Opéra—Trinite—Pigalle

PLACES OF INTEREST

Boulevard Haussman (*Au Printemps* and *Galléries Lafayette*)

Boulevards de la Madeleine, des Capucines and *des Italiens*

Églises Sainte-Trinité and *Notre-Dame-de-Lorette*

Hôtel Drouot (largest auction house in Paris)

Musée Grévin (wax museum)

Musée Gustave Moreau

"La Nouvelle Athens" (bordered by *Rues Saint Georges* and *Notre-Dame-de-Lorette*)

Passages Verdeau, Jouffroy and *du Havre*

Place Pigalle

Théâtre des Folies-Bergère

Théâtre National de l'Opera

AU PETIT RICHE 

M. LeJeune

Address: 25, rue Le Peletier, 75009 (off blvd. Haussman)
Open: Daily all year
Closed: Sun. and holidays
Price Range: Moderate
Tel: 47-70-68-68
Metro: Le Peletier and Richelieu-Drouot
Credit: All major credit cards
Remarks: Non-smoking room

An historic old bistro with authentic turn-of-the-century decor, serving classic fish and meat preparations with some specialties and wines from the Touraine and Anjou regions.

The Café Riche was opened as a *Grand Café* around 1865 but disappeared by 1873, leaving the "little Riche" to carry on alone. There is no main dining room; rather, there are a series of little dark-wood-paneled salons linked by corridors and kitchens. Painted ceilings, frosted glass, tall mirrors, brass overhead luggage racks, red upholstery and formally dressed waiters create a gracious atmosphere. The daily specials remain consistent with a few *plats du marché* prepared each day. The extensive wine list still specializes in wines from the Loire but no longer contains a portrait of Rabelais with the verse he put in Gargantua's mouth: "Refill your empty glass, empty your full glass; I cannot bear to see in thy hand thy glass neither empty nor full."

RECOMMENDED DISHES

Rillettes de Saumon à l'Aneth et Son Coulis de Concombre et Tomate. Preserved, mashed salmon pieces served as a spread with a purée of cucumbers and tomatoes.
Rillons de Vouvray en Gelée. Preserved potted pork cubes in aspic.
Pâté de Lapereau en Gelée aux Pruneaux. Rabbit pâté in aspic with prunes.
Assiette de Pecheur au Beurre Blanc. Assortment of poached fish in a white-wine butter sauce.

Filet de Turbotin à la Ciboulette. Grilled fillet of small turbot with chives.

Brandade de Morue. Creamed salt cod.

Magret de Canard Rôti au Poivre Vert. Fattened duck breast roasted with green peppercorns.

Boeuf Miroton. Slices of boiled beef simmered in a rich brown onion sauce.

Andouillette Grillée au Vouvray. Grilled pork sausage in Loire wine, served with a seasonal salad.

Petit Salé aux Lentilles. Lightly salted cooked pork with lentils.

Râble de Lapereau Farci aux Pruneaux. Saddle of hare roasted with a prune stuffing.

Tarte Fine aux Pommes Chaudes *(order in advance).* Thin, hot apple tart.

Crème Caramel. Vanilla-flavored flan.

WINE

Very large selection of first-quality wines from the Loire. Sauvignon de Cheverny *(en carafe)*, Gamay-de-Touraine *(en carafe)*, Vouvray Tranquille ou Pétillant *(en carafe)*.

LE ROI DU POT-AU-FEU 

M. Daniel Anée

Address: 34, rue Vignon, 75009 (off rue Tronchet)
Closed: Sun. and July 15 through August 15
Price Range: Moderate
Tel: 47-42-37-10
Metro: Madeleine or Havre-Caumartin
Credit: All major credit cards

Old musical instruments and cartoon-covered walls are part of the decor in this offbeat little spot specializing in a classic pot-au-feu. *A steaming bowl of golden bouillon is followed by a platter of tender cuts of boiled beef, vegetables and bone marrow. Crusty bread, a fresh Gamay d'Anjou and* crème caramel *complete the meal.*

Located in the busy shopping district off the Place de la Madaleine, this intimate art deco bistro with zinc bar and red-checkered tablecloths serves hearty plates of carefully chosen cuts of meat. Almost everyone orders the *pot-au-feu,* which comes with spicy Dijon mustard, coarse salt, *cornichons* and delicious bread freshly baked across the street at Fournil de Pierre. A branch of Le Roi du Pot-au-Feu (40 rue de Ponthieu, tel. 43-59-41-62), in the 8ᵉ near the Champs-Élysées, also serves a generous *pot-au-feu* along with other specialties such as a fine calf's head in vinaigrette and a tasty *hachis parmentier* (hash made from boiled beef leftovers and potatoes, served in a sauce). Reservations are not necessary, but both places are often crowded with well-heeled shoppers and their companions.

Recommended Dishes

Bol de Bouillon. Bowl of beef broth.
Terrine de Foies de Volaille. Chicken liver pâté.
Poireau Vinaigrette. Leeks in vinaigrette.
Pot-au-Feu. Enormous plate of boiled beef rib and shoulder with turnips, carrots, cabbage and bone marrow cooked in a rich broth accompanied by *cornichons,* Dijon mustard, coarse salt and crunchy bread.
Crème Caramel. Vanilla-flavored flan.
Mousse au Chocolat. Chocolate mousse.
Tarte-Tatin. Upside-down apple pie.

Wine

Gamay d'Anjou, Côtes-du-Rhône.

10ᵉ Arrondissement

Au Gigot Fin

La Grille

Gare-du-Nord—Gare-de-l'Est

PLACES OF INTEREST

Canal Saint-Martin

Gare du Nord, Gare de l'Est

Musée de l'Affiche et de la Publicité

Place de la République (3e, 10e, 11e)

Porte Saint-Denis

Porte Saint-Martin

Rue de Paradis

AU GIGOT FIN ★★

M. Rodrigue Lage

Address: 56, rue de Lancry, 75010 (Canal Saint-Martin area, Quai de Valmay)
Closed: Sat., Sun. and August
Price Range: Moderate
Tel: 42-08-38-81
Metro: Jacques-Bonsergeant
Credit: All major credit cards
Remarks: Non-smoking section

Located in a quartier populaire, *or working-class neighborhood, just steps from the Canal Saint-Martin, this substantial old establishment exhibits all the desirable characteristics for which the traditional bistro is revered.*

The most intriguing aspect of this corner restaurant is its authentic appointments and atmosphere that combine to transport any potential diner back to 1920 when this place was established. One is entranced by the sienna-painted façade, the polished wooden bar sporting a tempting oversized bottle of Bas Armagnac, the original wooden paneling beneath cream-colored walls, the pewter napkin rings set out under the stairs, and the beautiful grape-motif-decorated metal spiral staircase leading up to the bathrooms. All is original, honest, homey and good.

The fairly extensive menu, half-Bourgeois half-Gascon, is topped by the house specialty, leg of lamb, which may be had *au four* (roasted) and accompanied by white beans, or simply grilled. Lamb is also presented as *épaule d'agneau au four* (roast shoulder) or *côtes d'agneau grillées persillées* (parsleyed grilled lamb chops).

The amiable patron, M. Lage, aided by two experienced waitresses, insures that service is attentive and correct. He will probably advise you to choose a pitcher of Gamay wine to accompany your meal or something equally inexpensive and suitable.

This is a perfect spot to experience a delicious moderately-priced traditional meal, sitting elbow-to-elbow with average middle-class Parisian folks, in an authentic old-fashioned setting.

Recommended Dishes

L'Assiette Landaise (Foie Gras, Magret, Terrine). Platter of assorted Gascon duck specialties.
Salade Aux Gésiers Confits. Salad of preserved duck gizzards.
Magret d'Oie Fumé, Lit de Salade. Smoked goose breast in a bed of salad greens.
L'Assiette de Cochonnailles. Platter of assorted pork products.
Gigot d'Agneau Grillé. Grilled leg of lamb.
Gigot d'Agneau au Four, Haricots Blancs. Roast leg of lamb accompanied by white lima beans.
Côtes d'Agneau Grillées, Persillées. Grilled parsleyed lamb chops.
Épaule d'Agneau au Four. Roast shoulder of lamb (served for two).
Magret de Canard au Poivre Vert. Grilled breast of fattened duck with green peppercorns.
Sole Belle Meunière. Filet of sole, coated with flour, fried and served with brown butter.
Filet de Saumon Frais au Champagne. Salmon filet served cold in a Champagne sauce.
Tourtière Landaise aux Pruneaux. Gascon prune pie made in a molded tin.
Profiteroles au Chocolat. Ice-cream-filled pastries topped with chocolate sauce.

Wine

Saumur de Champigny, Muscadet, Sevre et Maine, Beaujolais Villages, by the pitcher.

La Grille

M. Yves Cullère
Mme. Geneviève Cullère

Address: 80, rue du Faubourg-Poissonière at the Intersection of rue de Montholon and rue des Méssageries, 75010
Closed: Sat. dinner, Sun., August and one week in February

Price Range: Fairly expensive
Tel: 47-70-89-73
Metro: Poissonière
Credit: All major credit cards
Remarks: Air-conditioning

One of the last old-time family bistros, where everything is carefully prepared and well looked-after. The setting is cozy with lots of lace, embroidery and damask, and the cuisine is fresh and of very good quality.

Mme. Geneviève Cullère puts as much into welcoming her guests and overseeing the dining room as her husband does into the superb specialties which have won him a glowing reputation. Perfectly grilled turbot, served for two, accompanied by a bowl of exquisite, tangy *beurre blanc* and a side of fabulous sliced potatoes baked in butter, is what brings people here, but the menu includes many other tempting choices. Excellent cuts of steak and little *andouillettes* (pork sausages) in mustard sauce, luscious scallops and salmon served with *beurre blanc* and a sumptuous *boeuf bourguignon* are all worthwhile. A crisp-white or fruity-red wine grown around the village of Ménétou Salon in the Loire Valley are fine choices with the food.

Recommended Dishes

Maquereau Frais au Vin Blanc. Whole fresh mackerel in white wine.
Filets de Sardine Marinés. Marinated sardine fillets.
Terrine de Canard aux Noisettes. Duck liver pâté with hazelnuts.
Terrine de Gibier. Various game pâtés in season.
Terrine de Fruits de Mer. Seafood terrine.
Saint-Jacques au Beurre Blanc. Pan-fried scallops in a white-wine butter sauce.
Turbot Grillé Beurre Blanc Avec un Gateau de Pommes de Terre au Lard *(for two).* Grilled turbot in a white-wine butter sauce. The outstanding specialty of the bistro. Served with a potato loaf cooked with bacon.
Boeuf Bourguignon à l'Ancienne. Beef stewed in red wine with mushrooms and onions.
Pavé de Boeuf à la Moutarde. Thick slice of broiled beef steak in mustard sauce.

Tête de Veau, Sauce Gribiche. Calf's head served hot with a mustard-mayonnaise sauce.

Poulet aux Écrevisses. Young chicken cooked with crayfish tails in cream sauce.

Mousse au Chocolat. Chocolate mousse.

Crème Caramel. Vanilla-flavored flan.

Oeufs à la Neige. Whipped, sweetened egg whites, poached in milk and served with a vanilla custard sauce.

WINE

Ménétou-Salon (white, rosé or red), Muscadet, Côtes-du-Rhône, Beaujolais.

11e Arrondissement

Anjou-Normandie

Astier

Auberge Pyrénées Cévennes (Chez Philippe)

Cartet

Le Chardenoux

Chez Fernand (Les Fernandises)

À Sousceyrac

Le Villaret

République—Nation

PLACES OF INTEREST

Cirque d'Hiver

L'Église de Sainte-Marguerite

Hôtel Tubeuf

Place de la Bastille (Opéra de la Bastille)

Place de la République

Rue du Faubourg St.-Antoine

Rue de Lappe

Rue Roquette

ANJOU-NORMANDIE 

M. Alain Langevin

Address: 13, rue de la Folie Méricourt, 75011 (off blvd. Voltaire)
Closed: Sat., Sun. and Mon. dinner; all of August
Price Range: Fairly expensive
Tel: 47-00-30-59
Metro: Saint Ambroise or Richard Lenoir
Credit: Visa
Remarks: Non-smoking room

A calm, delightful country-style inn, worlds away from the frenetic boulevards of the 11ᵉ where knowledgeable gastronomes pay homage to a chef that prepares the best homemade andouillettes *in Paris, perhaps in all France.*

Alain Langevin had the best introduction for his culinary career. He grew up in the provinces, in the area midway between Normandy and the Loire Valley, where his father was a skilled butcher. He also trained under famed dessert Chef Gaston Lenôtre. His regional cuisine, lighter than his Southwestern counterparts, does not display the customary overdose of dairy associated with Normandy cooking and everything is *fait maison,* that is, made in his own kitchen.

The much vaunted *andouillettes maison* (small chitterling sausages of tripe, pork or veal) are simply grilled with shallots and come out mellow and juicy. *Andouillettes* are an acquired taste, but if ever you wanted to experience this thoroughly French dish, this is the place.

It would be wrong to think of this regional bistro as a one-dish restaurant for other dishes here are superbly prepared, such as the generous *terrines* of chicken liver or duck, the Normandy-style veal chop, the exquisite little puff pastries *(feuilletés)* filled with either Roquefort cheese or mussels, the superb turbot served in a classic *beurre blanc* sauce or pan-fried with wild mushrooms, the salmon in sorrel sauce or the luscious desserts starting with a *tarte-Tatin* served for two or, if the spirit moves him (as stated on the menu), wonderful homemade puddings and cakes.

This quintessential bistro run by a husband and wife team displays great charm in its calm and colorful setting. It is an experience to look forward to.

Recommended Dishes

Terrines Maison, Foies de Voilaille, Canard. Chicken- and-duck-liver *terrines* accompanied by cornichons.
Foie Gras d'Oie. Goose liver foie gras.
Petits Feuilletés aux Moules. Tiny mussel puff pastries.
Petits Feuilletés au Roquefort. Blue cheese puff pastries.
Côte de Veau Normande. Veal ribs in a cream and white wine sauce.
Pintade Farcie. Guinea fowl stuffed with a pork and sage stuffing.
Les Andouillettes Maison. Grilled pork sausages with shallots.
Brochette de Gigot. Skewered lamb on the grill.
Turbot au Beurre Blanc. Grilled turbot in a white wine butter sauce.
Turbot Poêlé aux Pleurotes. Pan-fried turbot with oyster mushrooms.
Escalope de Saumon à l'Oseille. Sautéed slice of salmon in creamed sorrel sauce.
Sole Meunière. Filet of sole sautéed in butter and lemon juice.
Tarte Tatin Minute. Caramelized upside-down apple pie for two persons.
Millefeuille aux Framboises. Thin-layered puff pastry with cream and raspberries.

Wine

Gamay (Chez Marionnet), Anjou Rouge (Fern and Moron), Cahors (Clos Triguedina), Beaujolais (Duboeuf), Samur Champigny.

Astier

M. Vergnaud
M. Clerc

Address: 44, rue Jean-Pierre-Timbaud, 75011 (off ave. de la République)
Closed: Sat., Sun. and August

Price Range: Inexpensive
Tel: 43-57-16-35
Metro: Parmentier
Credit: Visa
Remarks: Air-conditioning

Superior home cooking at bargain prices brings a young, well-heeled, exclusively Parisian clientele to the heart of the 11e. Reservations are an absolute must, as this bustling place turns away as many people each night as it serves.

Decor is nonexistent and the elbow-to-elbow tables make service a bit strained, but no one seems to mind as they dig into heaping plates of shrimp, *terrines*, oysters, herring, foie gras, marinated leeks, salmon, sausages, turbot, veal stew, rabbit in mustard sauce, fillets of beef and pigeon *confit*. The astounding menu at 135F offers no less than nine *entrées*, ten *plats*, cheese and a half-dozen desserts, including a rich bittersweet chocolate cake and *fromage blanc*. There are two dining rooms and a constant flow of customers heading up the narrow stairs to the first floor. Downstairs, a tiny bar in the back serves as a waiters' station. The ambience is young, the room noisy and smoky, but everyone seems to enjoy themselves.

Recommended Dishes

Terrine de Lapin Maison. Rabbit pâté.
Terrine aux Foies de Volaille Maison. Chicken liver pâté.
Friture de Céteaux. Tiny fried sole.
Cassoulette d'Escargots aux Girolles. *Cassoulette* dish of snails and mushrooms.
Mousseline de Haddock, Beurre Blanc. Puréed haddock beaten with egg yolks and cream, poached and served with a white-wine butter sauce.
Brandade de Morue aux Brocolis. Creamed salt cod with broccoli.
Tête de Veau Ravigote. Calf's head served hot in a vinaigrette with capers, parsley and tarragon.
Brochette de Lotte aux Lard. Skewered monkfish wrapped in bacon and grilled.
Andouillette (A.A.A.A.A.) Grillée. Grilled pork sausage.
Magret de Canard à la Crème de Foie Gras. Fattened duck breast grilled and served with a creamy foie gras sauce.

-apin à la Moutarde Pâtes Fraîches. Rabbit in mustard sauce, served with fresh pasta.
Fricassée de Rognons et Ris de Veau au Poivre Vert. Light stew of veal kidneys and sweetbreads with green peppercorns.
Plateau de Fromages. Exceptional-quality cheese platter.
Gâteau au Chocolat. Chocolate cake.
Clafoutis. Baked custard fruit tart.
Crème Caramel. Vanilla-flavored flan.

WINE

Excellent selection of Burgundy and Bordeaux wines at bargain prices. Beaujolais (by the pitcher), Chinon Blanc, Mersault, Cabernet-de-Touraine, Saint-Nicolas-de-Bourgueil.

AUBERGE PYRÉNÉES-CÉVENNES (CHEZ PHILIPPE) ★★★★

M. Philippe Serbource

Address: 106, rue de la Folie-Méricourt, 75011 (off rue de la Fontaine, across from Canal Saint Martin)
Closed: Sat., Sun. and August
Price Range: Fairly expensive
Tel: 43-57-33-78
Metro: République
Credit: Visa and Amex
Remarks: Air-conditioning

A Pyrénéan-style auberge *where the atmosphere is intimate and gay. The menu offers superb Gascon food and spicy Basque specialties. These, accompanied by marvelous country wines, make this one of the most delightful and best regional bistros in the city.*

Owner Philippe Serbource, who bought the restaurant 29 years ago, added his own name to the old one but never changed the unpretentious exterior of this 65-year-old country-style inn located across the St. Martin Canal from the Place de la République. Beamed ceiling, ochre walls, red-tile floors, hanging sausages, hams and garlic, copper pots, shields and bull-fight posters make for cozy surroundings. The meal begins with a *Kir* offered by Mme. Serbource and a choice between generous portions of rich creamy pâté, a huge basket of assorted sausages or a deep tureen of herring fillets floating in vinegar brine with slices of pickles and onions, served with a crock full of fresh cream. Many order the *entrecôte,* in a rich sauce made with Burgundy and poached marrow served with crisp potatoes, or the lobster, served in two parts, the claws after the body, but one really ought to try the regional food. The *cassoulet* Toulousian-style, the *piperade Basquaise* and the paella *Valenciana* are as authentic as the country wines included on the excellent *carte des vins.*

Recommended Dishes

Foie Gras de Canard Naturel. Block of fresh duck foie gras.
Caille Confite au Foie Gras. Potted quail perserves with foie gras.
Cochonnailles de Pays. Large basket of assorted pork sausages.
Piperade Basquaise. Basque omelette with tomatoes, peppers and onions, served with sliced Bayonne ham.
Harengs Bismark. Marinated herring fillets brought to the table in a tureen with cream on the side.
Jambon Persillé de Bourgogne. Parslied ham molded in its own aspic.
Rougets Grillés au Beurre d'Anchois. Grilled red mullet with anchovy butter.
Sole Belle Meunière. Fillet of sole coated with flour, sautéed in butter and served with brown butter.
Homard Grillé à l'Estragon. Whole grilled lobster with tarragon.
Jambon Braisé au Gratin de Macaroni. Braised ham served with a *gratin* of macaroni.
Chou Farci. Stuffed cabbage.
Coq-au-Vin Bourguignon. Chicken stewed in Burgundy wine with mushrooms and onions.
Paella "Valenciana." Spanish dish of chicken, hot sausage and seafood with green and red peppers mixed with saffron rice. Extraordinary.
Cassoulet d'Oie Toulousain. Languedoc stew of white beans, pork, preserved goose, sausage and a generous addition of garlic and bread crumbs. An outstanding specialty of this bistro.

Confit d'Oie "Auberge." Preserved goose with white beans.
Petit Salé en Potée. Lightly salted pork stewed with vegetables.
Rognon de Veau en Cocotte. Veal kidneys served in a casserole.
Entrecôte à la Moelle. Sautéed ribsteak with bone marrow.
Profiteroles Glacées Sauce Chocolat. Ice-cream-filled pastry shells covered with melted chocolate.
Crème Caramel. Vanilla-flavored flan.
Vacherin Praliné. Baked meringue with almond flavoring.

WINE

Excellent selection of red Bordeaux and Burgundy wines. Cahors, Beaujolais Villages, Madiran, Aligoté de Bourgogne.

CARTET 

M. Raymond & Mme. Marie-Thérèse Nouaille

Address: 62, rue de Malte, 75011 (Place de la République area-off rue du Faubourg Temple)
Closed: Sat., Sun. and August
Price Range: Fairly expensive
Tel: 48-05-17-65
Metro: République
Credit: None

A small, unpretentious place made famous by Mme. Marie Antoinette Cartet. The kitchen is now in the capable hands of owners Raymond and Marie-Thérèse Nouaille, who carry on the traditions of fine, wholesome home-cooked cuisine.

You must reserve a few days in advance as there is only room for 25 or 30 people at the six or so little tables in the 1930s-style dining room. Vinyl banquettes, mirrors, wooden walls and pink damask linens add a quaint touch, evoking an intimate homey atmosphere. When Mme. Cartet arrived in Paris from Bourgen-Bresse she wanted a place where people could come to eat simply but well. She opened in 1936 and within a few years transformed an old *bougnat* (café), which also sold wood and charcoal, into a renowned bistro. She retired in 1980, but the Nouailles continue to serve abundant portions of meaty *terrines,* creamed pike dumplings, *boeuf à la ficelle* and a delicious lemon tart which Marie-Thérèse prepares twice daily.

Recommended Dishes

Charcuteries Maison (Cochonnailles). Assorted pork products.
Maquereau Marinés au Vin Blanc. Fresh marinated mackerel in white wine.
Jambon Persillé. Parslied ham in aspic.
Saucisson Chaud de Lyon. Large pork slicing sausage, served hot.
Frisée aux Lardons. Chicory salad with bacon.
Croûte aux Morilles. Puff pastry filled with wild mushrooms.
Quenelles de Brochet Sauce Nantua. Pike dumplings in a crayfish purée.
Baudroie Sauce Nantua. Monkfish in a crayfish purée.
Brandade de Morue. Creamed salt cod.
Pieds de Mouton, Sauce Poulette. Sheep's feet in a mushroom-flavored white sauce with lemon juice.
Palette de Porc à la Bourguignonne. Pork bladebone in a red-wine sauce with mushrooms and onions.
Gigot d'Agneau, Gratin Dauphinois. Roast leg of lamb with sliced potatoes baked in cream and browned on top.
Boeuf à la Ficelle. Slightly roasted fillet of beef tied and lowered into simmering broth. Served with *gratin dauphinois.*
Gras-Double. Scalded ox tripe cooked for hours in bouillon then sliced and sautéed with minced onions, vinegar and chopped parsley.
Tarte au Citron. Lemon tart.
Profiteroles aux Fraises. Chocolate-covered ice-cream-filled pastry shells with strawberries.
Bugnes. Sweet pastry fritters.
Gâteau au Chocolat. Chocolate cake.

Wine

Vin du Bugey (red, white and rosé), Morgon, Brouilly.

LE CHARDENOUX 

M. Bernard Passavant

Address: 1, rue Jules-Vallès, 75011 (at rue Chanzy)
Closed: Sat., Sun. and August
Price Range: Fairly expensive
Tel: 43-71-49-52
Metro: Charonne
Credit: Amex and Visa

Subtle and simple food in a Belle-Époque working-class café du coin, *where the new owner continues to offer unpretentious, good-quality cuisine.*

All the original fixtures are beautifully preserved in this charming corner bistro located in an up-and-coming, but out-of-the-way, part of town. An unrestored marble entrance leads into a small room divided by etched-glass and wood panels dating from the 1880s. Original paintings, mirrors, gilt ceiling appliqués and tulip lamps also remain untouched, but the bar, which is made of 17 different marbles, is the room's masterpiece. Even the original horse rings and polished brass spigot where customers used to water their horses are still at its front end. You don't come to Chardenoux by chance, but it is worth the trip for the authentic decor and cuisine lightened by modern touches.

RECOMMENDED DISHES

Oeufs en Meurette. Poached eggs in red wine sauce.
Poireaux Vigneronne. Cooked leeks and beef salad in vinaigrette.
Foie Gras de Canard Mi-Cuit Maison. Slightly cooked duck foie gras.
Crème de Lentilles à l'Ail et à l'Huile d'Olive. Lentils creamed with garlic and olive oil.
Gratin de Girolles. Dish of wild mushrooms in cream sauce with a crusted-cheese-and-breadcrumb topping.
Tripoux de Saint-Flour. Stuffed cushions of veal tripe, heavily seasoned as prepared in Auvergne.
Rognon de Veau Rôti Entier à la Moutarde de Meaux. Roasted

whole veal kidney in mustard sauce.

Pot-au-Feu. Boiled beef dinner of bouillon, meat and vegetables accompanied by mustard, cornichons and coarse salt.

Blanquette de Veau. Veal stew with onions and mushrooms.

Coq au Vin. Chicken stewed in red wine.

Côte de Veau Fermier Aux Morilles. Thick veal chop garnished with morel mushrooms.

Daube de Boeuf à la Provençale. Braised beef simmered in tomatoes, garlic and onions.

Onglet Poêlé aux Pleurotes. Pan-fried beef flank with oyster mushrooms.

Gibiers en Saison. Game dishes are available from October to January.

Morue à la Florentine. Salt cod served on a bed of spinach covered with cheese sauce.

Cerises à la Savoyarde. Hot cherries on home-made vanilla ice cream.

Fondant au Chocolat et aux Marrons. Frosted chocolate cake with chestnuts.

WINE

Well-chosen selection of wines from the Loire and Rhône regions, Beaumes-de-Venise (stand out).

CHEZ FERNAND (LES FERNANDISES)

M. Fernand Asseline

Address: 17, rue de la Fontaine-au-Roi, 75011 (off rue de la Pierre Levée)
Closed: Sun., Mon., and two weeks in August
Price Range: Moderate
Tel: 43-57-46-25
Metro: Goncourt or République
Credit: Visa

One of the only restaurants in Paris where you will find true Norman cooking. Each day owner-chef Fernand Asseline prepares crusty multigrain bread, his famous skate with Camembert, tripe with cider, crêpes, and an apple tart flamed with Calvados. Fernandise, next door, is a less expensive version of Fernand, but the two places share the same menu on Fridays and Saturdays.

Fernand moved to this location close to the Canal St. Martin, just off the Place de la République, in 1986. The little bistro-yellow dining room is scattered with a few paintings and pieces of copper. There is a bar along one side of the room and the ten tables are finely set with pink cloths and napkins. There is a *prix-fixe* menu at 130F, but the most outstanding dishes of the house, such as the grilled foie gras, the golden roast baby pig with garlic cream or the *emincé* of duck, Rouen-style, in a rich blood-thickened sauce, are listed à la carte. The only cheese is Camembert, but it is ripe and delicious served five ways: plain, or with pink peppercorns, hay, caraway or chopped walnuts. There are some fine crus from the Loire, including a red Valencay which is light in alcohol and fruity in flavor.

Recommended Dishes

Rillettes de Maquereaux. Cooked mackerel bits preserved in a jar, pounded to a pâté-like consistency and served as a spread.
Salade de Moules Fraîches aux Fines Herbes. Fresh mussel salad.
Foie Gras Frais de Canard. Fresh duck foie gras grilled and served with country bread.
Salade de Foies de Canard au Vinaigre de Cidre. Green salad with duck livers in a cider vinaigrette.
Raie au Camembert. Skate cooked with Camembert cheese.
Filets de Rascasse Vallée d'Auge. Scorpion fish fillets cooked with Calvados brandy and cream.
Porcelet Rôti à la Crème d'Ail. Roast baby pig with garlic cream.
Confit de Canard Pommes à l'Ail. Preserved duck, served with potatoes sautéed with garlic.
Emincé de Canard (Grillé, Cidre et Pomme, Rouennaise, au Foie Gras). Four distinct preparations of sliced duck, including the famous *"Rouennaise"* with its blood-thickened red-wine-and-duck-liver sauce.
Tripes au Calvados. Braised ox tripe, cooked with carrots, onions, garlic, tarragon, cider and Calvados brandy.
Plateau de Camemberts Affinés Par Fernand. Five versions of

Camembert cheese (plain, pink peppercorns, hay, caraway, chopped walnuts) prepared by the chef.

Tarte aux Pommes. Hot apple tart.

Crêpes aux Pommes Flambée Calvados. Thin pancakes stuffed with apples and flamed with Calvados brandy.

WINE

Well-chosen selection of country wines at attractive prices. Most from the Touraine, Auvergne and Bordeaux regions. Madiran, Sancerre, Côtes-de-Blaye, Valencay.

À SOUSCEYRAC

M. Gabriel Asfaux
M. Patrick Asfaux

Address: 35, rue Faidherbe, 75011 (off rue Chanzy)
Closed: Sat. lunch, Sun. and August
Price Range: Expensive
Tel: 43-71-65-30
Metro: Faidherbe—Chaligny
Credit: All major credit cards
Remarks: Air-conditioning

First-rate ingredients and careful preparation, with an emphasis on intensely rich specialties from the Quercy and Lot regions of Southwestern France, are the mainstays of this distinguished old bistro located in a remote corner of the 11e.

Sousceyrac is the name of a small village in the Quercy, and the cuisine here reflects the heartiness of old-fashioned Gascon cookery: delicious pâtés and *terrines* of foie gras, truffle salad, truffles and morels, sausages with morels in cream sauce, lamb sweetbreads, slices of duck breast, liver and kidneys in cream sauce with wild mushrooms and copious peasant stews. The house specialty is a wild hare preparation, *lièvre à la royale,* served on Fridays from mid-October to late December. This famous dish requires the hare to be marinated for several hours in red wine, herbs and onions then stewed for more hours with its liver, vegetables, herbs and seasonings all of which are finally blended with foie gras and truffles into a coarse mixture with a fine gamey flavor and rich texture. The small wine list includes some excellent choices including a fine Cahors by the pitcher and some old Armagnacs.

Opened in 1923 by Adolphe and Ida Asfaux, the restaurant is now run by grandsons Luc and Patrick. The decor is old-fashioned but comfortable and the paneled dining room is decorated with pictures and a collection of attractive country crockery.

Recommended Dishes

Foie Gras Frais de Canard. Fresh duck foie gras with truffles.
Foie Gras Frais d'Oie. Fresh goose foie gras.
Timbal Chaude de Lapereau aux Écrevisses. Hot rabbit *mousseline* with crayfish tails.
Mousse de Grouse au Foie Gras. Wild grouse mousse with duck liver.
Cul d'Artichaut Frais Garni de Langouste. Fresh artichoke bottoms garnished with crayfish.
Tourte aux Cailles. Hot quail pie.
Pavé de Saumon Sauvage Rôti au Coulis de Poivron Rouge. Thick slice of wild salmon roasted with a purée of sweet red peppers.
Andouillette au Four. Roast pork sausage.
Civet de Canard. Rich duck stew.
Cassoulet Comme à Sousceyrac *(Wednesdays and Fridays).* Languedoc stew with mutton, preserved duck and goose, sausage and white beans. A great favorite of this bistro.
Ris de Veau Entier Étuvé. Whole braised sweetbreads with mushrooms.
Foie de Veau Poêlé à la Forestière. Pan-fried calf's liver with wild mushrooms, bacon and potatoes.
Pieds de Porc Grillé Saint-Antoine. Grilled breaded pigs' feet.
Angus d'Ecosse à la Forestière. Grilled beef steak with mushrooms, bacon and potatoes.
Saucisson Chaud Pistaché. Hot pork sausage studded with pistachio nuts and served in a cream sauce with morel mushrooms.
Lièvre à la Royale *(Friday nights from early October through Christmas).* Stewed red hare. The outstanding specialty of the bistro when available.

Profiteroles au Chocolate. Ice-cream-filled pastries covered with melted chocolate.
Tarte Tiède aux Poires. Warm pear tart.
Pruneaux à l'Armagnac. Prunes stewed in Armagnac brandy.
Glace aux Marrons Confits. Vanilla ice cream with candied chestnuts.

WINE

Cahors (in the pitcher).

LE VILLARET

M. Michel Picard

Address: 13, rue Ternaux, 75011 (off rue Oberkampf)
Closed: Lunch every day, Sun. and August
Price Range: Moderate
Tel: 43-57-89-76
Metro: Parmentier or Oberkampf
Credit: Visa and MasterCard
Remarks: Open till 1 A.M.

In June 1992, finding it impossible to retire and having sold his very successful first restaurant Astier *to staff, Michel Picard opened this neighborhood bistro which succeeds in offering the same consistent quality with even better prices than his first venture.*

In an out of the way, untouristy, residential address a few blocks from the canal Saint Martin, M. Picard has transformed a tiny neighborhood bar into a neat twelve-table bistro which combines old half-timbering and exposed-stone walls with modern oak paneling. Narrow tables and terra-cotta tiled floors are discretely lit by unadorned light sconces.

Cab drivers will not find a sign indicating this establishment, for the name is only lightly marked on the entrance door. This does not mean, however, that the multitudes of Astier fanatics have not discovered this treasure which is open only for dinner from 7 P.M. to 1 A.M. and is always full-up.

The dishes tend to be simple, generous and hearty such as the huge country *terrines,* the pan-fried sausages, the hot foie gras salad, the thick steaks and veal chops. One can finish a meal with a perfectly executed *crème brulée,* and the exceptional cheese platter should not be passed up—it is supplied by the distinguished restaurant Fromager Anthès. The wine list, although consisting of no more than a dozen selections at present, are all under ten dollars and meticulously chosen.

Recommended Dishes

Terrine de Foies de Canard. Duck liver pâté.
Tarte au Saumon Fumé. Smoked-salmon tart.
Foie Gras Chaud au Salade. Hot duck liver served on a bed of greens.
Fond d'Artichauts Vinaigrette. Artichoke bottoms in an oil-and-vinegar dressing.
Oeufs Cocotte à la Crème de Foie Gras. Baked eggs with a duck liver thickened cream sauce.
Cervelle de Veau aux Câpres. Calf's brains with capers.
Hachis Parmentier. Minced meat Shepherd's Pie.
Confit de Canard au Frites. Preserved duck leg served with tasty french fries.
Canard Sauvage aux Figues. Roast wild duck with figs.
Râble de Lapin au Basilic. Roast saddle of hare seasoned with sweet basil.
Faux Filet Extra aux Échalotes. Sirloin steak in a butter and shallot garnish accompanied by french fries.
Filet de Haddock au Beurre Blanc. Filet of smoked haddock in a delicate sauce of vinegar, shallots and butter.
Médaillon de Lotte à la Crème d'Étrilles. Round filet of monkfish in a cream sauce flavored by little crabs.
Pruneaux au Vin Rouge. Prunes in red wine with spices.
Crème Brûlée à la Vanille de Tahiti. Rich custard dessert topped with caramelized brown sugar.
Clafoutis aux Pommes. Batter tart with apples.

Wine

Small selection of wines, all moderately priced. Chinon, Burgundy.

12e Arrondissement

À la Biche aux Bois

L'Ebauchoir

Chez Marcel (Antoine)

Le Quincy (Auberge Berry et Ardèche)

Les Zygomates

Gare-de-Lyon—Daumesnil—Reuilly Diderot

PLACES OF INTEREST

Place de la Bastille

Place de la Nation

Gare de Lyon (*Restaurant Le Train Bleu*)

Bois de Vincennes (*Château de Vincennes, Parc Zoologique, Parc Foral*)

Musée National des Arts Africains et Océaniens

Cimetière de Picpus

Place d'Aligre (flea market)

À LA BICHE AUX BOIS ★

M. Gérard Mettler
Mme. Monique Mettler

Address: 45, ave. Ledru-Rollin, 75012 (off rue de Lyon)
Closed: Sat., Sun. and July 15 to August 15
Price Range: Moderate
Tel: 43-43-34-38
Metro: Gare-de-Lyon or Bastille
Credit: All major credit cards

A charming restaurant located near the Gare de Lyon which one might think would be a fine place for a quick meal. Nothing could be further from the truth. Since 1989 M. and Mme. Mettler have maintained a traditional kitchen specializing in rarely encountered terrines, *foie gras, game and dishes from the Southwest. The service is professional, but slow, and the place filled with regulars.*

A terrace with little tables sheltered by a hedge and a green-and-yellow striped awning creates a pleasant impression as you pass it to enter the dining room, artfully decorated with mirrors on one wall and a large green wall hanging surrounded by hunting scenes on the other. Long benches, wooden booths and about twenty-five tables are divided between a small front room and a larger rear section separated by a wooden railing. The floors are of cracked marble tile and many green plants are scattered throughout.

Lamb sautéed with curry; *tournedos* Landais-style; *coq-au-vin* with lots of chicken, mushrooms and potatoes; and sea trout or sea bass in wine sauce are a few of the most popular specialties. Desserts are uninteresting except for the substantial chocolate cake *(l'opéra biche)* and the best wine buys are those offered as wines of the month.

RECOMMENDED DISHES

Salade Perigourdine. Mixed salad with tomatoes, truffles and a slice of foie gras.
Foie Gras aux Morilles. Fresh foie gras with morel mushrooms (for two or three).
Terrine de Sansonnets. Tiny prepared mackerel pâté (for two).

Pâté de Chevreuil. Venison pâté, in season, (for two).
Ballotine de Caille Fourrée au Foie Gras. Loaf of boned quail stuffed with foie gras (for two).
Escalope de Veau "Biche au Bois." Breaded veal chop.
Pavé de Cerf. Grilled venison steak (in season).
Sauté de Gigot au Curry et Riz Pilaf. Sautéed leg of lamb with curry on a bed of rice.
Coq au Vin "Maison." Chicken stewed in red wine with onions and mushrooms.
Rognons de Veau Grille Entier. Veal kidneys grilled whole.
Saumon Frais aux Champignons des Bois. Grilled fresh salmon with wild mushrooms.
l'Opera Biche (Gâteau au Chocolat). Rich chocolate ice cream cake.
Mousse au Chocolat "Maison." Chocolate mousse.
Crème Caramel "Maison." Vanilla-flavored flan.
La Poire Belle Helene. Cold poached pear with ice cream and hot chocolate.

Wine

Côtes du Rhône, Beaume de Venise rouge, Pinot Noir de Bourgogne (Cuvée Maison).

L'Ebauchoir

M. Yvon Levaslot

Address: 43, rue de Cîteaux, 75012 (off rue du Faubourg-Saint-Antoine)
Closed: Sunday
Price Range: Inexpensive
Tel: 43-42-49-31
Metro: Faidherbe-Chaligny
Credit: All major credit cards
Remarks: Non-smoking room

The bistro discovery of the year when famed food critic Claude Lebey honored this remarkable, simple establishment with his much-coveted award, the prize Lillet 1993, *for the best traditional bistro.*

The well-deserved accolades of customers and critics alike have not altered the cult-like appeal of this large, charmless new bistro located on a small, quiet street back of the bustling Faubourg-Saint-Antoine. The bargain basement decor is a cross between a Lyonais *buchon* and a 1950s Manhattan cafeteria. What draws the crowds of local artisans and shopkeepers here is the inexpensive but excellent quality *cuisine de ménage* (home-style cooking).

The *gâteau de riz* (vanilla-flavored rice cake covered with freshly made caramel) prepared each day by Madame Levaslot is beyond reproach. Other popular dishes are the light and flavorful *fricassee* stew of salmon and scallops and the generous and fragrant *soupe de favouilles* (crab soup). The tasty *tête de veau* (calf's head) is served in classic bistro style with a *gribiche* (mustard-mayonnaise) sauce. The stuffed fresh sardines served cold as an appetizer are another winner. These and more favorites are chalked each day on the blackboard and served in a totally informal atmosphere by helpful waiters in jeans. In the fall of 1994 the bistro still offered an extraordinary luncheon menu for 60F that included a pitcher of Beaujolais. Such generosity prompted Claude Lebey to state that L'Ebauchoir had the best quality–price ratio in Paris.

Recommended Dishes

Sardines Fraîches Farcies. Stuffed sardines.

Terrine de Foies de Volaille Maison. Chicken liver *terrine.*

Oeuf Mayonnaise. Hard-boiled egg with mayonnaise of exceptional quality and presentation.

Soupe de "Favouilles." Crab soup.

Tête de Veau, Sauce Gribiche. Calf's head served in a mustard-mayonnaise sauce.

Confit de Canard Moelleux. Grilled preserved duck accompanied by a savory potato cake.

Fricassée de Saumon et Coquilles Saint-Jacques. Salmon and scallop stew.

Médaillons de Thon aux Olives. Grilled round slices of tuna served with olives.

Saumon à l'Unilatérale. Salmon grilled on one side.

Foie de Veau, Miel et Coriandre. Sautéed calf's liver with honey and fresh coriander.

Entrecôte à la Moelle. Beef rib steak with marrow sauce.

Petit Salé Lentilles. Boiled salt pork in a casserole with lentils.
Boeuf Mode. Jellied braised beef.
Gâteau de Riz Grand-Mère. Rice pudding with fruit confit and whipped cream.
Paris-Brest. Creampuff ring split and filled with whipped cream.
Crème Brûlée. Rich custard dessert topped with caramelized sugar.

Wine

Beaujolais.

Chez Marcel (Antoine)

M. Trottet

Address: 7, rue Saint-Nicolas, 75012 (off rue Charenton, behind Opéra Bastille)
Closed: Sat., Sun., August and holidays
Price Range: Fairly expensive
Tel: 43-43-49-40
Metro: Ledru-Rollin
Credit: Visa
Remarks: Non-smoking room

If you are looking for authenticity you will find it in this wonderful old-fashioned bistro where the decor, the atmosphere, the service, the portions and the cuisine are absolutely traditional. A clientele of serious eaters is drawn here by the aromas of yesteryear.

In Chez Marcel there is a nice custom. As soon as you sit down three bottles are placed on your table: a Beaujolais Villages, a Muscadet, and a Crème de Cassis, the last two for making yourself a *Kir.* The red and the white remain throughout the meal, and are replaced if necessary; you pay for only what you drink. Located in a quiet neighborhood, the restaurant consists of a long room divided into two sections by beautiful etched glass. At the front is a bar, in the back red moleskin banquettes, large wall mirrors, a lovely tile floor and tables covered in white damask. Everything gives the impression that here good cooking will be found.

Appetizers come to the table in large bowls from which you can help yourself. *Cochonnailles* are brought back several times because the table is not big enough to hold them. Next, there are generous servings of beef, tripe and pork in old-fashioned sauces, quail with Chartreuse, grilled pigs' feet, Morteau sausage with lentils and delicious house desserts. The service is provided by the *patronne* and another woman dressed in cardigan sweaters and skirts. The bill will be expensive, but you will have received much more than you paid for.

Recommended Dishes

Terrines. Assorted pâtés (duck with hazelnuts, quail with raisins, thrush, rabbit with prunes, chicken liver, country style).

Cochonnailles. First-quality pork products.

Salade de Lentilles. Lentil salad with onion rings.

Pissenlits Blancs aux Oeufs Durs. Dandelion-leaf salad served with hard-boiled eggs.

Maquereaux Frais au Vin Blanc. Fresh mackerel fillets poached in white-wine bouillon, served chilled.

Harengs de la Baltique à la Crème. *Terrine* of marinated herring fillets, served with cream on the side.

Saumon Frais, Sauce Tartare (Froid). Thick slice of fresh salmon served cold with tartar sauce.

Selle d'Agneau à l'Aillade. Roast saddle of lamb served with a garlic-mayonnaise-herb sauce similar to *aïoli.*

Estouffade de Boeuf. Beef stewed in a sealed pot with vegetables and a remarkable wine sauce.

Boudin, Pommes en l'Air. Large pork blood sausage grilled and served with fried apples.

Deux Cailles Fraîches Perigourdine. Quails browned in sauce and garnished with sliced potatoes, onions and truffles.

Pieds de Porc. Pigs' feet served roasted *(au four)* or stuffed and grilled *(farci aux herbes).*

Tripes Maison, au Sancerre. Ox tripe cooked in white Loire wine.

Andouillette. Pork sausage, served poached *(à la ficelle)* or grilled with green peppercorns *(au poivre vert).*

Coq-au-Beaujolais. Chicken stewed in Beaujolais wine with onions and mushrooms.

Saucisson Chaud Poivre Vert Pommes à l'Huile. Large slicing sausage accompanied by hot potato salad.
Civet de Porcelet. Piglet stew.
Civet de Lièvre. Stewed hare with red wine and vegetables.
Poire au Vin. Poached pears in wine.
Pruneaux au Vin. Prunes in wine.
Glace Miel et Noix. Honey ice cream with walnuts.

Wine

Muscadet (Sèvres et Maine), Beaujolais Villages.

Le Quincy (Auberge Berry et Ardèche) ★ ★ ★

M. Michel Bosshard (Bobosse)

Address: 28, ave. Ledru-Rollin, 75012 (off rue de Lyon)
Closed: Sat., Sun., Mon., mid-August to mid-September
Price Range: Fairly expensive
Tel: 46-28-46-76
Metro: Quai de la Rapée or Gare de Lyon
Credit: None
Remarks: Air-conditioning

Sparkling wine, wonderful country ham, sausages, and provincial specialties from the Berry and Ardèche regions are served in a gay atmosphere encouraged by the owner, nicknamed "Bobosse," who divides his time between the kitchen and dining room. Reservations are suggested.

Le Quincy seems to be an Ardèche farmhouse deposited in the middle of Paris. An oak-and-glass-enclosed terrace is decorated with hand-painted pictures of farm animals. Red-and-white-checkered café curtains match the tablecloths inside. A pretty tile floor holds tables surrounded by ladderback chairs with wicker seats. Fresh and dried flowers add to the country atmosphere.

If you are a lover of tripe, try to arrive when *pieds et paquets* are on the menu—a dish which takes more than a day to make.

Another unique preparation is the *caillette Ardèchoise* (baked pork liver and vegetables), a great favorite of many regulars as the dish is rarely found outside the Ardèche region. More traditional plates of fish, veal and chicken are available along with some good wines. A rare *cornas,* almost black in color, with a rich, hearty aroma, is a delicious accompaniment to the stews and game.

Recommended Dishes

Assiette de Jambon de Pays. Plate of smoked country ham from the Ardèche.

Foie Gras Frais Maison. Fresh duck foie gras.

Panier de Saucissons. Basket of first-quality country sausages.

Oeufs Brouilles au Truffes Fraîches. Scrambled eggs with fresh black truffles.

Salade de Museau de Boeuf. Salad of vinegared brown beef muzzle.

Caillette Ardèchoise. Chopped pork liver, spinach, parsley and herbs rolled and baked, then served like a big sausage. A specialty unique to this bistro.

Pieds et Paquets. Mutton tripe and sheep trotters rolled in small parcels, stewed and simmered in broth with skin of veal, onions, carrots, celery and tomatoes.

Fine Caille des Dombes Forestière. Roasted quail garnished with mushrooms, bacon and fried potatoes.

Lapereau aux Échalots et Vin Blanc. Rabbit sautéed in white wine with shallots.

Chou Farci. Stuffed cabbage.

Cassoulet au Confit d'Oie. White bean casserole with sausages, pork, lamb and preserved goose.

Queues de Boeuf de la Camille Braisées. Braised ox tail in white wine with shallots.

Boudin aux Pommes. Large blood sausage with fried apples.

Morue à la Concarnois. Salt cod baked with onions, vinegar and herbs.

Panier de Crottins de Chavignol. Basket of first-quality, firm, little goat cheeses from the Berry region.

Marrons au Sirop. Candied chestnuts in syrup.

Mousse au Chocolat. Chocolate mousse.

Wine

Vin de l'Ardèche, Cornas, Saint-Joseph, Cahors, Brouilly, Sancerre blanc, Sancerre rouge.

Les Zygomates 

M. Patrick Fray

Address: 7, rue Capri, 75012 (at rue Claude-Decean)
Closed: Sat. lunch, Sun., and first 3 weeks of August
Price Range: Moderate
Tel: 40-19-93-04
Metro: Daumesnil
Credit: Visa and MasterCard

Located in an undistinguished neighborhood far out in the Daumesnil Quarter, this unusual bistro has a fanatical following, making reservations absolutely imperative.

Owner/Chef Patrick Fray has skillfully converted a turn-of-the-century *charcuterie* and butcher shop into a most delightful, friendly bistro, complete with marble countertops, huge etched-glass mirrors and full of fin-de-siècle adornments. Don't expect to hear English spoken as this is one of the most Parisian of places.

The menu is so well conceived and the prices so reasonable, it is no wonder people are instantly captivated by this incredible place. It is difficult to select any particular highlights since Chef Fray is equally successful with fish and meat dishes, however the two house specialties are considered the *amourette beurre noisette* (bone marrow in hazelnut butter) and *croustillant d'agneau au romarin* (lamb served in a crust infused with rosemary).

For a rewarding, nostalgic experience come seek out this rare find and enjoy classic bistro dishes, fresh and well prepared in a truly Parisian atmosphere.

Recommended Dishes

Amourette Beurre Noisette. Bone-marrow-filled pastry in hazelnut butter.

Quenelles de Brochet, Sauce Nantua. Small pike dumplings in a shallot-cream sauce.

Salade de Foie Gras Cru aux Pignons. Raw duck liver salad with pine nuts.

Ravioles de Fruits de Mer au Bouillon d'Algues. Seafood-filled raviolis in a seaweed broth.

Rognons au Vin Rouge et Cassis. Veal kidneys cooked in red-wine and black-currant cream sauce.

Croustillant d'Agneau au Romarin. Lamb cooked in a crisp pastry seasoned with rosemary.

Filet de Canette à l'Os. Filet of roast duckling served with the bone marrow.

Queue de Cochon Farcie aux Pâtés Fraîches. Stuffed pig tail accompanied by fresh pasta.

Suprême de Volaille au Jus et Chèvre Frais. Poached chicken breasts in a wine and cream sauce with fresh goat cheese.

Merlan au Coulis de Poivrons. Fried whiting in a puree of sweet peppers.

Saumon Rôti à la Croque au Sel et Beurre de Citron. Roasted salmon cooked in a salt crust and seasoned with lemon butter.

Fondant au Chocolat Amer. A bitter-chocolate mousse cake with icing.

Compote de Pommes et Rhubarbe et sa Grace Canelle. Stewed apples and rhubarb topped with ice cream.

Tartelette Coucher de Soleil aux Pruneaux. Little prune tarts.

WINE

Bouteilles du Moment—daily wine specials, fairly-priced Burgundy wines.

13^{e} Arrondissement

Le Petit Marguery

Place d'Italie

PLACES OF INTEREST

La Bièvre (small river which flows into the Seine)

La Butte-aux-Cailles

La Cité Floréale (artists' colony)

La Cité Verte

Gare d'Austerlitz

Manufacture des Gobelins

Les Olympiades

Place d'Italie

Le Quartier Chinois

LE PETIT MARGUERY ★★★

M. Alain, Jacques & Michel Cousin

Address: 9. blvd de Port-Royal, 75013 (off av. des Gobelins)
Closed: Sun., Mon., August and December 24–January 3
Price Range: Fairly expensive
Tel: 43-31-58-59
Metro: Gobelins
Credit: All major credit cards
Remarks: Non-smoking room

The Cousin brothers are perfect hosts, and you will enjoy delicious seasonal seafood and game in a gay and very stylish bistro atmosphere. Many of the dishes are changed daily and prepared with great imagination by chefs Michel and Jacques.

Marvelous tile floors, old-fashioned sconces and matching chandeliers, mirrors and terra-cotta-colored walls are part of the delightful turn-of-the-century decor in the two dining rooms charmingly accented by shades of red, pink and blue. Hand-painted frescoes create a festive backdrop within but, weather permitting, the outside terrace is most attractive. The mood is high-spirited, fostered by the amiability of the proprietor, Alain, and friendly waiters who bustle about in black waistcoats, their white shirt sleeves rolled to the elbow. You will want to begin with an aperitif as you sit trying to decipher the extensive handwritten menu. A special *degustation* menu of four varied *plats,* lime sherbert in a Gewurztraminer *marc,* cheese and a choice of desserts must be ordered by the entire table. Enticing fish specialties are carefully prepared and served in combinations to enhance their natural flavors: turbot with lobster sauce, fresh cod with crayfish and asparagus, little red mullets garnished with tiny vegetables and fillet of sole with fine herbs and light pasta. During the fall and winter there are succulent *"specialités de chasse"* such as wild boar prepared in pâté, grilled with pepper sauce or stewed and served with fresh noodles. Slices of wild duck or pigeon on a bed of green cabbage and foie gras, superb cuts of beef and veal in rich wine or cream sauces, wild mushrooms, *tagliatelle,* truffles and marvelous lightly salted duck with cabbage leaves are also delicious. A distinguished and expensive list of Burgundy wines includes a Hospices-de-Beaune, Chambolle-Musigny "Les Charmes," Charmes-

Chambertin and many others imported by the famous houses of Louis Latour and Jaboulet.

Recommended Dishes

Cochonnailles. Assorted pork products, especially *fromage de tête* (headcheese) and *saucisse sèche* (dry sausage).

Maquereau Marinés au Poivre Vert. Mackerel marinated with green peppercorns.

Foie Gras Frais de Canard "Maison." Fresh duck foie gras.

Salade Maraîchere Embaumée deTruffes Fraîches. Mixed vegetable salad scented with fresh truffles.

Cassolette d'Escargots de Bourgogne aux Champignons. *Cassolette* dish of sautéed vineyard snails with mushrooms.

Terrines. Exceptional *terrines: de canard au foie gras* (wild duck with foie gras), *de faisan au foie gras* (pheasant with foie gras), *de lièvre* (hare), *de volaille au foie gras* (fowl with foie gras).

Spécialités de Chasse. Large selection of outstanding game dishes available seasonally.

Petit Salé de Canard à la Poitevine. Duck cured in salt brine then poached and served in the style of Poitou with lentils.

Pintadeau Fermier aux Champignons Sauvages Suivant Season. Young farm fresh guinea fowl, roasted with wild mushrooms.

Quartier d'Agneau de Lait des Pyrénées au jus de Persil. Roast suckling Pyrénées lamb, served with parsley juice and garlic.

Civet de Lièvre "Vielle France" aux Pâtes Fraîches. Rich hare stew with red wine, served in a thickened sauce with fresh pasta. *Civet de marcassin* (wild boar) is also available in season.

Bourride de Coquilles Saint-Jacques au Fenouil. Scallop-and-fish stew flavored with fennel and served with a garlic-mayonnaise sauce (aïoli).

Blanc de Turbot au Coulis de Homard. Large grilled, white turbot served with a purée of lobster.

Raie Rôtie au Gingembre et à la Menthe Fraîche. Roast skate with ginger and fresh mint.

Tarte Amandine aux Poires. Almond-flavored pear tart.

Gâteau Chocolat à l'Alcool de Framboise. Chocolate cake infused with raspberry-flavored *eau-de-vie.*

Île Flottante. Poached meringue floating in vanilla custard sauce.

Wine

Very strong list of Burgundy wines fairly priced. Quincy, Bourgueil, Cornas, Saint Joseph, Sancerre.

14e Arrondissement

L'Assiette

Le Bistrot du Dôme

Le Bourbonnais

La Cagouille

La Régalade

Restaurant Bleu

Maine—Montparnasse

PLACES OF INTEREST

Boulevard du Montparnasse (*la Coupole, le Dôme, le Sélect, la Rotonde*)

Les Catacombes (tours leave from 1, pl. Denfert-Rochereau)

Cimetière du Montparnasse

Cité Universitaire

Parc de Montsouris, l'Observatoire

Place Denfert-Rochereau (Lion of Belfort by Bartholdi)

Puces de la Porte de Vanves (flea market)

Rue Daguerre (open-air market)

Les Villas (*Léone, Camélias*)

L'ASSIETTE ★ ★ ★

Mme. Lucette Rousseau

Address: 181, rue du Château, 75014 (off av. du Maine)
Closed: Mon., Tues., and August
Price Range: Expensive
Tel: 43-22-64-86
Metro: Mouton-Duvernet or Pernety
Credit: All major credit cards

Lucette Rousseau, a charming hostess, raises bistro cooking to an art. She creates fabulous seasonal game and seafood specialties and prepares tasty little accompaniments to compliment a succession of other sumptuous dishes, most with a Southwestern accent.

When Mme. Rousseau converted this 1930s *charcuterie* into a bistro she chose to keep most of the original fixtures intact. The wooden façade is now painted red and the front windows filled with green plants, but inside, the cozy room still has a lovely glass ceiling, yellow walls, columns, etched glass and fresh flowers. The place is usually filled with regulars who add to the tumult created by the animated "Lulu." Her cooking is faultless with earthy flavors leaning heavily toward Southwestern herbs and spices. Roasted garlic, buttery mushrooms, fresh tuna grilled with sea salt and a delicious *boudin* served with sautéed potatoes and garlic are some of the tempting choices.

A modern unadorned annex called Les Comestibles (10, rue de la Sablière, 75014, Tel: 45-45-47-12) where products of the Southwest are sold over-the-counter is an inexpensive place for lunch, also serving excellent country classics.

RECOMMENDED DISHES

Foie Gras de Canard Fait Maison. Whole duck liver with truffles (in season).
Giroles Fraîches de Sologne Poêlée. Pot-roasted wild chanterelle mushrooms in salad.
Terrine de Lièvre au Boudin Landais. Hare pâté with country sausage.
Rillettes de Maquereau. Preserved mackerel spread.

Fricassée de Cèpes Frais. Delicious wild mushroom stew (in season).
Petit Salé de Canard à la Poitrine. Slightly-salted duck stuffed with peas on a bed of braised cabbage.
Pintadeau Rôti. Roast guinea fowl.
Rognons de Veau aux Fines Herbes. Grilled veal kidneys seasoned with fine herbs.
Boudin de Campagne. Grilled black-pudding country sausage.
Hachis Parmentier de Boudin. Minced sausage hash served like a pie.
Boeuf à la Ficelle. Roasted beef tied with a string and lowered to poach in broth.
Suprême de Bar au Beurre Rouge. Sea bass cooked in a cream-butter sauce and red wine.
Saint-Jacques Fraîches en Blanquette. Scallop stew in a white cream-and-egg-yolk sauce.
Saumon en Papillote Fines Herbes. Salmon baked in a pouch with fine herbs.
Oeufs à la Neige. Egg whites poached in milk and served with vanilla custard.
Crumble aux Pommes avec Figues. Apple crumb cake with figs.
Marquise au Chocolat. Bavarian layered cream cake covered with whipped cream and jellied syrup.

WINE

Pachèrenc du Vic Bihl (blanc), Graves (rouge), extensive wine list, generally expensive.

LE BISTROT DU DÔME 

M. Maxime Bras
Chef: Liana Doyle

Address: 1, rue Delambre, 75014 (off blvd. du Montparnasse)
Open: Daily all year
Price Range: Moderate
Tel: 43-35-32-00
Metro: Vavin

Credit: Visa and American Express
Remarks: Air-conditioning, non-smoking room

The sparkling seafood annex of its elegant and pricey parent Le Dôme, *this lower-priced edition offers only the freshest of lightly seasoned fish, attractively presented and served whole with a minimum of fuss in a convivial setting.*

Opened in 1991, this Montparnasse bistro enjoyed instant success. So much so, it has now spun off another Bistrot du Dôme in the fashionable Bastille district (2, rue de la Bastille, 75004, Tel: 48-04-88-44). Aside from the obvious qualities that insure success such as an intelligent blackboard selection of the freshest seafood, a marvelous chef in Liana Doyle, an unusually attentive and jovial staff, a bright and cheerful decor (yellow with blue and white tiles and grape-cluster glass ceiling fixtures), the compelling factor here is price. Economy also shows up in the wine list. Twelve wines are offered (six white, six red), all priced identically at under twenty dollars and perfectly suited for fish and seafood. Any of the offered bottles are available by the glass for about four dollars.

One's choice of seafood will be dictated by individual taste, but a few of the most successful dishes include the grilled baby turbot, the thick slice of tuna steak grilled in anchovy sauce, the bouillabaisse and the two dishes which seem most popular with Parisians: *fricassée de patogos* (a creamed curry-based clam stew) and *encornet à la plancha,* the grilled squid platter.

Recommended Dishes

Fricassée de Potagos. Creamed clam stew spiced with curry.
Anchois Grillés. Grilled anchovies.
Encornet à la Plancha. Grilled squid platter.
Friture de Céteaux. Deep-fried tiny sole.
Turbotin Grillé. Grilled baby turbot.
Pavé de Thon Sauce Anchois. Thick grilled slice of tuna steak in anchovy sauce.
Bouillabaisse. Provençal fish soup.
Rascasse au Basilic. Grilled scorpion fish seasoned with basil.
Cabillaud à la Moutarde. Baked codfish in mustard sauce.
Chocolatine aux Griottes. Chocolate layer cake with sour cherries.
Riz Condé. Creamed rice topped with whipped cream and strawberries.

WINE

Vouvray (Gaston Huet), Chinon (Charles Joguet), Côtes de Gascogne (Domaine du Jariquet).

LE BOURBONNAIS 

M. Roger Le Meur

Address: 29, rue Delambre, 75014 (off blvd. du Montparnasse; entry can be gained through the "7 Parnassiens" arcade)
Closed: Sat. lunch, and Sun.
Price Range: Fairly expensive
Tel: 43-20-61-73
Metro: Vavin or Edgar-Quinet
Credit: All major credit cards

A true provincial Burgundy restaurant, solid and generous, run by a master of the repertoire and aided by his charming family.

Roger LeMeur opened this restaurant in 1976 after a stint in the splendid upscale bistro, Chez Pauline, in the 1er. It was here he perfected all the Burgundian classics he now offers in his own charming *auberge.* Le Bourbonnais is also one of the few places in Paris that excels in the preparation of game and wild mushrooms. Here you will also find a first-rate *coq au vin* (chicken stewed in burgundy wine with onions and mushrooms), tasty fat vineyard snails in garlic butter, poached eggs in red wine sauce and an incredibly rich *ris de veau aux morilles sauce crémée au foie gras* (concocted of sweetbreads and morel mushrooms blended in a thick cream sauce with foie gras). The cheese platter is exceptional coming from the famed cheese establishment Androuet.

The friendly welcome and impressive rustic dining room with its rough walls, dark red ceiling crossed with ancient massive wooden beams, comfortable tables covered in white linen, and the lovely arrangements of fresh flowers all add up to a most memorable bistro experience.

Recommended Dishes

Salade Landaise. Southwest salad with smoked duck breast.
Oeufs en Meurette. Poached egg in red wine sauce.
Foie Gras de Canard à la Façon du Chef. Duck foie gras, a specialty of the chef.
Poëlon d'Escargot de Bourgogne. Vineyard snails in garlic butter.
Terrine de Gibiers. Game pâté (in season).
Ragout de Homard Breton. Lobster stew.
Filet de Boeuf au Poivre Vert ou Moelle. Filet of beef in green-pepper sauce or with bone marrow.
Ris de Veau aux Morilles. Creamed sweetbreads with morel mushrooms.
Coq au Vin Garni de Pâtés Fraîches. Fowl stewed in red wine and served with freshly-made noodles.
Mousse au Chocolat. Chocolate mousse with whipped cream.
Plateau de Fromages "Androuet." Top-quality cheese platter.

Wine

Menetou-Salon, Saint Pourçain.

La Cagouille 

M. Gerard Allemandou

Address: 10, place Brancusi (25, rue de L'Ouest), 75014
Closed: The week between Christmas and New Years and the first two weeks in August
Price Range: Expensive
Tel: 43-22-09-01
Metro: Gaité
Credit: Visa and Amex
Remarks: Non-smoking room

Delicious ultra-fresh seafood is simply prepared with no heavy sauces or garnishes to spoil its natural flavor. The shrimp are cooked live, the salmon grilled on one side and the steamed mussels lightly sprinkled with pepper. Reservations are essential as this is the best seafood bistro in Paris.

Gerard Allemandou, the chef-patron, comes from the Charentes, a region of France's Atlantic coast north of Bordeaux. He attaches as much importance to wine and rare cheeses as he does to fresh seafood and has amassed one of the finest collections of Cognacs in Paris. The menu inscribed on a large slate offers a list of dishes which change daily according to what is available that morning at the Rungis market. Though the *cagouille* is a little snail from Charente, no snails are served here. Instead there are delicate dishes of fish seasoned with simple herbs, salt or pepper and garnished with steamed or lightly sautéed vegetables; baby squid roasted in hot oil; skate in mustard sauce; a stewed assortment of *fruits de mer* and pan-fried scallops with garlic. The desserts are sophisticated treats and there are over eighty Cognacs with which to complete your meal. The decor is clean and modern with stone floors, marble-topped tables, natural wood and a wall divider filled with bottles of Cognac. Bread and salted Charentais butter are on each table. The room can become a bit noisy and crowded, but there is a large terrace facing the Place Brancusi.

Recommended Dishes

Céteau Poêlés. Tiny pan-fried sole.

Coques Vapeur. Steamed cockles.

Pétoncle Nature. Queen (tiny) scallops cooked without seasoning.

Crevettes Roses Poêlées Vivantes. Pink shrimp pan-fried while alive.

Flan de Brocheton au Beurre Blanc. Pike dumplings served in a white-wine butter sauce.

Turbotin Grillé. Small grilled turbot.

Raie Sauce Gribiche. Skate grilled and served with a spicy mayonnaise sauce with capers, cornichons and herbs.

Saint-Jacques Poêlées à l'Ail. Scallops pan-fried with garlic and butter.

Rouget Barbet à l'Huile d'Olive. Grilled red mullet in olive oil.

Poire Super. Fresh pear served on pear sherbet.

Profiteroles au Chocolat. Ice-cream-filled pastries covered with a glaze of melted chocolate.

Tarte Maison au Citron. Lemon tart.

Wine

Well-chosen wine list of mostly whites from all the great areas, including many small-vineyard Champagnes. Quincy, Sancerre, Chablis.

La Régalade 

M. Yves Camdeborde
Mme. Claudine Camdeborde

Address: 49, av. Jean Moulin, 75014
Closed: Sat. lunch, Sun. and Mon.
Price Range: Moderate
Tel: 45-45-68-58
Metro: Alésia
Credit: Visa
Remarks: Air-conditioning, open until midnight

A chic little bistro orchestrated by the former second-in-command at the luxurious Hôtel Crillon restaurant, offering modern renditions of regional food at affordable prices.

This antique bistro, far out in the quiet Alésia residential area beyond Montparnasse, was opened in 1992 by Yves Camdeborde and his wife, Claudine. They set out to offer traditional bistro fare, reinvented by incorporating stylish flourishes of contemporary haut cuisine, all at remarkably moderate prices. The unpretentious yet attractive little dining room has as its centerpiece a tempting display of crusty country breads. When you are seated by Claudine, a generous *terrine* of homemade pâté is put at your disposal. Go easy for the three-course 150F menu offers a wide choice of mouthwatering dishes ending with fabulous desserts.

Each dish can be approached as an adventure in discovery and, as is the case with any great restaurant, can be ordered without hesitation. A mandatory starter, however, is the signature appetizer *pisaladière de thon, mi-cuit aux olives noires,* a thin pastry loaf topped with paper-thin slices of slightly cooked fresh tuna in a black olive sauce. Another exceptional appetizer is the *hure de veau,* a jellied mixture of veal head, tongue and brains—indescribably delicious. For a main dish, one may opt for the simple *hachis parmentier* (shepherd's pie) usually described as hash leftovers in an anonymous sauce, but here it is a masterful haut cuisine dish made from pork blood sausage and garnished with a shallot, tarragon, and white wine sauce. The skillfully executed desserts are topped by the *soufflé chaud au grand marnier* or the *figues rôties à la crème de vanille* (roasted figs doused in a sweet vanilla-flavored liqueur).

All the carefully chosen wines are available at giveaway prices. They are young wines, selected to accent the wonderful rich flavors that are the trademark of Yves' cooking. For a nice finish, try the *madeleines* (delicious little shell-shaped sponge cakes) served with perfectly brewed coffee.

Recommended Dishes

Cochonnaille de la Maison Familiale. Top-quality assortment of cooked and cured pork products.

Pisaladière de Thon, Mi-Cuit aux Olives Noires. Fresh tuna in black olive sauce.

Terrine de Poireaux et Queues de Boeuf au Vin Rouge. *Terrine* of oxtail and leek.

Hure de Tête, Langue et Cervelle de Veau. Jellied brawn of the head, tongue and brains of veal.

Pintade Rôtie sur l'Os. Whole roasted guinea hen.

Hachis Parmentier de Boudin Noir Béarnaise. Blood sausage rendition of shepherd's pie.

Filet de Biche. Grilled doe steak.

Épaule de Lapin Braisée. Braised shoulder of rabbit.

Gigot d'Agneau de Pauillac aux Flageolets. Roast leg of lamb with baby lima beans.

Saint Pierre Rôtie au Laurier. John Dory fish roasted with bayleaves.

Coquilles St. Jacques Rôties au Beurre Demi-sel. Pan-roasted scallops served on buttered toast.

Soufflé Chaud au Grand Marnier. Flamed orange liqueur soufflé.

Figues Rôties à la Crème de Vanille. Roasted figs in vanilla cream liqueur.

Wine

Béarn, (Domain Guilhemas), Beaujolais, Vignoble du Ronsay (J. Paul Brun), Viña Esmeralda Blanc (Torrès).

Restaurant Bleu 

M. Elie Bousquet

Address: 46, rue Didot, 75014 (off rue d'Alésia)
Closed: Sat., Sun., July and August
Price Range: Moderate
Tel: 45-43-70-56
Metro: Pernety
Credit: None

A simple but wonderful neighborhood bistro frequented mainly by Parisians who come for the hearty Auvergnat food and wine. Don't be misled by the casual appearance. The quality of the produce and cooking is first rate.

Owner-chef M. Elie Bousquet is an Auvergnat who insists on using only quality ingredients in his preparations. A meal here might begin with a glass of Sauternes and some fine regional pâté or ham, *andouillettes* from Vive or Guéméné or *cou d'oie farci* (the neck skin of goose stuffed as a sausage with meat and spices). Recommended main courses include a crispy grilled *boudin* (blood sausage), grilled Charolais beef, veal braised with *cèpes, tripoux* (mutton tripe) and a delicious *truffade* made with sautéed potatoes, tomatoes, herbs and garlic. The setting, entirely decorated in blue, is simple, with lace curtains, a beautiful zinc bar and old engravings on the wall.

Recommended Dishes

Plat de Cochonnailles. Platter of assorted pork products.
Jambon d'Auvergne. Smoked ham from the Auvergne region.
Terrine Rouergate. Country pâté.
Salade Frisée aux Lardons. Chicory salad with bacon.

Truffade Auvergnate. Potato cake with Cantal cheese and bacon.

Chou Farci. Stuffed cabbage.

Pièce de Charolais Grillée (for two). Finest-quality grilled beef.

Tripoux Auvergnats. Stuffed and heavily seasoned mutton tripe.

Rouelle de Veau Braisée aux Cèpes. Boned fillet of veal braised and served with wild mushrooms.

Confits de Canard et Oie. Grilled preserved duck or goose.

Boudin de Campagne Grillé. Large grilled blood sausage.

Charlotte au Chocolat. Molded lady fingers filled with custard and covered with chocolate.

Tarte aux Prunes. Prune tart.

WINE

Saint-Pourcain, Cahors, Marcillac.

15e Arrondissement

La Gitane

Le Petit Mâchon

Le Petit Plat

Restaurant du Marché

Porte de Versailles

PLACES OF INTEREST

Gare Montparnasse

Heliport de Paris

Institut Pasteur

Musée Antoine Bourdelle

Musée Postal

Palais des Sports, Parc des Expositions

Parc Georges Brassens

La Ruche (The Beehive, an artists' colony built by Gustave Eiffel)

Square Saint-Lambert

Statue de la Liberté

Tour Montparnasse

Le Village Suisse (antiques market)

LA GITANE ★

M. Francis Mouchet

Address: 53 bis, ave. de la Motte-Piquet, 75015 (École Militaire area, south side)
Closed: Sun.
Price Range: Moderate
Tel: 47-34-62-92
Metro: Motte-Piquet or École-Militaire
Credit: Visa and MasterCard
Remarks: Non-smoking room

A popular bistro of this quarter, serving solid bourgeois dishes in an unpretentious setting. There is a pretty, secluded, plant-bordered summer terrace, a nice alternative to the rather large, impersonal dining room.

Located across from the Village Suisse, an antiques-dealers' mart, this neighborhood spot is busy for lunch and dinner. Since there is no written *carte,* the menu is handwritten on wall tiles and often changed according to market produce. There are no unusual specialties, but the standard fare is well handled and nicely priced. Simmered *pot-au-feu, confit de canard,* calf's head in vinaigrette and stuffed cabbage are some of the favorites. Service is a bit slow, but it is worth a luncheon if you happen to be in the area.

RECOMMENDED DISHES

Moules de Bouchot à la Normande. Tiny mussels served in cream and cider.
Filets de Hareng Cotonneaux. Herring fillets in oil.
Fromage de Tête, Sauce Ravigote. Headcheese in a spicy vinaigrette with mustard, *cornichons* and capers.
Escargots de Bourgogne. Vineyard snails in garlic butter.
Pot-au-Feu. Boiled beef with vegetables and broth.
Chou Farci Paysanne. Stuffed cabbage with onions and carrots.
Manchons de Canard Confit. Small cakes of preserved duck.
Fricassée de Canard aux Pâtes Fraîches. Light duck stew served with fresh pasta.

Cassoulet Toulousain. White-bean stew cooked in an earthenware pot with pork, sausage and duck.
Mousse au Chocolat. Chocolate mousse.
Profiteroles au Chocolat. Small ice-cream-filled pastries, covered with chocolate.

WINE

Côtes-de-Saint-Mont (Gascogne).

LE PETIT MÂCHON ★

Mme. J. Moussié
Chef: Alain Besnard

Address: 123, rue de la Convention, 75015 (off av. Félix Faure)
Closed: Sun. and August
Price Range: Moderate
Tel: 45-54-08-62
Metro: Boucicaut or Félix-Faure
Credit: Visa

You will need to reserve in this splendid bistro elegantly decorated in faux *marble, leather and mirrors. This is the annex to the prestigious Bistro 121 and here, as next door, you will find typical Lyonnais food and wine served in high style.*

The Petit Mâchon has been described as the most Parisian of the Lyonnais *bouchons.* A Lyonnais *bouchon,* by the way, is a delicatessen-type restaurant serving hearty food at all hours. The Lyonnais are traditionalists and the menu is an anthology of classic regional dishes including *rosettes, andouillettes, cervelas* served with buttery hot potatoes, steaming tripe prepared in various ways and dishes of mutton, veal or pigs' trotters. The wines naturally come from Lyon's backyard, the Beaujolais.

A second Petit Mâchon was opened by the Moussié family convenient to the Palais Royal and the Musée du Louvre (158, rue Saint-Honoré, 75001, Tel: 42-60-23-37).

Recommended Dishes

Pâté de Canard Maison. Duck liver pâté.
Petits-Gris en Cassolette. *Cassolette* dish of tiny gray snails in cream sauce.
Salade de Pieds de Mouton, Foies de Volaille et Oeuf Dur. Salad of pigs' feet, chicken livers and a hard-boiled egg.
Caviar Lyonnais. Warm lentils with shallots.
Andouillette Sauce Moutarde. Pork sausage in mustard sauce.
Tripoux. Heavily seasoned stuffed tripe.
Gras-Double à la Lyonnais. Ox tripe sliced and fried with onions, vinegar and parsley.
Tablier de Sapeur. Ox tripe grilled with egg and breadcrumbs.
Confit de Canard. Grilled preserved duck.
L'Onglet de Boeuf à l'Échalotes. Beef flank grilled with shallots.
Pieds de Porc Farci. Stuffed pigs' feet.
Jambonneaux aux Lentilles. Small roast ham knuckle with lentil garnish.
Gâteau de Riz Crème Anglaise. Rice pudding with fruit *confit* in a light egg custard.
Tarte-Tatin. Upside-down apple pie.

Wine

Cahors, Côteaux Lyonnais, Saumur-Champigny, Beaujolais.

Le Petit Plat 

Victor Lampreia
Jean Lampreia
Clémentine Gault

Address: 45 av. Émile-Zola, 75015
Closed: Mon., Tues. lunch, and 10 days in March
Price Range: Moderate
Tel: 45-78-24-20
Metro: Charles-Michels
Credit: Visa

Overwhelming success of the first tiny modern bistro in the touristy Left Bank necessitated the opening of this second restaurant located in a sedate residential area.

It was only in July of 1992 that the two brothers of deceased Master Chef José Lampreia set up a homey little bistro in the heart of the Vieux Paris, half a block from the Quais of the 5th arrondissement. This first bistro (Le Petit Plat, 3 rue des Grands Degrés, 75005, Tel: 40-48-85-34) features provincially-inspired, moderately-priced home-style cooking coupled with remarkable little country wines. Victor Lampreia, married to Henri Gault's daughter (*Gault-Millau Magazine*), asked Henri to formulate a wine list of unusual *vins de pays.* These unexpected treasures are a delight to discover and set off the tasty dishes perfectly.

The new restaurant, with much of the same cuisine and wine, resides in an authentic 1930s art deco building on the broad residential lined avenue Émile-Zola. It has the feeling of a long-established neighborhood bistro with two small dining areas, tastefully wood-paneled, and a cool-looking stone-covered bar. Sepia-toned photos of old Paris decorate the walls and comfortable banquettes and curved period chairs grace both rooms. The inevitable chalkboard menu contributes to the bistro ambience. Weather permitting, tables are set out on the spacious sidewalk out front.

Although the menu changes daily, certain dishes found in both restaurants have become classics such as the *terrine de lapin en gelée* (rabbit pâté in its natural jelly), the deceptively simple *tomates à la provençale* (halved juicy tomatoes sprinkled with herbs, garlic and breadcrumbs, then fried), the *ragôut des joues de porc* (light stew of pork cheeks), the farm-bred roast chicken smothered in a blanket of sautéed wild mushrooms and bacon, and for dessert the superb rhubarb tart.

Tasty food, little prices, delightful ambience, and a very Parisian crowd all contribute to the success of Le Petit Plat.

Recommended Dishes

Terrine de Lapin en Gelée. Rabbit *terrine* in aspic.

Effilochée de Boeuf aux Legumes Tièdes. Thinly-sliced "frayed" beef served on a bed of warm vegetables.

Tomates à la Provençale. Tomatoes stewed with breadcrumbs and fresh garlic.

Saucisson de Lyon, Pommes à l'Huile. Dried pork sausage with potatoes in oil.

Nage de Moules et Coques. Garlicky cream broth filled with mussels and baby clams.

Estouffade de Veau à la Provençale. Veal stewed in a sealed pot with wine, garlic, herbs and vegetables.

Poulet Fermier Rôti, Champignons Sautés aux Lardons. Roast free-range chicken with sautéed sliced mushrooms and bacon.

Tendron de Veau Mijoté, Carottes et Oignons Confits. Roast veal ribs slow-stewed with carrots and preserved onions.

Rognons Rôtis au Thym, Gratin Dauphinois. Roasted veal kidneys accompanied by scalloped potatoes.

Daube de Joues de Porc. Braised pork cheeks stewed in wine.

Poisson du Jour. Market fresh fish-of-the-day.

Camembert au Lait Cru de Normandie. Raw milk Camembert cheese.

Mousse au Chocolat. Chocolate mousse with whipped cream.

Tarte à la Rhubarbe. Rhubarb tart.

Aumonière aux Abricots (ou Figues) et Glac à la Vanille. Thin crepe filled with apricot or fig compote, topped with vanilla ice cream.

WINE

Wine list created by Henri Gault of inexpensive but extraordinary country wines. Côte de Vaison-la-Romaine (stand-out).

RESTAURANT DU MARCHÉ

M. Michel Massia
Chef: Christiane Massia

Address: 57–59, rue de Dantzig, 75015 (off blvd. Lefebvre)
Open: Daily
Closed: August
Price Range: Fairly expensive
Tel: 48-28-31-55
Metro: Convention or Porte-de-Versailles
Credit: All major credit cards
Remarks: Air-conditioning

An old world atmosphere and the best traditions of French cooking reflected in fine specialties from the Southwest are found here. The singular menu features foie gras, ham, chicken, fruits and vegetables from the markets of Mont-de-Marsan, capitol of Landes, the region south of Bordeaux.

A lovely old 1930s dining room graced by lace table covers, multicolored tile floor, little oval mirrors, long drapery at the windows, old banquettes, and a pretty wooden bar adorned with a splendid bouquet of fresh flowers is the backdrop for remarkably high-quality cuisine, much appreciated by a sophisticated clientele. It thrives on delicate duck or goose *confits,* foie gras prepared in different ways, a delicious rustic pumpkin soup, beef braised in a robust Madiran wine sauce and plump farm chicken stewed in Armagnac.

Michel Massia is a charming host who is even more enthusiastic about the food than his guests, and Chef Christiane Massia supervises the kitchen. It is delightful to eat on the flowery terrace on a warm evening.

RECOMMENDED DISHES

Foie Gras d'Oie ou de Canard Maison. Exemplary goose or duck foie gras served cold in a terrine, or warm in salads.

Jambon Fermier. Country ham of rare quality from Mont-de-Marsan.

Omelette aux Peaux de Canard Croustillantes. Savory omelette with grilled, seasoned duck-skin bits.

Soupe aux Choux. White cabbage soup.

Soupe de Citrouille à la Bourgeoise. Puréed pumpkin soup.

Rillettes de Canard au Vinaigre de Miel. Potted duck spread with honey vinegar.

Piballes. Tiny fried young eels from Bordeaux region.

Cassoulet Mijoté au Confit. Slow-simmered Toulousian stew cooked in an earthenware pot with preserved goose and white beans.

Daube de Boeuf au Madiran. Braised beef slow-cooked in red Madiran wine.

Lièvre à la Royale. Boned hare stuffed with foie gras and truffles and braised in red wine and brandy.

Chartreuse de Perdreaux. Mold of young partridges and braised cabbage accompanied by a vegetable purée.

Estouffade de Poulet à l'Armagnac. Slowly stewed hen combined with vegetables, herbs and Armagnac brandy.

Magret de Canard. Grilled fattened duck breast.

Poule au Pot Farcie. Chicken stuffed with crumbs, egg and seasoning, poached in bouillon, and served with cream sauce and slices of stuffing.

Bar au Beurre Blanc. Sea bass in a creamed white wine and shallot sauce.

Carte de Desserts. Regional desserts prepared by the chef daily.

WINE

Madiran (Laplace), Tursan blanc et rosé (Dulucq), Côtes de Roussillon (Comtesse de Massia), Chalosse Rouge. In-depth selection of Bordeaux including very old bottles of Château d'Yquem, Sauternes.

16e Arrondissement

Auteuil—Passy—Muette—Trocadéro

PLACES OF INTEREST

Bois de Boulogne (*Longchamp* and *Auteuil* racetracks, *Jardin d'Acclimatation* children's park, *Fleuriste d'Auteuil* gardens, hothouses and arboretum, *Jardins de Bagatelle*)

Cimetière de Passy

Maison de la Radio France

Musée d'Art Moderne

Musée de la Mode du Costume

Musée des Arts et Traditions Populaires

Musée Balzac

Musée Guimet

Musée Marmottan (*Jardins du Ranelagh*)

Musée du Vin

Palais de Chaillot (*Musées de la Marine, de l'Homme, des Monuments Français, du Cinéma Henri Langlois*)

Palais de Tokyo (*Musée d'Art Essai*)

Place du Trocadéro (gardens and aquarium)

Rue la Fontaine (buildings by *Henry Guimard*)

La Butte Chaillot 

M. Guy Savoy

Address: 112, Avenue Kleber, 75016 (Place du Trocadero area)
Open: Daily all year
Price Range: Fairly expensive
Tel: 47-27-88-88
Metro: Trocadero
Credit: All major credit cards
Remarks: Air-conditioning, open till 1 A.M.

Two-star Chef Guy Savoy can now claim five bistros in his growing culinary empire. This recent entry is the most impressively designed and appears to be the most successful and popular to date.

An eighty-seat bi-level restaurant fashioned out of a former bank space has been brilliantly redesigned with polished hard wood floors, frosted glass walkways and terra-cotta-style beige and ochre walls. An impressive hi-tech steel-and-glass staircase leads down from the street level to the lower dining room in which comfortable turquoise leather chairs are reflected in handsome glass mirrors, giving the illusion of spaciousness. This is the contemporary concept of a bistro, built for the 90s, and works well in this posh, upscale neighborhood.

The magic touch of Chef Guy Savoy continues to offer a taste-filled menu of irresistible dishes including a delicious salad of tiny snails *(petits gris),* grilled salmon, *cassoulet,* spit-roasted farm chicken with mashed potatoes, and exceptional grilled *charolais* beef served with the lightest of deep-fried straw potatoes. The famous signature dessert, *tarte fine aux pommes* (thin apple tart), must be ordered at the start of the meal. The *plats du jour* are scrawled on a mirror in true bistro fashion. The small wine list is well chosen but pricey, though two inexpensive house wines are always available by the glass.

One may encounter similar bistro-chic cuisine at Guy Savoy's other three places all bearing the same name, Bistro de L'Étoile (13, rue Troyon, 75017, Tel: 42-67-25-95; 19, rue Lauriston, 75016, Tel: 40-67-11-16 and 75, av. Niel, 75017, Tel: 42-27-88-44) and Les Bookinistes (53, Quai des Grands Augustins, 75006, Tel: 43-25-45-94).

Recommended Dishes

Terrine de Joue et de Queue de Boeuf en Pot-au-Feu. *Terrine* of beef cheeks and tail.

Crème de Lentilles au Fumet de Langoustines. Cream of lentil soup flavored with crayfish.

Huîtres en Nage Glacé. Plate of fresh oysters in a cream mousse.

Salade de Petits Gris et Pommes de Terre. Tiny snails served with potato salad.

Raviolis du Royans aux Herbes Fines. Raviolis filled with cheese and tossed with fine herbs.

Volaille Fermière à la Broche, Pommes Purèes. Spit-roasted free-range chicken with mashed potatoes.

Poitrine de Veau au Romarin à la Broche. Spit-roasted breast of veal with rosemary.

Noix d'Entrecôte à la Moelle. Cushion of beef sautéed in marrow sauce, accompanied by scalloped potatoes.

Filet de Rascasse au Citron et Gingembre. Grilled fillet of scorpion fish with lemon and ginger.

Saumon Grillé sur la Peau. Grilled salmon fillet with the skin.

Mille-Feuille "Minute" à la Vanille. Thinly-layered puff pastry filled with whipped cream.

Tarte Fine aux Pommes. Thin apple tart (must be ordered at start of meal).

Tarte au Citron. Rich egg and butter tart made with whole lemons, topped with meringue and browned in the oven.

Wine

Bourgueil (Christophe Chasle), Pinot Noir d'Alsace (André Ostertag), Côtes du Rhône "Séguret" (Château de la Courançonne), Gamay de Touraine (H. Marionnet), Macon Villages blanc (Jean Manciat).

LE RELAIS DU PARC 

M. Joël Robuchon
Chef: Gilles Renault

Address: 55 av. Raymond-Poincaré, 75016
Open: Daily all year
Price Range: Fairly expensive
Tel: 44-05-66-10
Metro: Victor-Hugo
Credit: All major credit cards
Remarks: Air-conditioning, non-smoking room

This long-awaited entry of three-star Chef Joël Robuchon in the bistro sweepstakes is installed in the recently redone dining room of the Hôtel Parc Victor Hugo in the posh 16ᵉ arrondissement.

While waiting for his own restaurant to be relocated in the historic belle epoque building adjacent to the hotel, Chef Robuchon placed his talented second into the hotel dining room after extensive redecorating. The finished product resembles the clubby decor of an English colonial building with glossy white walls, polished marble floors, mahogany-stained fan-back chairs and mirrored French doors with a garden view. This is a bistro redefined in modern times, casually chic, unpretentious, and by first-class restaurant standards inexpensive. A three-course meal without drinks will run about fifty dollars, which is less than any first course in Robuchon's first restaurant.

The cuisine is always deceptively simple, yet excites the eye and palate. The cream of pumpkin soup is served in a hollowed-out squash or tiny pumpkin, the salad of baby vegetables is set out like a mosaic and is ultra-fresh and colorful, and the famous rabbit stew *(civet de lapin au lard)* is presented in a copper pot accompanied by the lightest of whipped potatoes. Many old bistro classics are updated and are sometimes unrecognizable by traditional standards. The simple herring filets with steamed potatoes are superb, the country chicken liver pâté is served copiously in its own *terrine* and the braised beef with carrots is served here as a wrapped sausage *(boeuf braisée en crèpine aux carottes)*. A simple apple tart *(tarte fine aux pommes)* is served thin as a wafer and topped with homemade vanilla ice cream.

This is a rare opportunity to sample great cooking at reasonable prices, served in a friendly yet dignified setting and should not be missed.

Recommended Dishes

Soupe Crémeuse de Potiron en Surprise. Cream of pumpkin soup.

Salade de Petits Légumes aux Saveurs Orientales. Baby vegetables salad.

Filets d'Hareng Marinées aux Pommes Tièdes. Marinated herring filets served with warm potato salad.

Hampe de Veau Poêlée au Citron. Flank of veal pan-fried with lemon.

Civet de Lapin au Lard. Rabbit stew with bacon accompanied by mashed potatoes.

Queue de Boeuf Braisée en Crèpine aux Carottes. Braised oxtail with carrots wrapped and cooked in a pig's membrane.

Pigeon Rôti à la Broche aux Endives Confites. Spit-roasted pigeon on a bed of braised chicory.

Barbue Grillée à l'Huile Épicée, aux Courgettes. Grilled sea brill with olive oil and spices served with zucchini.

Chartreuse de Sandre et Saumon. A mousse of salmon and pike served on a bed of cabbage.

Tarte Fine aux Pommes. Warm apple tart with ice cream.

Mikado au Chocolat. A layer cake of alternating dark and milk chocolate.

Oeufs à la Neige. Poached egg whites served with a vanilla custard sauce.

Wine

Côtes-de-Bordeaux (Domaine de Chastelet), Chinon (Olga Raffault), remarkable short list of wines priced between $15–$45.

Le Scheffer ★

M. Joël Chauvin
Mme. Joëlle Chauvin

Address: 22, rue Scheffer, 75016 (off av. Paul Doumer)
Closed: Sun.
Price Range: Moderate
Tel: 47-27-81-11
Metro: Pompe or Trocadero
Credit: Visa

An animated neighborhood bistro popular with a smart set of Passy regulars. The food is typical bistro with some regional dishes thrown in for good measure.

A red-lacquered facade and awning decked with colored lights are a gay welcome to this friendly spot a few blocks from the Trocadéro Gardens. There is a nice wooden bar at the front of a large dining room lined with several rows of little tables covered with red-and-white-checkered cloths protected by paper. A pretty floral-patterned white-tile floor is a nice contrast to the dark red ceiling. Lace curtains, old posters and photos scattered about the walls add a pleasant touch to the room. If you choose the *plat du jour,* posted on the window, with a pitcher of the Côtes-du-Rhone you will have eaten well for the price. The service is friendly but may be a little slow if it's crowded.

Recommended Dishes

Salade d'Epinards Frais et son Oeuf Poché. Fresh spinach salad topped by a poached egg.
Confit de Canard Maison. Grilled preserved duck.
Navarin d'Agneau Printanier. Lamb stew with spring vegetables.
Entrecôte Bordelais "Steak-Frites." Beef rib steak in a red wine and shallot sauce accompanied by french fries.
Côte de Boeuf Grillée au Gros Sel. Ribs of beef grilled in sea salt.
Saumon à la Crème de Ciboulette. Slices of steamed salmon in a white wine cream sauce with chives.

Crème Brûlée. Rich cream custard topped with caramelized sugar.
Soufflé Glacé au Grand Marnier. Chilled soufflé drizzled with orange-flavored liqueur.
Profiteroles au Chocolat. Ice-cream-filled cream puffs topped with melted chocolate.

WINE

Chinon, Cahors, Côtes-du-Rhône, Sancerre, Blanc.

17e Arrondissement

Aristide

Le Bistrot d'À Côté "Flaubert"

Chez Fred

Chez Georges

Les Gourmets des Ternes

Le Petit Salé

Batignolles—Ternes

PLACES OF INTEREST

Avenue de la Grande Armée

Musée de l'Air

Palais des Congrès

Parc Monceau

Place des Ternes

Sainte-Marie-des-Batignolles

Square des Batignolles

ARISTIDE ★★

M. Jean-Philippe Siegrist
Mme. Viviane Siegrist

Address: 121, rue de Rome, 75017 (near rue Legendre)
Closed: Sun., one week in August
Price Range: Moderate
Tel: 47-63-17-83
Metro: Rome
Credit: Visa

This truly traditional bistro with a classic Burgundian repertoire, located across the street from the old railroad tracks in a block of aging middle-class houses, is never mentioned in guidebooks yet is always filled to capacity.

"Cuisine au beurre et à la graisse d'oie—produits frais." This very unusual claim is conspicuous on the top of the menu. What it means is that all fresh produce is used and all cooking contains either butter or goose fat, no microwave cooking, no canned or frozen foods will be tolerated and that all dishes will be made to order and personally prepared by this fanatic of freshness and quality, Chef Philippe Siegrist.

People know Aristide "from the mouth to the ear." It has stood in this spot since its founding in 1893. A bastion of *cuisine bourgeoise,* it looks barely altered as you can see from the 1928 photo hanging in the entrance. The small enclosed glass terrace with original iron screens, the bamboo planters filled with geraniums, the friendly green-and-white-striped awning, the lace café curtains, the old seltzer bottles in the window, the well-spaced linen-covered tables, the old wooden bar with its antique pewter water fountain, the old wood-timbered ceilings, globe light fixtures and more, are evocative of the simple honesty of this genuine old-fashioned bistro. And best of all, the generous portions of splendidly-prepared food served by youthful waiters in correct long white aprons is above reproach.

RECOMMENDED DISHES

Rillettes de Herring. Minced, pounded and preserved herring

spread.
Foie Gras de Canard. Duck foie gras served cold.
Salade de Lentilles au Lard Fumé. Lentil and smoked bacon salad.
Poèlon d'Escargots à l'Armagnac. Casserole of vineyard snails flamed with Armagnac brandy.
Oeufs en Meurette. Poached eggs in red-wine sauce.
Soufflé au Roquefort. Savory blue cheese soufflé.
Blanquette de Veau. Veal in white wine cream sauce with onions, carrots and mushrooms.
Confit de Canard, Pommes à l'Ail. Grilled, preserved duck with garlic potatoes.
Filet de Boeuf Grillé au Poivre. Grilled filet of beef with green peppercorn sauce.
Andouillette A.A.A.A.A. au Sancerre. Grilled pork sausages accompanied by a savory potato cake.
Sole à l'Oseille. Filet of sole in creamed sorrel sauce.
Millefeuille "Maison." Cream-filled, thinly-layered puff pastry.
Clafoutis. Batter tart with seasonal fruit fillings.

WINE

Coteaux du Lyonnais (by the pitcher), Château Beaulieu.

LE BISTROT D'À CÔTÉ "FLAUBERT" 

M. Michel Rostang

Address: 10, rue Gustave-Flaubert, 75017 (at rue Rennequin)
Closed: Open every day
Price Range: Moderate
Tel: 42-67-05-81
Metro: Ternes or Courcelles
Credit: Visa, MasterCard, and Amex
Remarks: Air-conditioning

Flea market bric-a-brac decorate the walls of M. Rostang's "Bistro Next Door," the first of four new establishments operating under the same name. The menu includes traditional bourgeois fare with some interesting Lyonnais and modern specialties.

You will feel instantly at home in this small, colorful bistro installed on the premises of an old 1900s grocery store. The original shelves, tin ceiling and tile floor provide a perfect backdrop for the many interesting pictures and antiques used as decoration. Ten or so marble-top bistro tables fill the cozy room inside and several more crowd the sidewalk out front.

The waiters are young and attentive and will guide you through the menu and daily specials, which are chalked on a centrally located blackboard. Included on the list is a nicely prepared salad of warm lentils with sausages, a *carpaccio* of fresh tuna and basil in olive oil, and a tasty chicken liver *terrine.* The main courses include chicken in red-wine sauce and Lyonnais sausage with ravioli. A warm *clafoutis* is a good choice for dessert. The wine list is strongly oriented toward the Bordeaux and Rhone, and some of the less-expensive crus are very good.

Michel Rostang now counts four spin-offs, all serving lightened versions of classic bistro favorites and each called Le Bistrot d'À Côté. They are:

FLAUBERT 10, rue Gustave-Flaubert, 75017, Tel: 42-67-05-81

VILLIERS 16, av. de Villiers, 75017, Tel: 47-63-25-61

NEUILLY 4, rue Boutard / Neuilly 92200, Tel: 47-45-34-55

SAINT-GERMAIN 16, blvd. Saint-Germain, 75005, Tel: 43-54-59-10

Recommended Dishes

Boudin Noir aux Pommes Fruits. Blood sausage and apples served with a buckwheat flat cake.

Terrine de Foie de Volaille Campagnarde. Country-style duck-liver pâté.

Salade Tiède de Lentilles et Cervelas de Lyon. Warm lentil salad with smooth pork sausage.

Andouillette Tirée à la Ficelle. Poached pork sausage cut into long strips.

Gratin de Gras-Double "Léon de Lyon." Oven-browned tripe served in a *gratin* dish.

Sabodet Lyonnais aux Ravioles de Romans, Crème Vinaigrée. Hot pigs'-head sausage served in thick slices with tiny ravioli.

Poulet à la Fermière Rôti *(for two).* Roast chicken "farm-house"-style.

Joues de Cochon Confites au Vin Rouge. Pigs' cheeks preserved in red wine.

Fricassée de Volaille au Curry, Riz Blanc et Riz Sauvage. Curried chicken stew served with white and wild rice.

Gratin de Pommes aux Amandes et Calvados *(must be ordered at start of meal).* Browned apple dish with almonds and apple brandy.

Clafoutis Chaud aux Framboises *(must be ordered at start of meal).* Custard tart with raspberries.

Crème Brûlée à la Vanille. Custard, topped with brown sugar caramelized under the grill.

WINE

Crozes-Hermitage, Sancerre, Saint-Nicolas-de-Bourgueil, Brouilly, various Bordeaux.

CHEZ FRED 

M. Robert Marc

Address: 190 bis, blvd. Pereire, 75017 (off av. des Ternes)
Closed: Sun. and two weeks in August
Price Range: Moderate
Tel: 45-74-20-48
Metro: Ternes, Porte-Maillot or Pereire
Credit: All major credit cards

One of the most convivial neighborhood bistros, with all the trappings of a Lyonnais bouchon *(tap room). The* plats du jour *are always traditional meat preparations and complemented by a few Lyonnais bistro offerings.*

Fred, short for Alfred Peyraud, was the original owner of this famous bistro containing the actual table where fictional detective Inspector Maigret sat for lunch with his cronies from the Sûreté. The new *patron,* M. Marc, has not missed a beat since taking over in 1985. He kept the old 1930s decor and traditional *plats du jour* to the delight of regulars. An hors d'oeuvre table at the entrance displays tempting *terrines*, sausages, salads, beef headcheese and herring fillets. The *carte* is a roster of true bistro dishes featuring the specialties which for years have made this place popular. This is a good place to try the pork sausages *(andouillettes A.A.A.A.A.)* or the *tête de veau*. Freshly made *tartes*, chocolate cake and the candied chestnuts with *crème fraîche* are the most notable desserts. There is a nicely varied wine list.

Recommended Dishes

PLATS DU JOUR

***Gigot d'Agneau Rôti aux Flageolets** (Mondays).* Roast leg of lamb with small green kidney beans.

***Petit Salé** (Tuesdays).* Lightly salted cooked pork.

***Tête de Veau** (Wednesdays).* Calf's head.

***Pot-au-Feu** (Thursdays).* Boiled beef with vegetables and broth.

***Boeuf à la Mode** (Fridays).* Braised pot roast with vegetables.

***Sauté d'Agneau** (Saturdays).* Sautéed lamb.

Cochonnailles (Assiette de Saucisson Ailles). Assorted pork products.

Jambon de Campagne. Smoked country ham.

Saucisson Chaud Pommes à l'Huile. Hot Lyonnais sausage with potatoes in oil.

Andouillettes Grillées de l'A.A.A.A.A. Grilled pork sausages.

***Pavé de Rumsteak "Fred"** (for two).* Thick beef steak.

Confit de Canard. Broiled preserved duck.

Marrons Confits à la Crème Fraîche. Preserved chestnuts with slightly soured cream.

Tarte-Tatin. Upside-down apple pie.

Wine

Muscadet-Sur-Lie, Gamay-de-Touraine, Chénas.

CHEZ GEORGES ★ ★ ★ ★

M. Roger Mazarcuil
Chef: Jean Merle

Address: 273, blvd. Pereire, 75017 (Place de la Porte Maillot area)
Closed: August
Price Range: Fairly expensive
Tel: 45-74-31-00
Metro: Porte-Maillot
Credit: Visa and MasterCard

A famous old bistro that has remained unchanged for half a century. It lacks charm but has plenty of character. Here is an opportunity to enjoy old-fashioned cooking at its best.

Chez George, which was opened by the Mazarcuil family in 1926, has since been filled with members of a loyal following who come to this out-of-the-way spot in droves. This is one place that is absolutely worth the trip, but don't go without a reservation or a hearty appetite. The scene you'll enter is classic bistro: crowded tables, banquettes, etched glass, mirrors and lace curtains. Jostling waiters, balancing huge heavily laden trays over their heads, push through the line of customers waiting to be seated. Most come for one of the three famous specialties. Most sought after is the leg of lamb with *flageolets,* small tender green kidney-shaped beans. The second favorite choice is the ribs of beef with sliced potatoes, and the third is *petit salé* (salt-cured pork) with cabbage. Daily specials and a variety of tempting hors d'oeuvres add diversity to the menu. The most popular desserts are the giant eclair and the *tarte-Tatin.* There are several wine options but the best is a Cahors.

RECOMMENDED DISHES

Salade de Museau de Boeuf. Headcheese salad served in vinaigrette.
Tête de Veau, Sauce Vinaigrette. Calf's head served in a cold oil-and-vinegar sauce.
Saucisson Chaud Pistaché à la Lyonnaise. Large slicing sausage

studded with pistachio nuts, served warm.

Soupe au Chou. Cabbage soup.

Pied de Veau Vinaigrette. Veal foot in a cold oil-and-vinegar dressing.

Escargots Bourgogne. Vineyard snails served in garlic butter.

Baltique Hareng à la Crème. Marinated herring fillets served with thick sour cream.

Cochonnailles (Andouilles de Vire et de Guéméné). Two varieties of large, smoked pork sausage.

Saumon Cru Mariné à l'Aneth. Cured, marinated salmon with dill.

Gigot Rôti aux Flageolets Fins. Roast leg of lamb with small green kidney beans.

Petit Salé au Chou. Light salted pork with cabbage.

Train de Côtes de Boeuf, Gratin Dauphinois. Ribs of beef, served with sliced potatoes baked in cream and browned.

Plat de Côtes Gros Sel en Pot-au-Feu (Wednesdays). Boiled beef ribs with vegetables and broth.

Hachis Parmentier (Plat du Jour). Minced-meat-and-potato casserole (shepherd's pie).

Haricot de Mouton (Plat du Jour). Mutton stew with potatoes, turnips and onions.

Glace Café, Sauce Caramel. Coffee ice cream with caramel sauce.

Eclair Géant. Large cream-filled pastry with choice of chocolate or coffee topping.

WINE

Côte-de-Brouilly, Quincy, Cahors.

LES GOURMETS DES TERNES 

M. Francis Marie

Address: 87, blvd. de Courcelles, 75017 (Place des Ternes area)
Closed: Sat., Sun. and August
Price Range: Moderate
Tel: 42-27-43-04

Metro: Ternes
Credit: Visa
Remarks: Air-conditioning

This celebrated old bistro, with a reputation for serving excellent, no-nonsense food made from the finest ingredients, is always crowded and full of life. The owner selects the products, oversees the cooking and welcomes and seats the guests. For summer dining there are sidewalk tables just around the corner from the Place des Ternes.

It is almost impossible to get a reservation in this unpretentious establishment, soon to celebrate its centennial year, where yuppies, sophisticates, businessmen, tourists, professionals and interesting trendy types sit elbow-to-elbow at little paper-covered tables. Artificial flowers, aging wall mirrors, worn leather banquettes, old light fixtures and other relics of the past are part of the outdated 50's decor. Meats are exceptional, bought and aged by the owner who was once a butcher, and while you wait for a steak grilled exactly to your order you might try the celery root salad, the artichoke bottoms or the Burgundy snails. Salmon and sole are the only alternatives to meat and the *pêche melba* or *baba* with rum the best desserts. The service is professional but often brusque.

Recommended Dishes

Céleri Rémoulade. Raw shredded celery root in a spicy mayonnaise dressing.
Rosette du Beaujolais. Large dry pork sausage, sliced and served cold.
Museau de Porc Vinaigrette. Salad of pork brawn in a spicy vinaigrette.
Saint-Jacques à la Provençale. Pan-fried scallops served Provence-style with tomatoes, garlic and onions.
Boeuf Bourguignon au Vieux Vin. Beef stewed in vintage wine with tiny onions and mushrooms.
Andouillette de Campagne Grillée. Grilled country pork sausage.
Entrecôte à la Moelle avec Frites. Broiled rib steak with bone-marrow sauce, served with french fries.
Côte de Boeuf. Roast ribs of beef.
Crème Caramel. Vanilla-flavored flan.
Pêche Melba. Vanilla ice cream with sliced peaches covered in a black currant sauce *(cassis).*

Baba au Rhum. Yeast cake drenched in rum syrup and served with cream. A bottle of rum accompanies this dish and is at your disposal.

WINE

Côtes-du-Rhône, Beaujolais.

LE PETIT SALÉ ★

Mme. Laraki

Address: 99, ave. des Ternes, 75017 (off blvd. Gouvion, Porte Maillot area)
Open: Daily all year
Price Range: Moderate
Tel: 45-74-10-57
Metro: Porte-Maillot
Credit: All major credit cards
Remarks: Non-smoking room

A minuscule bistro with a charming patronne *where you can choose a robust Gamay or Côtes-du-Rhone to accompany a heaping plate of salt pork, vegetables and lentils served with crusty slices of bread. A selection of cheese and a* tarte-Tatin *complete this very substantial meal.*

Petit salé is one of the old-time favorite bistro specialties. Various cuts of pork, usually the shoulder, shank or breast, are pickled in brine for three to six days. The meat is then boiled and served with an aromatic vegetable garnish. In the classic preparation the lentils are served separately. In a restaurant so named, this is of course the specialty, but there are other good main-course choices on the menu such as leg of lamb, steak and Kakos, *jarret* of pork with potatoes. The house foie gras, marinated leeks, and herring with hot potatoes are tasty additions to this limited menu and you will be pleased with the liter of Gamay d'Anjou placed on your table.

Recommended Dishes

Foie Gras Frais Maison. Fresh duck liver.
Terrine du Chef Maison. Sumptuous house pâté.
Salade aux Lardons. Chicory salad with bacon.
Poireaux Vinaigrette. Leeks in vinaigrette.
Entrecôte. Grilled rib steak.
Confit de Canard. Preserved duck leg with sliced sautéed potatoes.
Côte de Boeuf. Roast rib of beef.
Cassoulet. White bean casserole with pork, sausage, and preserved duck.
Selle d'Agneau. Roast saddle of lamb.
Petit Salé aux Lentilles et aux Carottes. Lightly salted cooked pork with lentils and carrots.
Feuilleté de Turbot à l'Oseille. Pastry shell filled with turbot in sorrel sauce.
Tarte-Tatin. Upside-down apple pie.
Mousse au Chocolat. Chocolate mousse.
Crème Caramel. Vanilla-flavored flan.

Wine

Gamay d'Anjou, Sauvignon Blanc, Côtes-du-Rhône.

18e Arrondissement

Montmartre—Clichy

PLACES OF INTEREST

Basilique de Sacré-Coeur

Cimetière St.-Vincent

Marché aux Puces (Porte de Clignancourt)

Moulin de la Galette

Moulin Rouge, Lapin Agile

Musée d'Art Juif (Jewish Art Museum)

Musée du Vieux Montmartre

Place du Tertre

La Vigne (Vineyard)

Le Maquis (Bistrot de Clodenis) ★

M. Claude Lesage

Address: 69, rue Caulaincourt, 75018 (Place du Tertre area)
Closed: Sunday
Price Range: Moderate
Tel: 42-59-76-07
Metro: Lamarck-Caulaincourt
Credit: Visa

Owner/Chef Claude Lesage presents a short seasonal menu that changes five or six times a year. His smart, rather formal bistro is a short walk from the touristy Place du Tertre and one of the best in the area. Reservations are suggested.

Le Maquis is the bistro annex of the elegant little restaurant Clodenis, located just north of Sacré Coeur. The tasteful decor includes some old photographs, potted palms, fresh flowers and pink paper tablecloths. An old oak bar adds to the charm and in summer there is a tiny terrace along the front. The waiters, dressed in black, are friendly and courteous and will point out the specialties in season such as wild boar with prunes or pheasant with cabbage.

Desserts are delicious, freshly-made treats and include a wonderful orange mousse with chocolate sauce, a chocolate *charlotte* and a *dessert du jour* (of the day). A lunch menu at around 60F ($12) is a bargain and wine from the Gard region of the Languedoc is served in carafes.

Recommended Dishes

Mousseline de Poivron à l'Avocat. Creamed sweet pepper and avocado mousse.
Salade de Flétan Fumé. Smoked halibut salad.
Feuilleté au Roquefort. Puff pastry filled with roquefort cheese.
Briôche de Moelle. Rich bun filled with bone marrow.
Petit Salé aux Lentilles. Lightly-salted pork with lentils.
Sauté de Mouton aux Haricots. Browned mutton with beans.
Magret de Canard à l'Aigre Doux. Fattened duck breast with

sweet-and-sour sauce.
Lapin à la Moutarde. Rabbit in mustard sauce.
Caille au Raisin. Quail marinated in cognac and roasted with raisins.
Coq-au-Vin. Chicken stewed in red wine.
Sanglier aux Pruneaux. Roast wild boar with prunes (in season).
Jambonette de Volaille à l'Estragon. Poultry sausage, shaped like a small ham, flavored with tarragon.
Côte de Veau à la Normande. Broiled veal chop in a cream and Calvados sauce.
Brandade de Morue. Creamed salt cod.
Steak de Thon à la Provençale. Grilled tuna steak with tomato, garlic and parsley.
Filet de Flétan au Poivre Vert. Halibut fillet with green peppercorns.
Tarte Sablée Cannelle aux Framboises. Shortbread cinnamon tart with raspberries.
Mousse à l'Orange et au Chocolat Chaud. Orange mousse with melted chocolate.
Charlotte au Chocolat et Crème Anglaise. Bavarian cream sponge cake filled with chocolate.

WINE

Vin de Pays du Gard (in carafes)—white, red or rosé.

MARIE-LOUISE

M. and Mme. Jean Coillot

Address: 52, rue Championnet, 75018 (off rue de Clignancourt)
Closed: Sun., Mon., August and holidays
Price Range: Fairly expensive
Tel: 46-06-86-55
Metro: Simplon or Porte-de-Clignancourt
Credit: Visa, MasterCard and Diners
Remarks: Non-smoking room

An attractive, well-heeled, older clientele frequents this classic bistro serving perfectly executed bourgeois food, simply prepared and nicely presented. The house specialty is poularde Marie-Louise, *a traditional version of chicken in cream sauce.*

This very out-of-the-way old house near the Porte de Clingnancourt is definitely worth a trip if you are looking for absolutely classic food in intimate surroundings reminiscent of another time. There is a small room on each of two floors, adorned with copper pots, engravings, fresh flowers, white table linens, crystal and heavy cutlery. The waiters don't like new faces and will caution you that the portions are very large—and they are.

Chef Jean Coillot prepares simple but very tasty first courses followed by an excellent *boeuf à la ficelle, coq-au-vin,* veal chops, veal kidneys in Madeira sauce and, in season, a whole sea bass *(bar).* There are also seasonal desserts and the *crème caramel* is reputed to be one of the best in Paris.

Recommended Dishes

Terrine de Gibier. Wild game pâté.

Salade Maison. Melange of wild mushrooms, sliced ham and assorted greens in a creamy vinaigrette.

Saucisson Chaud. Hot garlic sausage served with potato salad.

Rognons de Veau au Madère. Veal kidneys cooked in Madeira wine.

Poularde Marie-Louise. Fattened hen in a cream-and-paprika sauce with rice. A specialty of the house.

Coq-au-Vin. Chicken stewed in red wine.

Côte de Veau Grandmère. Veal chop with onions, mushrooms, bacon and potatoes.

Boeuf à la Ficelle, Pommes Rissolées. Poached filet of beef, served with fried potatoes (for two).

Faux Filet Grillé, Sauce Béarnaise. Grilled sirloin filet accompanied by a thick sauce of egg yolks, vinegar, shallots, tarragon and white wine with butter.

Tête de Veau Sauce Gribiche. Poached parts of calf's head accompanied by a thick vinaigrette with chopped herbs and egg.

Lotte aux Pâtés Fraîches au Basilic. Fried monkfish served with fresh pasta in a tomato and basil sauce.

Crème Caramel. Vanilla-flavored flan.

Clafoutis aux Cerises. Deep-dish cherry batter cake.

Mousse au Chocolat. Whipped cream and chocolate dessert.

WINE

Excellent Loire Valley wines such as Chinon, Saint-Nicolas de Bourgueil, and Muscadet.

À LA POMPONNETTE 

Mme. Paulette Carteron

Address: 42, rue Lepic, 75018 (off rue J. de Maistre)
Closed: Sun. evening, Mon. and August
Price Range: Fairly expensive
Tel: 46-06-08-36
Metro: Blanche
Credit: None

The old-fashioned entrées *and generous home-style cuisine may be expensive but you will spend an unforgettable evening surrounded by fascinating photographs and a cast of colorful characters. Reservations are recommended.*

It is a scene out of the past as you make your way through the colorful bar, crowded with habitués smoking hand-rolled cigarettes and kibitzing with the bartender, to the dining room where Mme. Carteron is dishing out copious portions of fresh greens from a display table covered in oilcloth. The walls are filled with old prints, paintings and photographs, all having some connection with the family.

The large handwritten menu is supplemented by a list of daily specials and cautions a 5F charge for any change. The mackerel marinated in Muscadet is the thing to begin with, but the herring and the Burgundy snails are also good choices. Any of the poultry dishes will be well done, including perfectly roasted quail with cherries. If you feel in an adventurous mood, try the *tête de veau.* It is served here with enormous slices of tongue and brains. There are some fine desserts, including a selection of cakes, sherbets and ice cream.

Recommended Dishes

Lapin en Gelée aux Fèuilles d'Estragon. Rabbit *terrine* cooked with tarragon leaves.

Maquereau Mariné aux Aromates et Muscadet. Superb version of mackerel fillets poached in white wine and served cold as a first course.

Escargots de Bourgogne. Vineyard snails served in garlic butter.

Crudités. Varied and copious selection of raw vegetables served with a cold sauce.

Tête de Veau, Langue et Cervelle Sauce Ravigote. Calf's head, tongue and brains in a spicy vinaigrette with mustard, *cornichons* and capers.

Magret de Canard Sauce Moutarde au Poivre Vert. Fattened duck breast grilled in a mustard sauce with green peppercorns.

Confit de Canard Maison. Preserved duck grilled and served with sautéed potatoes in oil.

Blanquette de Veau à l'Ancienne. Veal stew in white sauce made from cream and egg yolks.

Charlotte au Fromage Blanc au Coulis de Framboise. Fruit custard mold with cream cheese and raspberries.

Vacherin. Baked meringue filled with ice cream, whipped cream and fruit.

Wine

Adequate selection of fairly uninteresting wines not up to the quality of the cuisine.

19e Arrondissement

Le Pouilly-Reuilly (Pré-St.-Gervais)

Buttes-Chaumont

PLACES OF INTEREST

Bassin de la Villette

Canal d l'Ourcq, Canal St.-Denis

La Cité des Sciences et de l'Industrie

Parc de la Villette (Inventorium)

Parc des Buttes-Chaumont

Le Pont de Crimée (last surviving drawbridge in Paris)

LE POUILLY-REUILLY (PRÉ-ST.-GERVAIS) 

M. Jean Thibault

Address: 68, rue André-Joineau, 93310 (off rue d'Estienne d'Orves)
Closed: Sun., and August through September 7
Price Range: Moderate
Tel: 48-45-14-59
Metro: Hoche
Credit: All major credit cards
Remarks: Non-smoking room

High-quality cuisine, half-bistro and half-regional, with specialties from the Berry, Auvergne, Nivernais and Solonge regions, is served in a warm and provincial atmosphere. Located on the outskirts of town, at the Porte de Pantin. Reservations are suggested.

A heavy, wooden, zinc-top bar, little tables covered in yellow cloths, fresh flowers, paintings and various other bric-a-brac brighten the decor of this famous old-time bistro which attracts a fanatically loyal, upscale clientele. Mme. and M. Thibault began the business many years ago, he in the kitchen and she in the dining room. Everyone receives a warm welcome and a taste of the very good freshly made foie gras to start, but after that one is on one's own in choosing from an extensive menu. All the down-to-earth basics are excellent: *boudin, andouillettes* in Pouilly wine, calf's sweetbreads, knuckle of ham with cabbage, chicken with crayfish, a stew of freshwater eel, veal kidneys in mustard sauce and *confit* of duck with small green kidney beans. The portions are enough to satisfy any appetite and may be accompanied by "little" wines from Berry, grand crus from Bordeaux or the outstanding Pouilly Fumé for which the house is famous.

RECOMMENDED DISHES

Oeufs en Meurette. Poached eggs in a red-wine sauce.
Pâté de Grenouilles Chaud. Pâté made from frogs' legs and served hot.
Andouillette Grillée au Pouilly. Grilled pork sausage cooked in

Pouilly wine.

Escargots en Coquilles. Snails with garlic butter served in shells.

Ris de Veau aux Morilles. Calf's sweetbreads in mushroom sauce.

Boudin Noir. Grilled blood sausage.

Rognon de Veau Dijonnaise. Veal kidneys in mustard sauce.

Paupiettes à la Morvandelle. Thin slices of beef, rolled and braised.

Queue de Boeuf Vinaigrette. Oxtail braised and served in vinaigrette.

Raie Beurre Noisette. Skate in brown butter sauce.

Éclair Géant Café. Eclair with coffee-cream filling, topped with coffee icing.

Gâteau de Riz au Coulis d'Abricots. Rice pudding filled with an apricot mixture.

WINE

Especially fine selection of small young growths from Bordeaux and Beaujolais. Excellent Pouilly-Fumé. Also a few great old vintage bottles of Burgundy and Bordeaux.

20ᵉ Arrondissement

Aux Becs Fins

Boeuf Gros Sel

Ménilmontant

PLACES OF INTEREST

Carrefour de Belleville—Café la Veielleuse
Cimetière de Belleville
Cimetière du Père Lachaise
L'Eglise de Saint-Germain-de-Charonne
Villa d'Ermitage
Villa Faucher

AUX BECS FINS 

Mme. Édith Lefebvre

Address: 44, blvd. de Ménilmontant, 75020 (across from main entrance to Père Lachaise)
Closed: Sun. lunch, Sept. 10–26
Price Range: Fairly expensive
Tel: 47-97-51-52
Metro: Père-Lachaise
Credit: All major credit cards

Delectable cuisine with the taste of the Perigord region is skillfully prepared by Mme. Lefebvre and served in a friendly rustic atmosphere. Fish appears daily on the menu but cassoulet *or* gras-double *(tripe) are the dishes to order.*

Wooden rakes hang from the ceiling in this well-known old *auberge* near the Père Lachaise cemetery. A pretty striped awning covers a little closed outdoor terrace. Inside, a long row of small tables faces the bar and an iron spiral staircase leads to another room above. The whole feeling is one of a country cottage. Copious house *terrines* and delicious foie gras are among the notable starters to be followed by either fish stew or tripe. Almost everything on the menu, though, is excellent and the helpings are generous.

RECOMMENDED DISHES

Foie Gras Maison. Exceptional, fresh duck liver.
Terrine de Foie de Canard. Duck liver pâté.
Terrine de Campagne. Coarse country pâté.
Truffade Perigourdine. Potato cake with Cantal cheese.
Gras-Double Lyonnais. Ox tripe sliced and fried with onions, vinegar and parsley.
Blanquette de Veau à l'Ancienne. Poached veal stewed in cream sauce and garnished with onions and mushrooms.
Pied et Tête de Veau, Sauce Gribiche. Calf's head and trotters in a mustard-mayonnaise sauce.
Cassoulet à l'Oie Perigourdin. Goose-and-white-bean stew cooked in an earthenware pot.

Rognons de Veau en Cassolette. Veal kidneys served in a small casserole dish.
Ragoût de Poisson Mère Edith. Light fish stew.
Pavé au Poivre. Thick slice of beef steak with pepper sauce.
Gâteau au Chocolat. Formidable chocolate cake.

WINE

Muscadet, Burgundy, Beaujolais.

BOEUF GROS SEL ★

M. Gilbert Brett

Address: 120, rue des Grands-Champs, 75020 (off rue du Volga)
Closed: Sat. lunch, Sun., July 15–Aug. 24
Price Range: Moderate
Tel: 43-73-96-58
Metro: Maraîchers
Credit: Visa

A unique menu, a congenial, countrified atmosphere and a mixed clientele with a common appreciation for hearty, rib-sticking food.

You'll know you are on the right block when you see the welcoming little red facade of Boeuf Gros Sel. Inside, the feeling extends to two rustic rooms, simply decorated with lace curtains and red-and-white cloths, an amiable *patron* and happy customers who know how to live. There is only one menu which lists ten appetizers including a choice of pâtés, salads, *boudins* and herring. You should go easy here because there is a gigantic *pot-au-feu* to follow—boiled beef with vegetables, marrow bones, coarse salt and *cornichons.* If you still have room there are cheese and dessert. If beef *gros sel* doesn't strike your fancy, *petit salé* is offered as an alternative.

Recommended Dishes

Des Saladiers et des Terrines. Abundant and varied selection of salads and pâtés served as hors d'oeuvres.

Petit Salé aux Lentilles. Lightly salted cooked pork served with lentil beans.

Boeuf Gros Sel (Pot-au-Feu). Boiled beef with vegetables and broth.

Brie de Meaux. Exceptionally good cheese cut from the center portion of the brie.

Tarte aux Pommes Maison. Apple tart.

Wine

Beaujolais or Côtes-du-Rhône.

PART II

Wine Bars

If any establishment epitomizes the current restaurant scene in Paris, it is the wine bar or *bistro-à-vin.* These little places, with their strong provincial flavor, have captured the hearts of sophisticated Parisians and travelers.

A decade or two ago, most people thought of wine bars as dimly lit, smoke-ridden haunts patronized by the owner's wine-loving cronies. In some places such a description is still pretty accurate, but in others you will find a substantial range of fine food and wine in a upscale, tasteful setting. This new-style establishment owes its existence to the influence of the English wine bars introduced to Parisians several years ago. The idea was to offer vintage wine by the glass and a selection of simple food to show off the wine to its best advantage. Robust pâtés, chunky *terrines,* garlicky sausages, cold meats, sourdough bread and cheese provided the basic fare. Only recently have menus been expanded to include hot meals.

Today's most popular wine bars are restauranty, serving food one might expect to find in a first-rate bistro. The chef offers his suggestion along side an *à la carte* menu. Good quality traditional cooking and a selection of regional preparations are made. The wines reflect the preferences of the owner, but most lists include fresh, dry, and full-bodied whites, fruity and more serious reds, a few stock favorites, and one or two more unusual *crus* from lesser known vineyards. The key is quality and variety. A wine list that is changed has the same appeal as a change of menu.

Each wine bar is the special creation of its owner. Many

bistrotiers (wine-bistro owners) have become leading wine experts, spending a large part of their time traveling throughout France hunting down new and obscure wines.

Every year an award, the "Coupe au Meilleur Pot" (best glass of wine trophy), is bestowed upon one Paris *bistrotier* by a jury of peers within the Académie Rabelais. Originally established in 1954 in Lyon by Marcel Grancher and a few of his friends, jury selection eventually moved to Paris where it remains today. The award was designed to encourage wine-bar owners to maintain a tradition of quality wine and buffet foods. The recipient is chosen for his merits and accomplishments as a promoter of wine. He must personally select and bottle the wine, then "help create an atmosphere of conviviality in which lasting friendships are likely to be forged." A winner will always be a celebrity in the world of wine and any bistro displaying the words "Coupe du Meilleur Pot" on the outside is considered a special place.

The first Meilleur Pot cup was awarded to Hubert Troquier, owner of the Café du Champ de Mars, in 1954. The bistro no longer exists and the *patron* is now deceased, but the cup continues, changing hands each year. The award is given to the *patron* and not to his establishment. If the title holder changes bistros or retires he takes the cup with him.

One of the myths about Paris is that you can eat well in any corner "zinc" on pâté, cheese and bread with a glass of good wine. Unfortunately, though the bread is usually fresh, the pâté and cheese can be pretty poor and the anonymous *petit blanc* or *ballon de rouge* pretty rough.

Like today's bistros, wine bars flourish throughout the city. Styles run from the belly-up-to-the-bar kinds to mini-chains to upscale restaurants. The standard of food varies from one to another, but most menus feature a brief selection of hot and cold dishes and desserts. Often a regional theme is apparent in both food and wine.

The list which follows includes only a few of the more popular and better-known places where you can enjoy a casual, quick and inexpensive lunch or dinner. But remember—Parisians frequent wine bars in the morning at breakfast, before and during lunch hours, and before dinner. These times are likely to be very busy, so reservations are suggested.

1er Arrondissement

Aux Bons Crus

La Cloche des Halles

Le Cochon à L'Oreille

L'Écluse des Halles

Juvenile's

Le Relais Chablisien

Le Rubis (Chez Prat)

Taverne Henry IV

Aux Tonneaux des Halles

Willi's Wine Bar

Aux Bons Crus

Address: 7, rue des Petits Champs, 75001
Tel: 42-60-06-45
Metro: Pyramides
Hours: Noon to 10 P.M., Sat. Noon to 6 P.M., Closed Sunday

Located in the heart of the trendy Place des Victoires area, this rustic 100-year-old bistro has recently undergone a facelift to keep up with its fashionable boutique neighbors. Food is basic *bistro* with a Lyonnais accent. The steak tartare served here is famous and the omelettes are perfectly prepared. A dozen wines are served by the glass favoring those of the Loire Valley with other regions represented. Although customers may eat or drink standing at the handsome marble bar, the low-ceiling upstairs dining room can be more peaceful.

La Cloche des Halles

Address: 28, rue Coquillière, 75001
Tel: 42-36-93-89
Metro: Les Halles or Louvre
Hours: 8 A.M. to 10 P.M., Sat. 10 A.M. to 6 P.M., Closed Sunday

A famous old wine bar named after the wooden bell that used to ring out across Les Halles. Here the wine is purchased directly from the growers and bottled by the knowledgeable owner Serge Lesage in his cellars. The wide choice available by glass or bottle is mostly from Beaujolais and the surrounding area of southern Burgundy. Cooked meats and homemade ham on the bone, quiches, open-faced sandwiches, and daily specials accompany the excellent wines. The Beaujolais wine is probably the best available in Paris.

Le Cochon à l'Oreille

Address: 15, rue Montmartre, 75001
Tel: 42-36-07-56
Metro: Les Halles
Hours: 4 A.M. to 4 P.M., Closed Sunday

An authentic *belle époque* working-class bistro featuring an extraordinary display of ceramic murals depicting the old Les Halles market. Smoked salmon, fish stew and a superb onion tart are served along with daily specials and hot meals sent over from the kitchens of the nearby bistro Le Brin de Zinc. The house wine served by the carafe is fine and other wines which may be sampled are nothing special but go to drink in the great atmosphere.

L'Écluse des Halles

Address: Rue Mondétour, 75001
Tel: 40-41-08-73
Metro: Etienne Marcel
Hours: Noon to 2 A.M., Closed Sunday in Jan. and Feb.
Credit Cards accepted.

One of a chain of five spread around the capitol, this was originally a British concept. The idea was to sample rare vintage wines by the glass at a fraction of the bottle price. Now taken over by the giant food and services company Groupe Accor, the Écluse wine bars, with their familiar burgundy-and-green façades, all feature superb vintage Bordeaux accompanied by sumptuous dishes. Top-quality foie gras, *terrines,* and smoked salmon highlight the à la carte menu, so expect to pay dearly.

Juvenile's

Address: 47, Rue de Richelieu, 75001
Tel: 42-97-46-49

Metro: Palais-Royal
Hours: 11 A.M. to 11 P.M., Closed Sunday

British owner, Tim Johnson, has turned a simple neighborhood café into one of the most chic and popular wine bars in Paris. Here the basic accompanying food is the Spanish snacks known as *tapas,* but a very British roast beef sandwich is always on the menu. Sherry wine of exemplary quality can be had at the *tapas* bar along with a fine selection of carefully chosen Rhône and Southern Burgundy wines.

LE RELAIS CHABLISIEN

Address: 4, rue Bertin-Poirée, 75001
Tel: 45-08-53-73
Metro: Châtelet
Hours: 8 A.M. to 10 P.M., Closed Sunday and August
Visa accepted

This friendly and cozy country *auberge* has been neatly installed by congenial host Christian Faure in a tiny street just off the Pont-Neuf. An outstanding selection of Chablis and other Burgundy wines can be had by the glass or bottle. The accompanying food, ranging from simple salads, cheeses and crusty sandwiches made from loaves of country bread, to the more elaborate dishes served in the upstairs dining room, are of exceptional quality and reasonably priced.

LE RUBIS (CHEZ PRAT)

Address: 10, rue du Marché-Saint-Honoré, 75001
Tel: 42-61-03-34
Metro: Tuileries or Pyramides
Hours: 7 A.M. to 10 P.M., Sat. 9 A.M. to 4 P.M., Closed Sunday and two weeks in August

A famous old wine bistro, one of the most picturesque in Paris, features Beaujolais and Côtes du Rhône wines skillfully chosen at the vineyards and bottled in the cellar by *patron* Albert Prat. Each day the kitchen features a hot *plat du jour* and fine assortments of *charcuteries, rillettes,* assorted cold meats, fillets of herring, and cheeses always served along with famous Poilâne bread. This extremely popular bistro once sold 1,000 bottles of Beaujolais Nouveau one fateful evening, effectively blocking downtown traffic all night.

TAVERNE HENRY IV

Address: 13, Place du Pont Neuf, 75001
Tel: 43-54-27-90
Metro: Pont-Neuf
Hours: Noon to 10 P.M., Closed Sat., Sun. and August

Strategically located on the tip of the Île de la Cité, in the Place Dauphine, Robert Cointepas—a true lover and expert on the wines of Beaujolais, Montlouis and Bordeaux—dispenses his "finds," along with good country produce in the form of ten appetizingly-prepared cold platters and a choice of open-faced sandwiches. Cointepas also features delicious tiny snails from the Charentes region, the perfect accompaniment to vintage Bordeaux wines.

AUX TONNEAUX DES HALLES

Address: 28, rue Montorgueil, 75001
Tel: 42-33-36-19
Metro: Les Halles
Hours: 7 A.M. to 11 P.M. (Tues. thru Fri.), Mon. 7 A.M. to 7 P.M., Sat. 5:30 P.M. to Midnight, Closed Sunday
Credit Cards accepted.

Don't be put off by the unremarkable decor; this is a classic zinc-bar bistro in the old Les Halles tradition, recently taken over by Patrick Fabre and his caring staff. The kitchen has been totally revamped and now skillfully prepares classic bistro dishes and exemplary desserts to go with an excellent wine list of Loire Valley and Beaujolais *crus*. The bistro is located on the pedestrian rue Montorgueil. Stop in and experience a delicious meal, a refreshing glass of fresh fruity wine, and a nostalgic trip in a convivial atmosphere.

WILLI'S WINE BAR

Address: 13, rue des Petits Champs, 75001
Tel: 42-61-05-09
Metro: Palais-Royal
Hours: 11 A.M. to 11 P.M., Closed Sunday
Visa accepted.

Willi, short for Mark Williamson, runs the perfect, elegant and snobish "English Type" wine bar which, despite its British origin, is very *Parisien*. Over 300 *crus* may be found here with an emphasis on the finest Rhône Valley wines. This assortment is most eclectic, with many countries represented, especially Spain and Italy. An imaginative menu of hot and cold dishes is ideally prepared to accompany the extraordinary choice of fine wines.

2^e Arrondissement

La Côte

L'Entre-Deux-Verres

La Côte

Address: 77, rue de Richelieu, 75002
Tel: 42-97-40-68
Metro: Bourse
Hours: 7:30 A.M. to 8:30 P.M., Closed Saturday and Sunday
Visa accepted

Just steps away from the Bourse (stock exchange), Marc Fabre has transformed a simple 1930s traditional bar into a highly successful *bistro à vin* that was awarded the title "Best Bistro" for the year 1991. A thoughtful choice of Rhône, Loire Valley and Beaujolais wines is offered, many of which are bottled in the cellar rooms beneath the bistro. A small set menu of hot, hearty bistro specials and cold platters served by Marc's wife, Primrose, accompany the wines.

L'Entre-Deux-Verres

Address: 48, rue Sainte-Anne, 75002
Tel: 42-96-42-26
Metro: Quatre-Septembre
Hours: Noon to 3 P.M., Closed Saturday, Sunday and August
Visa accepted

Everything in this ancient converted *hôtel des postes*—food, wine and patron Loïc de Roquefeuil—hails from Bordeaux. This is the perfect spot to sample *foie gras de canard* accompanied by a glass of Sauternes. Regional specialties such as *lamproie au vin* (eel in wine sauce), excellent cheeses, and dainty sweet desserts enhance the wines grown in the family vineyards around Entre-Deux-Mers and Fronsac in Bordeaux.

4e Arrondissement

Le Coude Fou

L'Enoteca

La Tartine

Le Coude Fou

Address: 12, rue du Bourg-Tibourg, 75004
Tel: 42-77-15-16
Metro: Hôtel-de-Ville
Hours: Noon to 4 P.M. and 6 P.M. to 2 A.M.
Credit Cards accepted

Located in a quiet corner of the Marais, this agreeable little bistro with its long wooden bar and reputation for simple well-priced dishes stays open till all hours. The interesting selection of little wines is personally "found" by *patron* Patrick Segall and changes monthly. If you prefer to sit at the handsome bar rather than a table you will be offered a generous assortment of Lyonnaise sausages and a dozen wines by the glass. Fish dishes and poultry with a touch of "nouvelle" predominate at the table.

L'Enoteca

Address: 425, rue Charles V, 75004
Tel: 42-78-91-44
Metro: Saint-Paul
Hours: Noon to 2 A.M., Closed the last three weeks in August
Visa accepted

L'Enoteca is considered by many to be one of the premier wine bistros of Paris and, interestingly, both the food and wine are 100 percent Italian. Here one finds more than one-hundred-twenty good and rare wines accompanied by delicious *trattoria* cuisine. Located in an ancient building in the heart of the Marais, we can't think of a better place for Sunday dinner

LA TARTINE

Address: 24, rue de Rivoli, 75004
Tel: 42-72-76-85
Metro: Saint-Paul
Hours: 8 A.M. to 10 P.M., Closed Tuesday, Wednesday morning, and August

Follow the rue de Rivoli to its eastern end and it spills out into the Marais. Here, La Tartine remains untouched by time or fresh paint, run by octogenarian and passionate wine devoté Jean Bouscarel. M. Jean took over this ancient café in 1941 and has always offered cold meats and *tartines* (open-faced sandwiches) but one comes here to drink, not eat. There are 3,000 bottles of wine in La Tartine's cellar, including some 60 vintage Beaujolais wines and thirty *crus* served by the glass. This must be a mandatory stop for any serious wine imbiber.

5e Arrondissement

Les Pipos

Au Soleil d'Austerlitz

Les Pipos

Address: 2, rue de L'École-Polytechnique, 75005
Tel: 43-54-11-40
Metro: Maubert-Mutualité
Hours: 8 A.M. to 9 P.M., Saturday 8 P.M. to 1 A.M., Closed Sunday

A tiny wine bar with the look of a corner café, Les Pipos features a classic 1930s period bar, aged wooden bistro tables, and funky fake vines running down the walls. Jean-Michel Delhoume and his wife set up shop here in 1990 opposite the school. Because of their combined years of experience they have met with outstanding success. The couple delight in playing the nostalgic songs of Edith Piaf and Aristide Bruant on their antique record player. This is the real thing, no tourists here, just regulars enjoying Jean-Michel's passion for wine, fun and good, simple country food.

Au Soleil d'Austerlitz

Address: 18, blvd. de l'Hôpital, at rue Nicolas-Houël, 75005
Tel: 43-31-22-38
Metro: Gare d'Austerlitz
Hours: 6 A.M. to 9 P.M., Saturday 7 A.M. to 6 P.M., Closed Sunday and August
Visa accepted.

There is not much to distinguish this outstanding wine bistro from the countless family cafés and simple *brasseries* that cover Paris, but the diversity and quality of the rare country wines selected and bottled by André Calvet lifts this establishment far above the ordinary. Knowledgeable people combine a visit to the nearby Jardin des Plantes (botanical gardens) with a detour to Au Soleil d'Austerlitz for an Auvergne-fix of cooked ham, pâtés, *fritons,* sausages, and copious daily specials of regional dishes.

6e Arrondissement

Bistrot des Augustins

L'Écluse Saint-Michel

Bistrot des Augustins

Address: 39, Quai des Grands-Augustins, 75006
Tel: 43-54-41-65
Metro: Saint-Michel
Hours: 11 A.M. to 2 A.M.

Just past the upscale English wine bar L'Écluse, along the *quai,* is this remarkable little *bistro à vin.* A dozen Beaujolais and Côtes-du-Rhône wines are offered by the glass and served along with delicious omelettes, homemade daily specials, and delightful fruit tarts. Noëlle Oiry and her daughter Marie oversee the kitchen, tables, and diminutive oak-and-marble bar. It is rare to find so appealing and relaxing a situation so close to the incredible tumult of Boulevard Saint-Michel.

L'Écluse Saint-Michel

Address: 15, Quai des Grands-Augustins, 75006
Tel: 46-33-58-74
Metro: Saint-Michel
Hours: Noon to 1:30 A.M., Closed Sunday
Credit Cards accepted
See page 239, 1er arrondissement, L'Écluse des Halles.

7e Arrondissement

Le Sancerre

Au Sauvignon

Le Sancerre

Address: - 22, av. Rapp, 75007
Tel: 45-51-75-91
Metro: École-Militaire or Alma-Marceau
Hours: 7:30 A.M. to 8:30 P.M., Closes at 4 P.M. on Saturday, Closed Sunday and one week in August
Visa accepted

Alphonse Mellot designed his rustic wine bar in the style of a country *auberge,* reminiscent of his home in Sancerre. It is remarkably unpretentious but comfortable, and rates highest marks for home-grown Sancerre *cru* wine and *crottin de Chavignol* goat cheese, considered some of the finest in Paris. Creamy cheese or herb omelettes with home-fried potatoes accompanied by a fresh salad are always available. Don't fail to note the fanciful Art Nouveau façade just across the street, the best-preserved in Paris.

Au Sauvignon

Address: 80, rue des Saints-Pères, 75007
Tel: 45-48-48-02
Metro: Sèvres-Babylone
Hours: 8:30 A.M. to 10:30 P.M., Closed Sunday and August

Marie-Françoise, daughter of the founder, and her husband, Michel, run this stylish wine bar that caters to an affluent crowd located in a boutique-intensive, upscale neighborhood. The decor of floor-to-ceiling wine-related pictures, frescoes, and caricatures, combined with the warm welcome of the entire Vergne family, make for a relaxed and amusing visit. No hot dishes are served but a selection of *tartines* are prepared on the wonderful sourdough bread of Lionel Poilâne. Classic, fruity Quincy wine is the drink of choice but there is a good selection of little-known country wines from the Loire Valley and Burgundy.

8e Arrondissement

Le Bistrot du Sommelier

Ma Bourgogne

L'Écluse François

L'Écluse Madeleine

Le Val D'or

Le Bistrot du Sommelier

Address: 97, blvd. Haussmann, 75008
Tel: 42-65-24-85
Metro: Saint-Augustin
Hours: Noon to 3 P.M. and 7 P.M. to 10:30 P.M., Closed Saturday evening, Sunday, and the last week of July through the first three weeks in August
Credit Cards accepted

Philippe Faure-Brac is a connoisseur of wines and considered one of the top sommeliers of the world, but no less impressive are his culinary talents. This is the only place in Paris that offers a *dégustation* of great wines with complimentary dishes personally chosen by M. Faure-Brac. Rare vintages of Rhône and Bordeaux wines may also be enjoyed by the glass.

Ma Bourgogne

Address: 133, blvd. Haussmann, 75008
Tel: 45-63-50-61
Metro: Miromesnil
Hours: 7 A.M. to 8:30 P.M., Closed Saturday and Sunday
Credit Cards accepted

The atmosphere here is that of a bustling *brasserie* and, as expected, lunch is always a mad scramble as customers fill the spacious restaurant/wine bar to sample the hearty Burgundian food and excellent selection of Mâcon region wines representing the best of Beaujolais and Burgundy. Owner Louis Prin purchases all his wines directly from the producers and bottles most of them himself. His intense Pouilly-Fumé is a standout and the Chenas from Beaujolais is superb.

L'Écluse François 1er

Address: 64, rue François-1er, 75008
Tel: 47-20-77-09
Metro: George V
Hours: Noon to 1:30 A.M.
Credit Cards accepted

See page 239, 1er arrondissement, L'Écluse des Halles.

L'Écluse Madeleine

Address: 15, Place de la Madeleine, 75008
Tel: 42-65-34-69
Metro: Madeleine
Hours: Noon to 1:30 A.M.
Credit Cards accepted

See page 239, 1er arrondissement, L'Écluse des Halles.

Le Val D'or

Address: 28, av. Franklin D. Roosevelt, 75008
Tel: 43-59-95-81
Metro: Saint-Philippe-du-Roule
Hours: 7:30 A.M. to 9 P.M., Closes Saturday at 5 P.M., Closed Sunday
Visa accepted

The most popular wine bar in this highly fashionable district is Le Val D'or, where owner Géraud Rongier has amassed some 13,000 bottles. Customers at the street-level bar sit elbow-to-elbow enjoying a glass or two of Beaujolais and a thick slice of *jambon à l'os* carved off the bone and served on Poilâne bread. If you choose to eat downstairs in the small dining room, opt for a copious serving of *boeuf bourguignon* or the *plat du jour.* Wine down here must be ordered by the bottle but you pay only for what you drink.

9e Arrondissement

Les Bacchantes

La Cave Drouot

L'Oenothèque

Les Bacchantes

Address: 21, rue Caumartin, 75009
Tel: 42-65-25-35
Metro: Opéra or Madeleine
Hours: 11:30 A.M. to 5:30 A.M., Sunday: 11:30 A.M. to 10 P.M.
Closed: Les Bacchantes closes for a few hours each morning for cleaning purposes, otherwise it is always open.
Credit Cards accepted

Owner Raymond Pocous has crafted a true wine bistro, that is, a place to relax, communicate, and have a good time unencumbered by the pressures of the day. Here one may enjoy steak and *frites,* remarkable home-made foie gras, *charcuteries* and superb cheeses. If you allow M. Pocous to guide you through his selection of little *vins des pays* you will be in for a treat.

La Cave Drouot

Address: 8, rue Drouot, 75009
Tel: 47-70-83-38
Metro: Richelieu-Drouot
Hours: 7:30 A.M. to 9 P.M., Closed Sunday
Credit Cards accepted

Ever since 1980 when Jean-Pierre Cachau bought the *brasserie* Le Bossuet and changed the name to La Cave Drouot, this wine bar/restaurant has become a mecca for the art dealers of the famous Drouot auction house and the brokers from the nearby Bourse. Cold meats are served in the bar and substantial *plats du jour* are featured in the restaurant section. In the fall one may sample the famous hare stew, *liévre à la royale.* Although wonderful Loire Valley and Beaujolais wines are a specialty we urge the adventurous to taste the Basque country wines, in particular the white Béarn wine Pacherenc du Vic Bihl and the slightly rough but delicious Madiran.

L'OENOTHÈQUE

Address: 20, rue Saint-Lazare, 75009
Tel: 48-78-08-76
Metro: Notre-Dame-de-Lorette
Hours: Noon to 10:30 P.M., Closed Saturday, Sunday, and last three weeks in August
Credit Cards accepted

This fine establishment operates more as a quality restaurant than *bar-a-vin.* The refined cuisine served in tasteful surroundings is in the hands of owner/chef Daniel Hallée, formerly sommelier of the three-star Chez Jamin. Wines of the Jura are of particular interest here but one may also discover treasures from other regions, including a selection of more than fifty superb cognacs. The upscale decor, service, and quality of the food and wine makes the somewhat elevated prices understandable.

10e Arrondissement

L'Enchotte

Le Rallye (Chez de Conquans)

Le Réveil du Xe

L'Enchotte

Address: 11, rue de Chabrol, 75010
Tel: 48-00-05-25
Metro: Gare-de-l'Est or Poissonnière
Hours: Noon to 2:30 P.M., and 6 P.M. to 11 P.M., Closed Saturday evening and Sunday

We believe the most unappreciated and ignored *bistro à vin* in Paris is this unpretentious establishment of Richard Bartoszynski. The lovely blue façade and long wooden bar face the superb architecture of the Saint-Quentin covered market. Very reasonably priced menus feature the freshest the market has to offer and at least a dozen wines by the glass may be accompanied by an assortment of *charcuteries* or *tartines* on Poilâne sourdough bread. On Thursday evening one can enjoy *le jazz hot.*

Le Rallye (Chez de Conquans)

Address: 267, rue du Faubourg-Saint-Martin, 75010
Tel: 46-07-22-83
Metro: Stalingrad or Louis Blanc
Hours: 7 A.M. to 8:30 P.M., Closed Sunday

Why, you may ask, would anybody venture to a lonely street corner facing an elevated subway in a deteriorating quarter of northern Paris? The answer is to visit with the generous and jovial Antoine de Conquans. Hailing from Cantal, his Auvergnat background favors a cuisine of regional specialties such as stuffed cabbage, *Tripoux* and *andouillettes.* The wine selection though modest in scope is headed by an outstanding Pouilly and a superb Côtes de Brouilly. Here you may also sample the almost mythical wine of the Côtes-d'Auvergne, the Chanturgues Rouge, a rich, tannic Gamay wine produced in infinitesimal quantities, an outstanding accompaniment to any heady dish.

LE RÉVEIL DU X^E

Address: 35, rue du Château-d'Eau, 75010
Tel: 42-41-77-59
Metro: Jacques Bonsergent or Château-d'Eau
Hours: 7 A.M. to 9 P.M., 7 A.M. to 11 P.M. on Tuesdays, Closed Saturday and Sunday
Credit Cards accepted

If you did not know that an awakening (*réveil*) beckoned you on the corner of the tiny rue du Château-d'Eau, you would pass by this rather ordinary-looking zinc bar. Here you will find very special wines selected and bottled by the young Daniel Vidalenc and an authentic regional Auvergnat cuisine prepared by the charming Marie-Catherine Vidalenc. Stuffed cabbage, veal knuckle with lentils, *aligot* and tripe are among the menu choices.

11e Arrondissement

L'Ange Vin

Bistrot Lyonnais (Patrick Cormillot)

Le Clown Bar

L'Écluse Bastille

Jacques Mélac

Le Passage

L'Ange Vin

Address: 24, rue Richard-Lenoir, 75011
Tel: 43-48-20-20
Metro: Voltaire or Charonne
Hours: 10:30 A.M. to 8:30 P.M., Monday, Wednesday, and Friday, 11 A.M. to 2 A.M. Tuesday and Thursday, Closed Saturday and Sunday
Credit Cards accepted

Nowhere can you better sample the rich, sweet regional wines of Anjou and Touraine than in Jean-Pierre Robinot's wine bar. Ever since its opening in 1989, these special wines coupled with the skill of chef Daniel Bourguelat, has brought immediate praise from critics. His steady customers who pack the place from noon to night come to taste his homemade *rillons,* substantial soups, and exquisite *terrines.* The slightly *pétillant* Vouvray and Anjou wines complement the perfectly-executed dishes such as *blanquette de veau* (veal stew) and *gigot d'agneau* (leg of lamb).

Bistrot Lyonnais (Patrick Cormillot)

Address: 8, rue de la Main-D'Or, 75011
Tel: 48-05-77-10
Metro: Ledru-Rollin
Hours: 10 A.M. to 8 P.M., Closed Saturday, Sunday and August

An authentic Lyonnaise *bouchon* atmosphere (complete with wood-burning stove), enhanced by some of the finest Beaujolais wines in Paris, may be enjoyed at Patrick Cormillot's charming little bistro. Here the self-taught chef prepares mouthwatering calf's liver, slow-cooked rabbit stew, roasted Bresse chicken, breast of veal with sautéed potatoes and onions, flavorful house *terrines* and first-quality *charcuteries* from the Ardoise.

Le Clown Bar

Address: 114, rue Amelot, 75011
Tel: 43-55-87-35
Metro: Filles-du-Calvaire
Hours: Noon to 3:30 P.M. and 7 P.M. to 1 A.M., Closed Sunday and August

The current owner of the Clown Bar, Joe Vitte, discovered this historically-listed monument around 1987. At the time it was closed but the superb turn-of-the-century circus-theme wall ceramics caught his fancy. It reopened in 1989 and is now so popular that even the bar seats must be reserved. Surrounded by extraordinary decorations, you will enjoy herring fillets, hot sausages, copious *terrines* and reputedly the best beef shank in Paris. The wines representing the Southwest, Rhône and Burgundy regions are not exceptional but are above reproach.

L'Écluse Bastille

Address: 13, rue de la Roquette, 75011
Tel: 48-05-19-12
Metro: Bastille
Hours: Noon to 1:30 A.M., Thursday, Friday and Saturday this branch stays open till dawn.
Credit Cards accepted

See page 239, 1er arrondissement, L'Écluse des Halles.

Jacques Mélac

Address: 42, rue Léon-Frot, 75011
Tel: 43-70-59-27
Metro: Charonne
Hours: 9 A.M. to Midnight, Monday till 6 P.M., Closed Saturday, Sunday, and August

Visa accepted

Jacques Mélac is regarded by many as the most famous wine bar *patron* in Paris. His establishment, just off the Place de la Bastille, enjoys a worldwide reputation. Mélac proudly serves his own Lirac wine along with a selection of country *crus* that are near perfection. The moderately-priced meals feature Auvergnat *charcuterie, pot-au-feu, andouillettes,* omelettes with Cantal cheese, and tripe.

Le Passage

Address: 18, Passage de la Bonne-Graine, 75011
Tel: 47-00-73-30
Metro: Ledru-Rollin
Hours: 8 A.M. to 10:30 P.M., Closed Saturday lunch and Sunday
Visa accepted

Hard to find, this extraordinary *bistrot à vin* is tucked away in an alley between av. Ledru-Rollin and rue du Fg. Saint-Antoine. Mademoiselle Soizik de Lorgeril has a unique offering of five superb varieties of *andouillettes* served pot-roasted with *gratin dauphinois.* Other specialties feature the slow-cooked dishes of Provence, such as *pot-au-feu, blanquette de veau,* stuffed cabbage, and rabbit with polenta. The wine list, vast in scope and quality, runs nine pages with an ever-changing selection of unusual wines sold by the glass.

12ᵉ Arrondissement

Le Bastidien

Address: 1, av. Saint-Mandé, 75012
Tel: 43-43-37-73
Metro: Nation
Hours: 7:30 A.M. to 7 P.M., Closed Saturday and Sunday

More a friendly neighborhood café with an extensive wine collection than a *bistro à vin,* this inviting place is literally in the shadow of the Bois de Vincennes. Third-generation owner Jean-Marie Bernauer was awarded the highest wine honor, the Meilleur Pot, for 1991. Here an interesting assortment of wines including those of central France and Corsica can be tasted. Should you find yourself in this quiet, rather provincial section of Paris, you would do well to drop in.

14e Arrondissement

Les Caves Solignac

L'Énchanson

Le Rallye (Bernard Péret)

Au Vin des Rues

Les Caves Solignac

Address: 9, rue Decrès, 75014
Tel: 45-45-58-59
Metro: Plaisance
Hours: Noon to 2 P.M. and 7:30 P.M. to 10 P.M., Closed Saturday, Sunday, and two weeks in May, Sept. and Dec.
Credit Cards accepted

Tucked away on a back street of Montparnasse, Les Caves Solignac is quintessentially Parisian. Owner/chef Jean-François Banéat welcomes and serves his clients tasty specialties such as roasted duck breast, thinly-sliced beef smothered in green pepper sauce, and some of the best foie gras in the city. Rare old wines will be expertly decanted at your table and his selection of superior-quality little-known wines is famous.

L'Echanson

Address: 89, rue Daguerre, 75014
Tel: 43-22-20-00
Metro: Denfert-Rochereau or Gaîté
Hours: Noon to 2:15 P.M. and 8 P.M. to 10:45 P.M., Closed Sunday, Monday, and August 10th to Sept. 10th
Visa accepted

Luc Desrousseaux, aided by his charming wife, runs a perfect little modern bistro at the far end of the rue Daguerre, which is rapidly becoming a pedestrian street. Luc expertly prepares rather elaborate dishes with a light touch. He serves game in the winter and the usual meat dishes, but his seafood preparations are where he really excels. His *pot-au-feu de la mer* is most successful, as is his superb salmon. Luc grew up tasting wines in the Loire Valley and the selection from that region is outstanding. He offers twelve examples of Bourgueil wines alone. Other featured wines are from the Rhône Valley.

Le Rallye (Bernard Péret)

Address: 6, rue Daguerre, 75014
Tel: 43-22-57-05
Metro: Denfert-Rochereau
Hours: 9:30 A.M. to 8 P.M., Closed Sunday and Monday
Visa accepted

Le Rallye's large terrace spills out onto the incredibly active pedestrian mall near the start of rue Daguerre. Here Bernard Péret, honored wine merchant, operates a tiny bistro with an enormous cellar containing more than 200 *appelations.* Péret offers salads and cold meat platters, assortments of cheeses and outstanding open-faced sandwiches on Poilâne bread dressed with the famous butter *échire.* Two special highlights of his menu are the extraordinary Cantal cheese *laguiole,* and the *saucisson de montagne,* a delicious provincial slicing sausage. All the above can be accompanied by some forty-odd wines sold by the glass.

Au Vin des Rues

Address: 21, rue Boulard, 75014
Tel: 43-22-19-78
Metro: Denfert-Rochereau
Hours: Monday, Tuesday, and Saturday 10 A.M. to 8 P.M., Wednesday and Friday 10 A.M. to 11 P.M., Closed Sunday, Monday, and August

Jean Chanrion describes his working-class bistro as a café that offers an excellent choice of Beaujolais and Mâcon wines. His famous daily specials might include braised *andouillettes,* tripe Lyonnaise-style, *petit salé, boeuf ficelle* or *blanquette de veau.* All are rich, delicious and generous. Located on a quiet street just off the lively rue Daguerre, Au Vin des Rues is always packed so reservations are advisable, especially on Wednesday and Friday evenings when dinner is available.

15e Arrondissement

Au Père Tranquille

Au Père Tranquille

Address: 30, av. du Maine, 75015
Tel: 42-22-88-12
Metro: Montparnasse-Bienvenue
Hours: 10 A.M. to 8 P.M., The bistro frequently stays open later in the evening according to the wishes of the owner. Closed Saturday and Sunday.

This tiny wine bistro is practically impossible to find. There is no sign on the outside and it is squeezed between two large buildings behind the monumental 70-story Tour Montparnasse. Opened in 1906, its present owner, Jean Nouyrigat, is an incredible character. He selects and bottles all the wines, does the cooking and engages in the spirited conversation which is this bistro's hallmark. Assisted only by his longtime barman, Ibrahim de Mayotte, Nouyrigat serves daily meals to twenty lucky diners. No choice is allowed, but the menu is always prepared from quality ingredients and is good and inexpensive.

16e Arrondissement

La Bergerie

La Bergerie

Address: 21, rue Galilée, 75016
Tel: 47-20-48-63
Metro: Boissière
Hours: 8 A.M. to 8 P.M., Closed Saturday and Sunday
Visa accepted

On a quiet embassy street, about midway between the Arc de Triomphe and the Trocadero gardens, award-winning owner Christian Baudy maintains the only true wine-bar bistro in the highly fashionable 16e arrondissement. The "Sheep Fold," with its strange kitschy decor of pseudo feeding-troughs and life-size sheep photos, is noted for superb Bourgueil and other delightful Loire Valley wines. Since La Bergerie is always closed by 8 P.M., the bistro is packed at lunchtime by an enthusiastic, upscale crowd enjoying simple, delicious cuisine such as *pot-au-feu* and similar hearty *plats du jour.*

17e Arrondissement

Pétrissans

Le Verre Bouteille

Pétrissans

Address: 30bis, av. Niel, 75017
Tel: 42-27-83-84
Metro: Ternes or Pereire
Hours: Noon to 10 P.M., Closed Saturday, Sunday, and August
Credit Cards accepted

For one hundred years Pétrissans has been considered one of the best stocked *caves* in Paris and has now evolved into a deluxe wine bar, probably the most chic in Paris. The great-granddaughter of the founder, Christine Allemoz, and her husband, Jean-Marie, are perfect hosts and Pétrissans is considered a veritable institution in the area around the Place des Ternes. The 1930s retro decor suggests an English-style wine bar but the choice and quality of the cuisine reveals a very elegant Parisian bistro.

Le Verre Bouteille

Address: 5, boulevard Gouvion-Saint-Cyr, 75017
Tel: 47-63-39-99
Metro: Porte-de-Champerret or Ternes
Hours: Noon to 3 P.M. and 7:30 P.M. till dawn.
Credit Cards accepted

After receiving a doctorate in management and gaining experience working at the well-known Paris brasserie L'Hippopotamus, Patrick Ameline now pursues his passion for wine. He has opened his second wine bistro, handsomely decorated with bric-a-brac and antique corkscrews. Le Verre Bouteille stays open till five in the morning serving a nice little menu of familiar bistro dishes, salads, *tartines,* sausages, and desserts. The extensive selection of wines is extremely varied, containing such unusual *crus* as a *Vin de Paille du Jura* and the extraordinary Château Grillet. Service is attended by attractive young women and the wines may be had by the glass or bottle.

18e Arrondissement

Le Moulin à Vins

Aux Négociants

Le Moulin à Vins

Address: 6, rue Burq, 75018
Tel: 42-52-81-27
Metro: Abbesses or Blanche
Hours: 11 A.M. to 2 A.M., Closed Sunday and Monday
Credit Cards accepted

The "Wine Mill," appropriately located on the side of Montmartre, is run single-handedly by the charming young hostess Danièle Bertin-Denis. In 1990 Dany converted an old run-down café into an authentic wine bistro. Generous portions of bistro cuisine such as *boeuf mode* or *petit salé* are served along with Lyonnaise sausages and *tartines.* The wines are bought directly from the vineyards by Dany from longtime friends. Southwestern *crus* are featured but the Beaujolais and Côtes du Rhone wines are impeccable. An accordionist plays the old songs of France during evening meals.

Aux Négociants

Address: 27, rue Lambert, 75018
Tel: 46-05-15-11
Metro: Château-Rouge or Lamarck-Caulaincourt
Hours: Monday and Wednesday Noon to 8 P.M., Tuesday, Thursday and Friday Noon to 10:30 P.M., Closed Saturday, Sunday and August

At the foot of Montmartre, Jean Navier, an experienced wine *patron* and remarkable self-taught chef, runs a friendly and unpretentious wine bistro. With his wife tending bar, Jean cooks and serves simple tasty dishes. His omelettes are outstanding, as are the homemade *rillettes* served in an earthenware jar accompanied by tart, crispy gherkins. No attempt at decorating is in evidence but the wines are of impeccable quality and uniformly inexpensive. They include the rare aperitif from Touraine, Jasnières, and other outstanding Loire Valley wines.

20e Arrondissement

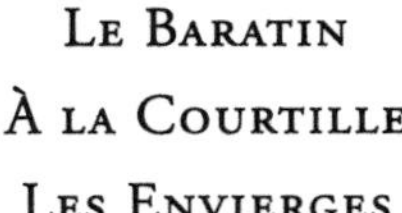

Le Baratin

À la Courtille

Les Envierges

Le Baratin

Address: 3, rue Jouye-Rouvé, 75020
Tel: 43-49-39-70
Metro: Pyrénées or Belleville
Hours: 11 A.M. to 1:30 A.M., Closed Monday, Tuesday, and Sunday lunch

Olivier Camus, with twelve years experience working in the distinguished cave of Hédiard, decided to open his own wine bar close to the lovely Belleville park. Some of Olivier's wines are rare discoveries such as the fruity Mondeuse, an outstanding red wine of the Savoie, and a Clos-de-Coulaine originating in the Maine and Loire regions. Other good and correct wines are showcased by a really extraordinary selection of cheeses. However the young crowd that frequents "the good chat" comes for the exquisitely-prepared *plats-du-jour* put out by Olivier's wife, Rachel. The decor is practically nonexistent but the consistently high quality of the cuisine, coupled with reasonable wine prices, explain the popularity of this bistro.

À la Courtille

Address: 1, rue des Envierges, 75020
Tel: 46-36-51-59
Metro: Pyrénées
Hours: Noon to 2 P.M. and 8 P.M. to 1 A.M.
Visa accepted

It is hard to describe this establishment. It could be a nouvelle cuisine restaurant, or brasserie, but we think of it as an unusual upscale wine bistro. The wines take precedence and are chosen by the two partners, Bernard Pontonnier and François Morel, with great discrimination. In order to allow for tastings the wine is served in glasses rather than by the bottle. Open every day, À la Courtille is always formally set out with fresh table linen and the customers are served by waiters dressed in traditional *brasserie*-style garb. The sophisticated, modern decor is accented by marvelous photographs by Willy Ronis. A lovely terrace, much sought after in summer, offers a breathtaking view of Paris down below.

Les Envierges

Address: 11, rue des Envierges, 75020
Tel: 46-36-47-84
Metro: Pyrénées
Hours: Noon to 1 A.M., Saturday and Sunday, Noon to 8 P.M., Closed Monday and Tuesday

François Morel, with degrees in art history and philosophy, is also passionate when it comes to the subject of wine. He runs this small unpretentious neighborhood bistro, widely considered one of the best in Paris, assisted by Nadine who conceives wonderful Lyonnaise-inspired dishes such as slow-cooked stews, succulent *terrines* and outstanding *plats-du-jour.* François matches the cuisine with skillfully selected wines from the old province of Roussillon and the vineyards along the foothills of the Jura, making them available by the glass or bottle. From dinner to closing the bistro is jammed so it is prudent to reserve.

PART III

Bistro Cuisine

As much a part of the bistro tradition as family involvement, a faithful clientele, and an intimate, hospitable atmosphere, is the heart-warming food in which the French take such pride and pleasure. There are no ambitious or sophisticated preparations. Perfection is found in the simplicity of old-fashioned recipes developed over time by generations of frugal housewives who sought to feed their families palatable meals by relying on their own inventiveness. Very often the deficiencies of a region led to its culinary assets. Women cooked with whatever was plentiful in their part of France, so it is not surprising that several completely individual styles of cuisine developed. Each of the provinces earned a reputation for producing and preparing certain foods and one region's specialties cannot be confused with another's.

Part of the special appeal of bistro cooking is its tremendous regional variety. There are the sausages of the Lyonnaise, the *gigots de pré salés* of Brittany, the *gratins* of Dauphine, the *brandades* of Provence, the *choucroutes* of Alsace, the *cassoulets* of Languedoc, the open tarts of Lorraine, *entrecôte* from Bordeaux, *bouillabaisse* from the Riviera, and from Burgundy *coq-au-vin, escargots* and beef *bourguignon.* Less well known are the *marmites* and *andouilles* from Normandy, *rillettes* and *matelots* from the Loire, *truffades* and *aligots* from Auvergne, *garbures* from the Pyrénées and the *poulets au vin jaune* from the mountains of the Jura.

The hallmarks of bistro cooking are its simplicity and its balance between the food's natural flavors and the creativity of the person preparing it. Talented cooks and chefs come to Paris, bringing with them recipes and flavors remembered from their grandmothers' kitchens. They may update and refine them to satisfy modern tastes but innovation is always tempered by tradition. Today's bistro menus are quite diversified. There are hundreds of dishes that are considered authentic bistro fare and of these, standard classics such as *pot-au-feu* and *boeuf bourguignon* are prepared in dozens of different ways. Menus change from season to season reflecting the freshest products available at Paris markets brought in daily from the various regions. It is well worth some time to become acquainted with the menu items described in this section as many are virtually unknown outside of France. *Tête de veau sauce ravigote, blanquette, boudin, gratin dauphinois, gigot, onglet, fricassée de poulet, gras-double, boeuf môde,* and *petit salé aux choux* are the sorts of lusty foods appreciated by those who love to eat. As French law requires that the menu and prices be posted on the door or window of every restaurant, you will have an idea of what you will encounter before entering.

You will not be surprised to find there is nothing more satisfying than a well-prepared bistro meal. A bottle of crisp white wine with thick slices of sturdy duck pâté, or silvery fish marinated in brine with chunks of pickles and onions, whet your appetite for roast leg of lamb seasoned with garlic and served with tiny green kidney beans or grilled duck breast, tender and rare, accompanied by turnips no bigger than spring onions, and washed down with hearty red wine. Farm-fresh goat cheese or a fruit tart may follow, along with strong coffee and perhaps an Armagnac. "The truth is," wrote Brillant-Savarin in *The Physiology of Taste,* "that at the end of a well-savored meal, both soul and body enjoy an especial well being."

La Carte

La Carte. The menu.
Prix-Fixe. A set meal at a fixed price, including a choice for each of several courses *(au choix).* Sometimes a drink is included *(boisson compris).*
Menu Dégustation. A tasting menu. Usually a small sampling of the restaurant's specialties.
Apéritif. A before-dinner drink.
Kir. An apéritif made by adding Crème de Cassis (black currant) or Framboise (raspberry) liqueur to a glass of dry white wine or champagne (Kir Royal).
Pousse-Rapière. An apéritif made by adding Armagnac brandy to sparkling white wine; served with a slice of orange. A specialty of Gascogny in Southwest France.
Hors d'Oeuvres. Appetizers.
Potages. Soups.
Sur Commande. Available by request though possibly not on the menu.
Marée. Seafood (all kinds).
Coquillages/Crustacés. Shellfish.
Fruits de Mer. Seafood. Usually shellfish and crustaceans.
Poissons. Fish.
Entrées. May or may not mean the main course. Usually the *entrées* refer to "appetizer" courses, before the main course.
Chaud(e). Hot.
Froid(e). Cold.
Un Plat. A course.
Plats du Jour. Specials of the day.
Maison (à la). A specialty of the chef or restaurant.
Viandes. Meats (*bleu:* very rare; *saignant:* rare; *à point:* medium; *bien cuit:* well done).
Grillades. Grilled meats.
Volailles. Fowl.
Légumes. Vegetables.
Garnitures. Garnishes (additional vegetables or sauces may be

offered at an exra charge).

Salade. Salad.

Fromages. Cheeses.

Le Plateau de Fromages (Variés). A cheese platter. Usually a large selection of assorted cheeses.

Assiette de Fromages. A small plate of three or four cheeses.

Desserts. Desserts.

Desserts (à commander au debut du repas). Desserts must be ordered at the beginning of the meal.

Délices. All sorts of pastries and sweet desserts.

Entremets. Sweet or cooked desserts, usually served after the cheese course.

Carte Des Vins

Carte des Vins. Wine list.
Sommelier. Wine steward.
Doux. Sweet.
Mousseaux. Sparkling wine.
Sec. Dry.
Vins Blancs White wines.
Vins Rouges. Red wines.
Vins Rosés. Rosé wines.
Vin de la Maison. House wine.
Vin Ordinaire. Non-vintage table wine.
Vins du pays. Local wines: fresh and palatable. Usually a local luxury, must be drunk at an early age.
Alcools. A general term for spirits, after-dinner drinks and digestives.
Alcools Blancs. White alcohols. Clear brandies that are colorless because they are distilled in glass, not wood. They are not sweetened, so the flavor is very strong.
Eaux-de-vie. Fruit brandies. White alcohols distilled from fruit, e.g., raspberry *(framboise)*, pear *(poire)*, or plum *(mirabelle)*.
Marcs. Brandies distilled from the skins, stems, pips and liquid not drained off after the wine has been pressed. They are colorless, dry and very strong, e.g., Marc de Bourgogne or Marc de Champagne.

HORS D'OEUVRES/ ENTRÉES

Anchois. Anchovy, usually preserved fillets.

Andouille. A type of smoked sausage generally containing pork tripe, although there are good veal, mutton and beef versions. They are ready-cooked, highly seasoned and served cold as any salami-type sausage or saveloy. The best come from Normandy and Brittany.

de vire. A smoked pork-tripe sausage from Normandy which is well-seasoned and marbled. It is tender and has a mild flavor.

Andouillettes. A smaller version of the above, but which must be cooked before eating and is generally grilled or fried. Usually served hot with mustard and vegetables such as potatoes, cabbage or white beans. There are different varieties, distinguished by their seasonings. Most are rich, pungent and have an overripe sweet flavor which may not appeal to all tastes. The best come from Caen and Cambrai in Flanders and from Troyes in Champagne.

A.A.A.A.A. The *Association Amicale des Amateurs d'Authentique Andouilletes* (The Amicable Association of Appreciators of Authentic Pork Tripe Sausages). An exclusive gourmet group who award their diploma to a few restaurants serving what they consider to be the best tripe sausages. The ideal is made of pig's intestines filled with strips of choice innards mixed with pork fat and seasonings. It is fleshy without too much fat.

À la Ficille. Steeped *à point* in a light broth or wine, giving them a subtle and aromatic flavor.

Au vin blanc. Grilled in butter and garnished with pan juices de-glazed with white wine.

Artichaut. Artichoke.

Asperges. Asparagus.

Assiette. Plate.

Anglaise. A plate of cold meats, e.g., veal, roast beef, ham, etc.

Assorti(e)s. Assorted.

Avocat. Avocado.

Belons. A white-fleshed oyster from Brittany (see *Huîtres*).

Betteraves. Beets/Beetroot.

Boeuf en Salade. Slices of cold beef served on lettuce. Sometimes other items are added, such as hard-boiled eggs, tomatoes and potatoes.

Salade tiède de boeuf. Warm beef salad.

Bouquet. Large reddish shrimp, prawn (see *Crevettes*).

Carottes Rapées. Grated carrot salad. Finely grated carrots in a vinaigrette dressing.

Céleri Rémoulade. Celery root salad. Grated raw celery root garnished with tangy mayonnaise or creamy vinaigrette dressing. (*Céleri-rave* is a type of celery cultivated for the root.)

Cervelas. A closely textured, lightly smoked pork sausage with a smooth skin and mild garlic flavor; usually poached in a light broth and served either cold in slices with a vinaigrette, *tartare* or *rémoulade* dressing, or hot with sliced potatoes or lentils. The best come from Lyon, Nancy and Paris.

Aux Pistaches. Stuffed with pistachio nuts and whole spices.

Aux Truffles. Stuffed with truffles.

Champignons à la Grècque. Mushrooms marinated "Greek style" in olive oil, lemon juice and spices. Served cold in the marinade.

Chou(x). Cabbage.

Chou-fleur. Cauliflower.

Chou Rouge. Red cabbage.

Cochonnailles. Assorted pork products such as sausages, hams, *terrines, rillettes,* headcheese, etc. Served with mustard and *cornichons.*

Concombres. Cucumbers.

Cornichons. Tart gherkins.

Crevette(s). Shrimp.

Grises. Small shrimp, grayish in color. They can be eaten whole with the shell.

Roses. Medium-sized pink shrimp; served cold. The larger ones are called *bouquets.*

Crudités. Assorted raw vegetables.

Écrevisse. Crayfish.

Endives: Endives.

Épinards. Spinach.

Escargots. Snails.

De Bourgogne. With garlic butter and parsley.

Petit Gris. Small gray garden snails.

Foie Gras. Lit. "Fat Liver." Liver of a goose or duck which has been force-fed with maize. Cooked either whole or in slices and served hot in a sauce, or cold. (See *Pâté.*)

Frisée aux Lardons. A salad of chicory garnished with crisp bacon bits in a vinegar, hot bacon-fat and garlic dressing. Sometimes pieces of fried bread are added.

Fritons. Leftover pieces of pork, duck, or goose skin slowly cooked in fat until their own fat is rendered and they are tender. They are then quickly fried until they bubble and become crisp, drained and pressed to extract all the fat, then salted and left to cool. They may also be pressed into a mold turning them into a kind of coarse pâté. They should not be confused with *rillettes,* which are made differently. (See *Rillettes.*)

Fromage de Tête. Headcheese, usually pork. (See *Hure de porc.*)

Grillettes. Pieces of fatty meat, usually goose, pork or duck, grilled until crisp.

Hareng. Herring. Usually herring fillets marinated with herbs and seasonings and served with cream.

Huîtres. Oysters.

Belons. From Brittany; round and flat with white flesh.

Marennes. From near Bordeaux; long and naturally colored green from algae.

Fines de Claires. A designation of oyster indicating they are raised in *"Claires"*—oyster beds in salt marshes rich in seaweed, where they are fattened up for a few months before going to market. Usually from Brittany and Arcachon.

Spéciales. These are the largest. They are immersed in the *claire* basins for six to eighteen months before harvesting.

Hure de Porc. Headcheese. This is usually sold in butcher shops ready to eat. The entire head of a pig or boar is steeped in brine for several days, drained, then braised for several hours. The best parts of the skin are removed and spread out. The head, ears, tongue and brains are cut into pieces and seasoned with spices and shallots. They are arranged in such a way as to mix the various meats, folded into the skin and replaced in the braising liquid (wrapped in a napkin) to cook. The contents are then removed from the napkin, put into a brawn mold, pressed and left to cool in their own aspic.

Jambon. Ham.

Blanc. A boiling or cooking ham. The meat is lightly salted and unsmoked, or only lightly smoked. This ham is also called *jambon demi-sel, jambon glacé* and *jambon de Paris.*

De Campagne/Du Pays. Country ham. These hams carry

the name of the place of origin such as those from the Auvergne, Brittany, Burgundy, Bayonne, the Vosges, Alsace-Lorraine, Touraine, etc. They are cured (salted and smoked, or salted and dried) according to local methods. They are eaten raw or used in cooking, but not boiled.

Cru. Raw. Ham that has been cured but not cooked, such as Jambon de Bayonne. This is a famous raw ham that is cured in a pickling mixture that includes wine, and is delicious eaten raw in postcard-thin slices or fried with tomatoes and pimientos.

Cuit. Cooked. *Jambon cuit à l'os* is a country ham cooked on the bone. Served in slices with bread, butter, mustard and pickles.

Fumé. Smoked. *Jambon fumé de Savoie* is a particularly fine raw smoked ham from the Savoy region. Eaten alone in thin slices.

de Montagne. Mountain ham (see *Jambon de Campagne*).

Persillé/De Bourgogne. Parslied ham. A specialty of the Morvan in Burgundy. The ham is shredded into large chunks and cooked in heavily seasoned and parslied aspic and wine. It is then placed in a mold, chilled and pressed. Sliced and served cold in its own aspic.

Sec. Dried ham. Raw ham, salted and dried.

Jésus (Gésu) de Morteau. This smoked sausage comes from the Franche-Comté. It is made of coarsely chopped pork and fat, flavored with cumin. It has a mild, sweet flavor and is generally poached in wine with shallots and served with hot potatoes in oil or buttered string beans.

Maquereaux au Vin Blanc (au Cidre). Mackerel fillets poached in white wine, cider, or cider vinegar and marinated with herbs. Served chilled with a sauce, or mustard, and chopped parsley. (Sometimes the entire mackerel is served.)

Mâche. Lamb's lettuce.

Moules. Mussels.

Farcies. Mussels stuffed with a mixture of chopped garlic, shallots and parsley, butter and sometimes breadcrumbs. Browned in the oven and served on the half-shell.

Marinières. Mussels steamed in white wine, shallots, parsley-butter and herbs. Served in the shell.

Museau de Boeuf (de Porc). Beef (or pork) headcheese/muzzle brawn, vinegared ox muzzle (pig's snout). These brawns are usually sold ready-made in a *charcuterie.* The meat is cut into thin slices seasoned with a vinaigrette, chopped herbs, onions, pickles and parsley, and served cold.

Oeuf Dur Mayonnaise. Cold hard-boiled eggs, sliced in half lengthwise and often served on a bed of lettuce, garnished with fresh mayonnaise and a sprinkling of finely chopped parsley.

Oeuf Meurette.* Eggs poached in red wine seasoned with onions, garlic and herbs. Served on fried toast, covered with a sauce made from the poaching liquid, enriched and thickened with flour and butter, then garnished with bacon bits.

Pamplemousse. Grapefruit.

Pâté. Minced meat (poultry, game or fish) and spices molded and baked in a *terrine* or pastry shell. Usually eaten cold in thick slices.

De Campagne. Country pâté; often made with pork, liver and veal.

De Fois Gras. Goose liver pâté.

Pissenlits. Dandelion greens.

Aux Lardons. With bacon bits.

Poireaux Vinaigrettes. Leeks vinaigrette. The whites of leeks are poached in salted water and marinated in an oil-and-vinegar dressing.

Potage. A thick soup.

Radis Beurre. Red radishes served with fresh butter and salt.

Rillettes. A spread of minced pork. (Some varieties can be greasy, bland and stringy.) Pieces of fat and lean pork are cooked slowly with lard and herbs, cooled, pounded together in a mortar to form a paste, then preserved in jars. *Rillettes* may also be made with goose, duck, fish or rabbit. They are served cold with rolls, bread or toast.

De Tours. A finer variety than most others.

Rillons. A variation of *rillettes.* Pork belly is cut into chunks and cooked in seasoned lard until crisp, then drained of fat and preserved. Rillons can also be made of duck, goose or rabbit.

Rollmops. Herring fillets prepared in a highly seasoned white-wine base marinade, rolled around *cornichons,* and pinned with a wooden skewer. Sometimes served with cream.

Rosette. Dry pork sausage. Pork is soaked in a *marc* and seasoned with pepper and herbs, then chopped and stuffed into a pig's large intestines. During the curing process, the thick, fat skin nourishes the meat and gives it a rich, moist quality. Served in thin slices with butter. The best come from Lyon,

---

**Meurettes.* A general term used for all the wine sauces used in Burgundian cooking. They are usually red-wine sauces, well spiced and thickened with flour and butter. They appear in various forms, depending on the foods they accompany (e.g., meat, fish or eggs).

the Ardéche, Beaujolais and the Morvan.

Salade. Salad.

Blettes. Leaves of the beet-root plant (similar to Swiss chard).

Cervelas. Sausage salad.

D'Epinards. Spinach salad.

De Foies de Volaille. Chicken-liver salad.

Marche–Betteraves. Lamb's lettuce and shredded beets.

Panachée. Mixed salad.

Verte. Green salad.

Sardines à l'Huile. Sardines in a vinaigrette dressing.

Saucisse. Usually refers to a small sausage that must be cooked before eating. The majority of fresh or partly cured sausages are made of pork and carry the name of the place where they are made.

D'Alsace Chaudes au Raifort. Hot Alsatian sausage with horseradish.

De Campagne. Small country sausages.

Sèche de Vans. A small dry sausage from Vans, well seasoned with a firm texture. Served in thin slices with bread and butter.

Sèches à Vouvray. Small, dry red sausages. The pork is mixed with Vouvray, a dry, rich, slightly crisp wine from the Loire Valley.

De Strasbourg. Smoked beef-and-pork sausage usually eaten with *choucroute.*

De Toulouse. A fresh pure-pork and garlic sausage coarsely cut with a good deal of fat. It is poached to stiffen it, then grilled or fried in butter and placed in the oven to finish. Served with mashed potatoes, stewed white beans, or cabbage. In another preparation it is sautéed in garlic and butter and served with tomatoes, parsley and capers.

Saucisson. Usually refers to an air-dried sausage, sliced and eaten cold as a first course, but others are cooked and served hot (see below).

À l'Ail. Garlic sausage. Large saveloy-type sausage, cooked and served warm with hot potato salad.

De Campagne (Fumé). Thick (smoked) country sausage. Served hot with fried potatoes or cold.

Chaud. Hot garlic sausage poached in water and served plain with hot potato salad.

Chaud à l'Huile. (See *Pommes à l'Huile,* below.)

Chaud à la Lyonnaise. Sausage from Lyon, usually poached and served with hot sliced potatoes. (See *Cervelas.*) Also called *Saucisson Chaud de Lyon.*

Chaud au Macon. Hot sausage simmered in white Macon wine.

En Croûte. Any cooking sausage, coarsely cut and interlaced with cubes of fat, may be used. It is first poached in water and skinned. Then it is encased in brioche dough, glazed with cream, baked to a golden brown and served in thick slices.

Cru. Raw.

Pommes à l'Huile. Sliced hot sausage tossed in oil with warm potatoes.

Sec. An air-dried sausage which is hung to ripen naturally. The composition and seasoning vary according to region. The coarser the grain, the milder the flavor. The best known come from Arles (made of pork and beef and mildly seasoned with pepper, garlic and paprika), Lyon (a cured salami-type sausage—which tastes nothing like salami—flavored with garlic and pepper and studded with cubes of fat), the Ardèche (see *Rosette*) and the Morvan.

Terrine. Usually refers to a meat, game or fish mixture cooked in a rectangular earthenware dish and eaten cold in thick slices. (See *Pâté.*)

De Foie de Volaille. A coarse pâté made with chicken livers.

De Lapereau en Gellée. Rabbit potted in aspic.

Tomate. Tomato.

Thon. Tuna, eaten fresh or canned.

À l'Huile. Chunks of canned tuna in olive oil. Served with lemon, bread and butter.

Les Plats

Agneau. Lamb. The principal cuts of lamb are: *Baron:* Saddle and both legs. *Carré:* Rack. *Côte:* Chop. *Côtelette:* Cutlet, lamb chop. *Épaule:* Shoulder. *Gigot:* Leg. *Médaillon/Mignonette:* (See *Noisette.*) *Noisette:* Small round boned cutlet. *Poitrine:* Breast. *Selle:* Saddle.

Aiglefin (Églefin). Haddock.

Aiguillette. Usually refers to long, thin slices cut from the breast of game or poultry. (See *Boeuf.*)

Ail. Garlic.

Aile. Wing (of poultry or game birds).

Aïoli. Garlic-flavored mayonnaise. (See *Bourride.*)

Aligot. Puréed potatoes with cheese, usually fresh Cantal cheese from Auvergne.

Alose. Shad.

Alouette. Lark.

Anguille. Eel. Freshwater eel as opposed to *Congre* sea eel. (See *Matelote.*)

Anis. Aniseed.

Anisé. Flavored with aniseed or caraway.

Aromates. Herbs and spices.

Aubergine. Eggplant.

Bar. Sea bass.

Barbue. Brill, a sea fish similar to turbot.

Basilic. Sweet basil.

Bavette. Flank steak.

  Aux Echalotes. With shallots.

  Poêlée. Pan fried.

Béarnaise. A butter sauce made with egg yolks, white wine, sometimes vinegar, tarragon and minced shallots which melt into the sauce as they are cooked.

Bécasse. Woodcock.

Beurre. Butter.

  Blanc. White butter. A thick creamy sauce of butter, white wine, "melted" shallots and vinegar. The making of this sauce is an art, depending as much on the hand of the chef as on the ingredients.

Meunière. Melted herb-butter flavored with lemon juice and parsley.

Noir. Black butter. Melted butter blackened with vinegar and flavored with lemon juice, parsley and sometimes capers. (See *Raie.*)

Noisette. Brown butter. Melted butter, lightly browned with lemon juice and parsley.

Bifteck. Steak. An inexpensive cut which is often made into hamburger.

Blanquette de Veau (d'Agneau). Veal (lamb) stewed in a white cream sauce with mushrooms and onions. The sauce is enriched with egg yolks and flour. *Blanquettes* are also made with chicken and seafood.

Boeuf. Beef. The principal cuts of beef are: *Aiguillette:* A thin steak from the end of the loin (rump), also called *pièce de boeuf* or *culotte. Aloyau:* Tenderloin, the long strip around the loin. *Bavette:* Flank steak. (See *Bavette.*) *Bifteck:* Steak (See *Bifteck.*) *Châteaubriand:* Steak cut from the fillet. *Contre Filet:* Sirloin steak, also called *faux-filet. Côte:* Rib. *Entrecôte:* Rib steak, from between the ribs and loin. (See *Entrecôte.*) *Faux Filet:* Sirloin steak. (See *Faux-filet.*) *Filet:* Fillet steak. *Filet de Boeuf Poêle:* Sautéed beef tenderloin. *Onglet:* Mitre-joint, a cut similar to flank steak. (See *Onglet.*) *Pavé:* A thick slice of beef steak. *Romsteck/Rumsteak.* Rumpsteak. *Tournedos:* Steak from the best part of the fillet. (See *Tournedos Rossini.*)

Boeuf Bourguignon. Beef stewed in red wine, bacon, onions, mushrooms and herbs.

Boeuf Carotte. Pot roast with carrots.

Boeuf en Daube. Chunks of marinated beef braised in red wine with aromatic vegetables.

Daube. A method of braising meat, poultry, game or fish in wine, stock, herbs and vegetables. The exact mixture is a matter of choice. A special earthenware pot called a *daubière* is often used. In some *daubes* the meat is cut up; in others it is cooked whole.

Boeuf à la Ficelle. A fillet of beef is wrapped tightly with string, quickly browned in a hot oven, then placed, suspended, into an herbal bouillon made from aromatic vegetables. The meat is then poached for several minutes until tender and served rare in slices with or without vegetables.

Boeuf Gros Sel. Chunks of boiled beef in the stockpot broth, with vegetables. Served with coarse salt and other condiments such as mustard, *cornichons,* horseradish, etc.

Boeuf Miroton. Left-over *pot-au-feu* meat that has been chilled, sliced and reheated by simmering in a sweet brown sauce made with butter, flour, onions, seasonings and a dash of vinegar.

Boeuf Mode (á la mode). Pot roast marinated in herbs and brandy, larded, then braised with red wine, carrots and onions. Sometimes other vegetables such as mushrooms and turnips are included. Served hot from the pot or cold, when it becomes a sort of jellied meat dish.

Boudin. A type of soft sausage.

Blanc. White pudding. Today this sausage is stuffed largely with bread, eggs, onions, fat and herbs, and can be poached, grilled or fried. In some areas the bread is replaced by veal, chicken *(Boudin Blanc Touraine),* or pork *(Boudin Blanc Lyonnais).*

Noir. Blood sausage/black pudding. A soft sausage made with pork, pig's blood, fat, herbs and garlic. It is usually grilled and served with roasted potatoes and sautéed apples. When well prepared, it is crisp on the outside and moist on the inside.

Bouillabaisse. Mediterranean fish stew traditionally made with *rascasse, congre* and *grondin* plus other fish, shellfish, onions, tomatoes, garlic, saffron and herbs. Served with *rouille,* a hot pepper mayonnaise.

Bourride. Mediterranean fish stew traditionally made with white fish only. Served with *aïoli,* a garlic-flavored mayonnaise.

Brandade. A mousse-like blend of fish, garlic and oil.

De Morue. Purée of desalted salt cod, cut into pieces and mixed with cream, olive oil and garlic. The mixture is pounded in a mortar while a thin thread of olive oil is poured in, transforming it into a purée with the consistency of cream cheese. Sometimes mashed potatoes are added. Served warm with fried bread.

Brochet. Pike. (See *Quenelles.*)

Au Beurre Blanc. Poached and served with white-wine butter sauce.

Burbot. (See *Lotte.*)

Cabillaud. Fresh codfish.

Caille. Quail.

Calamars. Cuttlefish, squid.

Canard. Duck.

Aux Choux. With cabbage.

Aux Navets. Braised and served with small turnips in a brown butter sauce.

Au Poivre Vert. Roasted, and served in a sauce made with green peppercorns.

Sauvage. Wild duck, mallard.

Caneton. Duckling (male).

Canette. Duckling (female).

Carré. Rack (Lit. "square"). Usually rack of lamb, but also pork or veal.

Cassoulet. A casserole of white beans and varying fresh or preserved meats such as sausage, pork, mutton, lamb, *confit* of duck, goose, etc. The ingredients are different in each region.

Cèpes. Wild flat mushrooms.

Cervelles. Brains. Usually calf or lamb brains, sautéed and served in a butter sauce.

Meuniere. Floured and fried in butter. Served with a sauce of brown butter, lemon and parsley.

Champignon. Mushroom.

Chanterelle. A yellow, trumpet-shaped mushroom with a fragrant flavor. Also known as *Girolle.*

Chapon. Capon.

Charolias. A region in Burgundy whose breed of light-colored cattle produces high-quality beef.

Cheveuil. Venison.

Choucroute (Garnie). Sauerkraut (garnished) with an assortment of sausages, bacon, pork, ham and served with boiled potatoes.

Chou Farci. Leaves or small heads of cabbage, scalded then stuffed and cooked in various ways. A common preparation stuffs scalded cabbage leaves with minced pork or beef, bacon, onions, herbs, cream, and eggs, then bakes or boils them in bouillon with onions, cloves and parsley. In another variation, small cabbage heads are stuffed with minced pork, veal and mushrooms then simmered for several hours in white wine.

Civet. In the past, a *civet* was simply a stew with onions *(cives).* Today, it usually refers to a game stew (unless otherwise indicated) in a rich red wine sauce made with onions, mushrooms, spices and thickened with the animal's blood.

Cochon. Pig

De Lait. Suckling pig.

Colin. Hake, a kind of codfish. (See *Merlin.*)

Colombe. Dove

Congre. Sea eel, an ocean fish resembling eel.

Confit. Meat that has been salted to draw out the moisture then cooked and preserved in its own fat.

De Canard. Preserved duck, usually grilled and served in large pieces.

Contre Filet. Sirloin steak.

Coq. Cock, cockerel.

Coq-au-Vin. Chicken braised in red wine with onions, pork, mushrooms, herbs and sometimes tomato paste.

Coquelet. Young (male) chicken.

Coquilles Saint-Jacques. Sea scallops.

Côte. Rib, chop.

Cotriade. Brittany fish stew.

Cou d'Oie. Stuffed neck of goose. A goose neck skin is marinated in brandy and spices, stuffed with force meat, duck liver or foie gras, chopped truffles, spices, tied up and cooked. Served like a sausage.

Coulis. A general term for a thick sauce or purée, often of vegetables or fruit.

Cru. Raw, uncooked.

Cuisse. Leg, thigh.

De Grenouilles à la Provençale. Frogs' legs in garlic and oil.

De Poulet. Chicken drumstick.

Daube. (See *Boeuf en Daube.*)

Daurade. Sea bream, a gilt-head fish similar to porgy. Not to be confused with *dorade* or red sea bream, which is not as good.

Dauphinois. Layers of thin sliced potatoes, baked in milk with grated cheese and nutmeg. *(Gratin Dauphinois.)*

Dinde. Turkey (hen).

Dindon. Turkey (cock).

Dodine. A preparation of poultry (or meat) boned, stuffed and braised; often refers to duck.

Dorade. Red sea bream. (See *Daurade.*)

Échalote. Shallot.

Échine. Lit. "spine." Backbone of loin of pork, pork shoulder.

Écrevisse. Freshwater crayfish.

Entrecôte. Steak from between the ribs and loin.

Bercy. Pan-fried or grilled steak served with chopped shallots, marrow, lemon juice, parsley and butter creamed with a reduction of white wine.

Marchand de Vin. Steak grilled or pan-fried and served in a reduction of red wine with brown sauce *(demi-glace)*, butter, chopped shallots and parsley.

À la Moelle. Steak grilled or pan-fried with bone marrow. Served in a sauce of wine, pan juices, marrow and herbs and garnished with poached marrow.

Épaule. Shoulder. Refers to lamb, pork, or veal. Beef shoulder is called *paleron.*

Éperlan. Smelt. Usually fried, as in *Friture d'Eperlans.*

Escalope. A thin slice of meat.

Escalope Panée. Breaded veal cutlet.

Espadon. Swordfish.

Estragon. Tarragon.

Faisan. Pheasant.

Faisandeau. Young pheasant.

Faisane. Pheasant (hen).

Farci. Stuffed. (See *Chou Farci.*)

Faux-filet. Steak sirloin, lit. "false fillet."

Fenouil. Fennel.

Foie. Liver.

De Veau (Rôti). Calf's liver (roasted).

De Veau au Vinaigre de Xérès. Calf's liver with sherry vinegar from Jerez, Spain.

Flageolet. A small, tender pale-green kidney-shaped bean (baby lima bean).

Flétan. Halibut.

Fricandeau.* Thinly sliced veal or rump roast larded with bacon and braised with white wine and vegetables. Served on a bed of braised vegetables such as chicory and sorrel or celery, lettuce and spinach.

Fricassée. A light stew usually consisting of meat in a cream sauce. The meat is first sautéed, which distinguishes it from a *blanquette.*

De Poulet aux Morilles. Chicken sautéed, then braised in a sauce containing crinkled black wood-mushrooms, and thickened with egg yolks and cream.

De Veau à l'Oseille. A stew of veal with mushrooms and onions in cream sauce seasoned with sorrel.

Frites. French fries. (Short for *Pommes Frites.*)

Friture. Fried food. Usually refers to tiny deep-fried fish. (See *Éperlan.*)

Gibier. Game.

À Plume. Refers to game birds. (Lit. "with feather.")

À Poile. Refers to deer, rabbit, hare, wild boar, etc. (Lit. "with fur.")

Gibelotte de Lapin. Rabbit stewed with onions, garlic, herbs and white wine; served on fried toast.

Gigot. Leg (usually) of lamb or mutton.

---

* *Fricandeau* also applies to pork-liver pâté cooked in a casing made with the lining of a sheep's stomach.

Aux Flageolets. Roast leg of lamb seasoned with garlic, served with pan juices and tomato purée and accompanied by small, pale-green kidney-shaped beans.

De Pré-Salé. Salt-marsh mutton, often served with white beans. (See *Pré-Salé.*)

Girolles. Wild curly mushrooms. (See *Chanterelle.*)

Gras-Double. Ox tripe. (Refers to 3 stomachs of ox as opposed to *tripe,* which includes all four.) Tripe (from the inner belly; tender and juicy) is scalded, cooked for several hours in bouillon, drained, braised with lard, then sautéed with white wine, minced onions and butter. Served sprinkled with vinegar or lemon and chopped parsley.

À la Lyonnaise. Poached tripe, sliced, breaded and fried. Served with snail butter or a sharp sauce.

Aux Haricots Blancs. Tripe with white beans.

Gribiche. A thick creamy vinaigrette made with oil, vinegar, hard-boiled-egg yolks and chopped pickles, capers and herbs.

Gros Sel. Coarse salt. (See *Boeuf Gros Sel.*)

Hachis Parmentier. Mincemeat hash with potatoes. Best when made with leftovers from a good *pot-au-feu* and quality potatoes. Ground beef (or pork) and puréed potatoes are sprinkled with breadcrumbs and grated cheese, then browned in an oven. Sometimes served in potato jackets.

Haddock. Haddock, a sea fish of the cod family but smaller than cod.

À l'Anglais. Haddock sautéed English-style with egg and breadcrumbs.

Au Beurre Blanc. Haddock poached in water or milk and served in a white-wine butter sauce.

Emincée à la Crème de Raifort. Haddock with horseradish cream.

Hake. A sea fish of the cod family. It is called *merlin* in Provence and *colin* in Paris, and sometimes referred to as *saumon blanc* (white salmon).

Haricot. Bean.

Blanc. White bean.

Vert. String bean.

Haricot de Mouton. A stew of white beans and lamb. Today the word *haricot* replaces the obsolete word *halicot* (meaning stew). The latter traditionally included mutton, turnips, potatoes and onions but no beans. The former contains white beans as well, and is seasoned with garlic and herbs.

Hochepot (le). A northern version of *pot-au-feu* with a variety of meats and vegetables. The famous version is *Queue de Boeuf en*

Hochepot, made with oxtail, pig's trotters, ears, cabbage, carrots, onions and turnips.

Homard. Lobster.

Jambon. Ham. (See *Hors d'Oeuvres.*)

Jarret. Shin, knuckle of veal, beef, etc.

De Porc aux Lentilles. Pork shank with lentils.

De Veau. Veal shank (stew).

Jambonneau. Pork knuckle/shoulder of pork.

Jésus Lyonnais. A small dried sausage.

Jésus (Gésu) de Morteau. A smoked pork-sausage from the Franche-Comté.

Au Vin Blanc. Smoked pork-sausage sautéed in butter until brown then simmered with small whole potatoes, onions, garlic, parsley, tomato paste and white wine. The sausage is sliced and served with the potatoes and reduced pan juices, then garnished with parsley.

Langouste. Spiny lobster.

Langoustine. A delicate pink crustacean (scampi) resembling a small lobster.

Langue. Tongue. Usually beef *(langue de boeuf)* unless otherwise designated. Served in a sauce of butter, minced *cornichons,* white wine, vinegar, parsley and cayenne pepper *(sauce piquante).*

Lapereau. A young rabbit.

Lapin/Lièvre. Rabbit/hare.

Chasseur. Rabbit sautéed with white wine, mushrooms, shallots, brown sauce *(demi-glace)* and tomato sauce, then sprinkled with parsley.

Grandmère. Rabbit sautéed with butter, onions, mushrooms, bacon, potatoes, Madeira wine, herbs and seasonings.

À la Moutarde. Rabbit in a mustard sauce enriched with cream and seasoned with lemon juice, salt and pepper.

À la Royale. Rabbit, boned and stuffed with foie gras and truffles, then braised in red wine and brandy.

Limande. Lemon (usually sole).

Lotte. Monkfish

Aux Poireaux. With leeks.

Loup (de mer). Mediterranean sea bass, lit. "sea wolf."

Magret de Canard. Duck breast. Boned and sliced, usually grilled or gently pan-fried. Served rare.

Maquereaux. Mackerel.

Matelote. A stew of different freshwater fish, particularly eel and carp, pike or perch; in wine with mushrooms and onions.

Merlin (frit). Whiting (fried).

Meurette. Red wine sauce.
Meunière. Herb-butter sauce. (See *Beurre.*)
Moelle. Bone marrow, usually beef.
Morilles. Wild mushrooms, morels.
Morue. Codfish. (Salt cod, as opposed to *cabillaud,* which is fresh codfish.)
Mousseline. A light, creamy purée.
Nantua. A light crayfish-flavored cream sauce.
Navarin. Lamb or mutton stew with vegetables. Usually served with turnips and potatoes.
D'agneau Printanier. Lamb stew with a variety of spring vegetables such as new potatoes, onions, carrots, turnips, tomatoes, peas, string beans. Seasoned with garlic and herbs.
Navet. Turnip.
Noisette. Hazelnut. But also refers to anything small and round, especially a medallion of meat.
Noix. Nut, especially walnut. But also refers to the topside of veal. (See *Fricandeau* and *Veau.*)
Oie. Goose.
Oignon. Onion.
Ombre. A freshwater fish similar to trout.
Onglet. Steak (mitre-joint from the strip encasing the ribs). Like strip steak, the cut is juicy and flavorful. Usually grilled or sautéed with shallots.
Os. Bone.
À l'Os. With bone marrow.
Oreille. Ear, usually pig.
Oseille. Sorrel.
Panée. Coated with breadcrumbs.
Palette. Blade bone. A thin circular cut from the top of the shoulder blade, usually pork.
Palombe. Wild dove, wild pigeon.
Pavé. A term for various thickly sliced items, lit. "paving stone," e.g., thickly sliced beef steak.
Perdreau. Young partridge.
Perdrix. Adult partridge.
Petits Pois. Green peas.
Petit Salé. Lightly salted pork tenderloin.
Aux Choux Braisés. Salt pork poached and served with braised cabbage.
Aux Lentilles. Salt pork simmered with garlic, onions, and herbs. Served with green lentils, and garnished with butter and chopped parsley.

De Canard. Duck that has been marinated for several days in salt brine, herbs and spices, then cooked and served with vegetables.

Pieds. Feet or trotters.

De Mouton. Sheep's trotters. Prepared in ways similar to those described below for pigs' feet.

Poulette. Poached sheep's trotters in a rich sauce made with pan juices, cream and egg yolks flavored with lemon and parsley. Sometimes mushrooms are added.

De Porc (pané). Pigs' feet (breaded). Usually grilled.

Farci et Pané. Poached pigs' feet, stuffed, breaded and grilled. Served with potatoes and a spicy sauce or mustard.

Ste. Menehould. Pigs' feet poached for 24–36 hours in a stock of white wine, cloves and herbs to soften the bones, making them edible. They are then breaded and grilled until crisp. Served plain with mustard or a pungent sauce and often accompanied by potatoes or lentils.

Pieds et Paquets. Stuffed lamb's trotters and tripe. The "packets" are little rolls made from a sheep's stomach stuffed with a seasoned salt pork mixture. These are braised with lamb's feet in white wine, onions, tomatoes, garlic, herbs, parsley and orange peel. This is a specialty of Marseilles.

Pigeon. Pigeon.

Pigeonneau. Squab.

Pintade. Guinea fowl.

Pinteaudeau. Young guinea fowl.

Pipérade. A Basque preparation consisting of an omelette or scrambled eggs with onions, Bayonne ham, sweet peppers and tomatoes.

Piquant(e). Spicy, pungent.

Poêlé. Pan-fried.

Poivre. Pepper.

Pomme de Terre (pomme). Potato.

Porc. Pork. The principal cuts of pork are: *Carré:* Rack, ribs. *Côte:* Chop. *Échine:* Shoulder. *Filet:* Tenderloin. *Jambon:* Ham. *Jamboneau:* Knuckle/shoulder. *Longe:* Top half of the loin. *Palette:* Shoulder. *Pied:* Trotter. *Poitrine:* Breast.

Porcelet. Piglet.

Potage. A thick soup which may be a purée of vegetables, a creamy soup made with cream or milk, or a soup based on creamy white velouté sauce made with stock, eggs and cream.

Pot-au-Feu. Boiled dinner (soup, meat and vegetables). Usually various cuts of beef simmered with bone marrow, turnips, leeks, cabbage and carrots. A *pot-au-feu* is traditionally served with the soup first followed by a platter of the vegetables and meat garnished with marrow. Served with mustard, *cornichons* and coarse salt. No two chefs agree on the ingredients. Sausage, ham, fowl, mutton, bacon, etc., may be used.

Potée. A substantial soup of meat and vegetables. The basic ingredients are fresh or salt pork with cabbage, beans or lentils and sausage, but there is a wide latitude as to what may be included and the ingredients vary according to region.

Alsacienne/aux Haricots Rouges. Soup made with red kidney beans, sausage and pork.

À l'Auvergnate. Soup made with sausage, bacon, cabbage, onions, carrots, garlic and sometimes lentils or other beans.

Bourguignonne. Cubes of beef, chicken, salt pork, garlic, sausage, cabbage, potatoes, leeks, celery and turnips. The soup is poured over slices of bread and the meat and vegetables are served separately.

Poularde. A roasting chicken, fattened hen, pullet. Often used interchangeably with *capon, coq* and *poulet.*

À la Crème au Vinaigre de Xérès. With sherry vinegar from Jerez.

Au Riz. With rice.

Poule. Hen (boiling).

Poule au Pot. Chicken stuffed with a mixture of its own liver, ham, bread, eggs, garlic and herbs, then poached in bouillon made with aromatic vegetables. The vegetables (turnips, carrots, leeks and celery) are removed before poaching the chicken and transferred to a skillet where they are simmered in stock. Meanwhile some of the stuffing ingredients are wrapped in cabbage leaves and cooked with the chicken. The chicken is served accompanied by the vegetables and a sauce made from some of the stock, thickened with cream and egg yolks. The rest of the stock is served separately as a soup. Coarse salt and *cornichons* may also accompany this dish.

Poulet. Chicken.

De Bresse. Corn-fed free-range chicken from Bresse in Eastern France. Very high in quality.

Fermier. Free-range.

À l'Estragon. Roasted or sautéed chicken with tarragon. Served with either a cream sauce or a brown sauce flavored with tarragon.

Rôti. Roasted.

Poulette. A rich white sauce made from stock thickened with egg yolks and cream. Sometimes button mushrooms, onions and white wine are added. *Poulette* is also the name for a young chicken.

Poulpe. Octopus.

Poussin. Young spring chicken, baby chicken.

Pré(s) Salé(s). Salt marsh mutton. This is the most prized mutton in France because the sheep are grazed in meadows saturated with salt from ocean winds, giving the meat a special salty taste.

Quenelles. Forcemeat dumplings. A purée of meat, poultry or fish is mixed with fat, eggs and pastry dough or crumbs, then made into light dumplings. These are usually poached and served with a simple cream sauce.

De Brochet. Pike dumplings, often served in a *beurre blanc* sauce.

Nantua. Dumplings served with a crayfish-flavored cream sauce made with white wine, fish stock, a few drops of cognac, and cayenne pepper. Sometimes mushrooms or truffles are added.

De Volaille. Chicken dumplings.

Queue de Boeuf. Oxtail.

Queues et Oreilles de Cochon Grillées. Grilled pigs' tails and ears.

Râble de Lièvre (Lapin). Saddle of hare (rabbit). The word *selle* is used for larger animals.

Raie. Skate.

Au Beurre Noir. With black butter. Poached or grilled skate served in a sauce of blackened butter, vinegar, lemon and parsley. Sometimes garnished with capers.

Raifort. Horseradish.

Rascasse. Scorpion fish.

Ravigote. A thick, spicy vinaigrette mixed with vinegar, chopped *cornichons*, herbs, capers and onions.

Rémoulade. Spicy mustard mayonnaise mixed with chopped herbs, capers, *cornichons* and sometimes anchovies.

Ris. Sweet breads, usually braised or sautéed.

D'Agneau. Lamb.

De Veau. Calf.

Riz. Rice.

Rognons (d'Agneau, de Veau). Kidneys (lamb, veal), usually grilled or sautéed.

Poêle de Rognons. Sautéed kidneys.

Rôti. Roasted.

Rouget. A mediterranean fish similar to red mullet.

Rouille. Hot red-pepper mayonnaise. (See *Bouillabaisse.*)

Saint-Pierre. John Dory, a firm, white-fleshed ocean fish with dark spots (the thumb marks of St. Peter!) on each side.

Sandre. Pike-perch, a freshwater river fish.

À l'Oseille. With sorrel.

Sanglier. Wild boar.

Sauge. Sage.

Saumon. Salmon.

Fumé. Smoked.

Grillée à l'Unilateral. Grilled on one side.

Mariné. Marinated.

Saumuré. Salted.

Sauté. A preparation of meat, game, fish or fowl lightly pan-fried in oil and butter over high heat. The pan juices are used as a garnish and sometimes vegetables are added. In some *sautés* the meats are braised or baked to complete the cooking.

Selle. Saddle, back (of meat).

Sole Meunière. Sole (pan-fried) with butter sauce.

Soupe. Soup, usually refers to a thick country-style soup with pieces of meat and vegetables.

Sucré(e). Sweetened.

Tabliers de Sapeur. Pan-fried tripe. Ox tripe is pounded into a flat sheet, cut into small squares, breaded and pan-fried until crisp. Served with garlic butter, tartar sauce or béarnaise. This is a specialty of Lyon.

Tête. Head, especially calf's head, usually served hot with vinaigrette (see *Tête de Veau*). Can also mean brawn, as in *fromage de tête.*

Tête de Veau. Head of veal, poached in an herbal stock with spices, white wine, carrots and onions. It is boned, sliced and served hot or cold in a sauce, often with slices of the tongue and brains. When the head is lean and tender and served very hot in a tasty warm vinaigrette, it can be quite good. Otherwise, it can have a repellent and gristly texture.

Sauce Gribiche. With a creamy vinaigrette flavored with tarragon, chopped hard-boiled egg yolks, capers, and *cornichons.*

Sauce Ravigote. With a vinaigrette seasoned with *chervil,* tarragon, capers, and onions.

Thon. Tuna.

Thym. Thyme.

Tiède. Warm, tepid.

Tomate. Tomato.

Farci. Stuffed.

Topinambour. Jerusalem artichoke.

Tournedos. Steak from the best part of the fillet.

Rossini. Tournedos sautéed and served on a crust topped with a slice of foie gras, then covered with pan juices mixed with red wine.

Tranche. A slice.

Tripe. Ox tripe.

À la Mode/À la Mode de Caen. The classic Norman preparation for tripe, in which it is boiled and braised for several hours with calf's foot, salt pork, carrots, onions, herbs and seasonings in apple cider, wine, and Calvados.

Tripous/Tripoux. Pieces of veal or mutton tripe wrapped round a stuffing mixture of minced pork and veal seasoned with cloves. The stuffing ingredients may vary, but cloves are always used. The tripe is then made into small rolls and simmered for several hours in an airtight casserole.

Truffade. A large fried pancake made with layers of potato, Cantal cheese, bacon and garlic. A specialty from Auvergne.

Truffe. Truffle.

Truite. Trout.

Au Bleu. A method of cooking trout by first plunging it into boiling water with vinegar, then removing it to a court bouillon to finish the cooking.

Turbot. Turbot, a flat white sea fish with a subtle flavor.

Vapeur (à la). Steamed.

Veau. Veal. The principal cuts of veal are: *Carré:* Rib, rack. *Côte:* Chop. *Cul:* Rump. *Escalope:* Thin slice from the fillet. *Jarret:* Knuckle. *Longe:* Top half of the loin. *Noisette:* Medallion, small round steak. *Noix:* Topside, from the upper part of the leg. *Poitrine:* Breast. *Tendron:* Cartilage from the end of the breast. *Tête:* Head (see *Tête de Veau*).

Vert(e). Green.

Poivre Vert. Green peppercorns.

Sauce Verte. Green herb mayonnaise.

Volailles. Poultry.

Xérès: A dry white sherry produced in Jerez de la Frontera, Spain.

Vinaigre de. Vinegar made from this wine.

DESSERTS

Abricot. Apricot.

Ananas. Pineapple.

Au Kirsch (Rhum). Sliced pineapple sprinkled with sugar and Kirsch (rum).

Baba au Rhum. Sponge cake with rum-flavored syrup.

Banane. Banana.

Bombe. A moulded, layered ice cream dessert. Usually two flavors layered together in a spherical mold.

Café (Chocolat) Liégeois. Cold coffee (chocolate) poured over coffee (chocolate) ice cream. Served in tall glasses topped with whipped cream.

Caprice. A dessert, lit. "whim."

Cerises. Cherries.

Charlotte. A molded dessert of which there are two kinds. One is a pudding mixture made from fruit and sugar, baked in a mold lined with white buttered bread or sponge cake and served hot. The other is a cold custard cream or mousse (e.g., chocolate) chilled in a mold lined with lady fingers.

Citron. Lemon.

Clafoutis. A thick custard tart made with egg yolks and a kind of pancake batter poured over preserved fruit (traditionally cherries but any available fruit may be used), and baked. This is a specialty from the Limousin.

Compôte. Fresh or dried fruit stewed in wine.

Corbeille. A basket of fresh fruit.

Coupe. A glass or bowl. Often refers to one serving, e.g., one scoop or *boule,* of ice cream.

Crème Anglaise. Light egg and vanilla custard sauce.

Crème Brûlée. Egg custard topped with brown sugar which is "burnt" to form a hard dark coating.

Crème Caramel. Egg custard in a sauce of caramelized sugar.

Cremet. Fresh unsalted cream cheese eaten with fruit, jam or cream and sugar.

Crème de Marrons. Sugar-sweetened chestnut purée.

Crème Renversée. Upside-down *crème caramel.*

Délice. Lit. "Delight," a menu description of a dessert.

Douce (Doux). Sweet(s).

Flan. A baked custard tart or open pie; sometimes refers to *crème renversée.*

Frais/Fraîche. Fresh.

Fraises. Strawberries.

Framboises. Raspberries.

Au Sucre. With sugar.

Fromage. Cheese.

Blanc. Fresh cream cheese with a salty taste and the consistency of smooth cottage cheese. Served plain or with sugar, cream, fruit or salt and pepper.

Brebis. Sheep's milk cheese.

Cervelle de Canut. A soft, fresh cream cheese made with herbs, vinegar, white wine, oil and garlic. A specialty of Lyon.

Crottin (de Chavignol). A small dry goat's milk cheese with a strong sharp taste.

Au Fruits Rouges. With berries.

Gâteau. Cake.

Gâteau de Noix. Walnut cake.

Gâteau de Riz. Rice is cooked in vanilla-flavored milk, moulded into a cake and served with whipped cream and/or sauce. Sometimes fruit is added to the rice.

Glace. Ice cream.

Île Flottante. "Floating island." Poached egg whites are caramelized with sugar and vanilla beans and served in a vanilla custard sauce. Sometimes used interchangeably with *Oeufs à la Neige.*

Marquise au Chocolate. A mousse-like chocolate sponge cake with a butter cream filling.

Marrons Glacés. Candied chestnuts.

Mille-Feuille. A Napoleon. Layers of puff pastry, filled with cream or custard, cut into rectangles, glazed and frosted.

Mirabelle. A kind of yellow plum.

Mont Blanc. A mound of puréed chestnuts topped with whipped cream.

Mousse au Chocolat. A light chocolate pudding, often served with whipped cream.

Mûres. Mulberries/blackberries.

Myrtilles. Huckleberries/blueberries.

Mystère. A "mystery." An ice cream dessert, often vanilla ice cream in meringues with chocolate sauce.

Oeufs à la Neige. "Snow eggs." Caramelized egg whites served in a vanilla custard sauce. (See *Île Flottante.*)

Oranges. Oranges.

Panaché(e). Mixture.

Parfum. Flavor.

Pâtisseries. Pastries.

Pêches. Peaches.

Melba. Poached peaches with vanilla ice cream and raspberry sauce.

Poires. Pears.

Belle Helène. Poached pears with vanilla ice cream and chocolate sauce.

Au Vin. Pears poached in sugar and red wine or Port.

Pommes. Apples.

Au Four. Baked apples.

Profiteroles. Small cream puffs filled with ice cream (or pastry cream), covered with chocolate or coffee sauce and served with whipped cream.

Pruneau(x). Prune(s).

Raisins. Grapes.

Riz au lait. (See *Gâteau de Riz.*)

Sorbet. Fruit ice, sherbet.

Tarte-Tatin. Caramelized upside-down apple tart, served hot or cold.

Tartes. Open-faced pies. Fruit tarts may or may not be made with pastry cream but are usually coated with an apricot or currant glaze.

Tartelettes. Small or individual tarts.

Glossary

Afternoon	*Apres-midi*
An amusement—something to nibble while waiting for food to be served	*Amuse-bouche*
Ashtray	*Cendrier*
Beer	*Bière*
Draft Beer	*À la pression (bière)*
Beverages	*Boissons*
Bread	*Pain*
Breakfast	*Petit déjeuner*
Butter	*Beurre*
The check	*l'addition*
Cider	*Cidre*
Closed*	*Fermé*
Coffee	*Café*
black	*noir*
decaffeinated	*déca/décafeiné*
espresso	*express*
very strong, black	*filtre*
with milk	*au lait/crème*
Cover charge	*Un couvert***
Cup	*Tasse*
Dinner	*Dîner (8:00–10:30)*
Evening	*Soir*
This evening	*Ce soir*
Every day	*Tous les jours (TLJ)*
An extra charge	*Supplément*

---

*Most restaurants close for a summer holiday and for one or two days a week throughout the year.

**This charge is for a place setting. Sometimes, but not always, bread is included.

Fork	*Fourchette*
Full, no more room for customers	*Complet*
Glass	*Verre*
Half bottle	*Demi-bouteille*
Head waiter	*Maître d'hôtel*
Horseradish	*Raifort*
Jug, pitcher	*Pichet*
Juice (fruit juice)	*Jus (des fruits)*
Fresh squeezed orange (lemon) juice	*Orange (citron) pressé*
Orange (lemon) fruit drink	*Jus d'orange (de citron)*
Knife	*Couteau*
Large bottle	*Grande bouteille*
Lemon	*Citron*
Lunch	*Déjeuner (12:30–2:00)*
Midday/Noon	*Midi*
Milk	*Lait*
Mustard	*Moutard*
Napkin	*Serviette*
Night	*Nuit*
Oil	*Huile*
Open	*Ouvert*
Pepper	*Poivre*
Pepper mill	*Moulin de poivre*
Pickle	*Cornichon (small, tart gherkin)*
Plate	*Assiette*
Please	*S'il vous plaît*
Proprietor	*Patron(ne)*
Reservation	*Réservation*
Salt	*Sel*
Serving until (9:30)	*Jusqu'à (21h30)*
Spoon	*Cuillère*
Sugar	*Sucre*
Tea (Chinese)	*Thé (de Chine)*
Herb tea	*Infusion*
Thank you	*Merci*
Tip included	*Service Compris*
Tip not included	*Service Noncompris*
Today	*Au jour d'hui*
Tomorrow	*Demain*
Toothpick	*Cure-dent*
Vinegar	*Vinaigre*

Waiter	*Garçon*
Waitress	*Serveuse****
Water	*Eau*
Hot water	*Eau chaude*
Ice water	*Eau glacé*
Mineral water(s)	*Eau(x) minerale(s)*
Non-Sparkling/flat	*Non-gazeuse/plate (e.g., Vittel, Evian)*
Pitcher of tap water	*Une carafe d'eau*
Plain tap water	*Eau fraîche*
Sparkling	*Gazeuse (e.g., Perrier, Vichy, Badoit)*
Week	*Semaine*
Monday	*Lundi*
Except Monday	*Sauf Lundi*
Tuesday	*Mardi*
Wednesday	*Mercredi*
Thursday	*Jeudi*
Friday	*Vendredi*
Saturday	*Samedi*
Sunday	*Dimanche*
Wine steward	*Sommelier*

***Not a form of address. "Madame" or "mademoiselle" is appropriate.

PART IV

Ratings of the Best Bistro Dishes

The dishes that follow portray a cross section of the most typical bistro cuisine. These are the foods for which bistros are famous and, while many establishments may serve these items, the restaurants appearing under each heading offer outstanding versions and are listed in order of their preparation's merit. In each case our favorite is listed first, however, all may be considered part of an honor roll of restaurants where meals of exceptionally high quality or originality—truly the great bistro classics of Paris—may be enjoyed.

Andouillette

(Smoked Pork Sausage)

Anjou-Normandie 11^{e}
Restaurant Pierre au Palais Royal 1er
Le Cochon d'Or des Halles (Chez Beñat) 1er
Chez Marcel (Antoine) 12^{e}
Le Pouilly-Reuilly 19^{e}
Joséphine (Chez Dumonet) 6^{e}
Moissonnier 5^{e}
Chez Fred 17^{e}
À Sousceyrac 11^{e}
Le Petit Plat 15^{e}
Les Gourmets des Ternes 17^{e}
Berrys 8^{e}
Le Vieux Bistrot 4^{e}
Au Gourmet de l'Isle 4^{e}
Astier 11^{e}
Aristide 17^{e}
Aux Charpentiers 6^{e}
Au Petit Riche 9^{e}
La Tour de Monthléry (Chez Denise) 1er
Le Chardenoux 11^{e}
Perraudin 5^{e}
Au Petit Tonneau 7^{e}
L'Auberge Bressane 7^{e}
Au Moulin à Vent (Chez Henri) 5^{e}
Le Bistro d'à Côté 17^{e}

Baba

(Yeast Cake with Rum Syrup)

Chez André 8^{e}
Les Gourmets des Ternes 17^{e}
Chez Janou 3^{e}
Chez Georges 2^{e}

Beurre Blanc

(White-Wine Butter Sauce for Seafood)

La Grille 10^{e}
Au Petit Tonneau 7^{e}
Allard 6^{e}
Anjou-Normandie 11^{e}
L'Assiette 14^{e}
Restaurant Pierre au Palais Royal 1er
Restaurant du Marché 15^{e}
Chez Maître Paul 6^{e}
Au Petit Riche 9^{e}
Savy 8^{e}

Blanquette de Veau

(*Veal Stew in White Cream Sauce*)

Savy (Thursdays) 8^{e}
Au Becs Fins 20^{e}
À l'Impasse (Chez Robert) 4^{e}
Benoît 4^{e}
Aristide 17^{e}
À la Pomponnette 18^{e}
Chez Germaine 7^{e}
Chez René (Fridays) 5^{e}
Polidor 6^{e}
Le Chardenoux 11^{e}
Au Pied de Fouet 7^{e}

Boeuf Bourguignon

(*Beef Stew with Red Wine*)

Chez René 5^{e}
Le Vieux Bistrot 4^{e}
Chez Pauline 1er
La Grille 10^{e}
Joséphine (Chez Dumonet) 6^{e}
Lescure 1er
Chez Germaine 7^{e}
Au Petit Tonneau 7^{e}
Perraudin 5^{e}
Les Gourmets des Ternes 17^{e}
Polidor 6^{e}
Restaurant des Beaux-Arts 6^{e}
Au Moulin à Vent (Chez Henri) 5^{e}

Boeuf en Daube

(*Beef with Red Wine and Vegetables*)

Chez la Vielle 1er
Restaurant du Marché 15^{e}
Baracane 4^{e}
Le Chardenoux 11^{e}
Campagne et Provence 5^{e}
Le Caméléon 6^{e}
Aux Charpentiers 6^{e}

Boeuf à la Ficelle

(Poached Filet of Beef)

Marie-Louise 18e
L'Assiette 14e
Restaurant Pierre au Palais Royal 1er
Cartet 11e
Benoît 4e
Au Moulin à Vent (Chez Henri) 5e
Aux Charpentiers 6e

Boeuf Miroton

(Leftover-Beef Stew with Onions)

Chez la Vielle 1er
Le Brin de Zinc . . . et Madame 2e
Moissonnier 5e
Au Petit Riche 9e

Boeuf à la Mode

(Pot Roast with Vegetables)

Benoît 4e
Chez René (Thursdays) 5e
L'Ebauchoir 12e
Chez la Vielle 1er
Chez Fred (Fridays) 17e
Allard 6e
Aux Charpentiers (Tuesdays) 6e

Boudin

(Sausage)

La Fermette du Sud-Ouest 1er
Auberge D'Chez Eux 7e
La Quincy 12e
Benoît 4e
L'Assiette 14e
Aux Charpentiers 6e
Moissonnier 5e
Chez Marcel (Antoine) 12e
Le Pouilly-Reuilly 19e
Le Petit Zinc 6e
Au Gourmet de l'Isle 4e
Chez André 8e
Thoumieux 7e

Brandade

(Purée of Cod)

Le Cochon d'Or des Halles (Chez Beñat) 1er
L'Oeillade 7^{e}
Campagne et Provence 5^{e}
Cartet 11^{e}
Astier 11^{e}
Le Maquis 18^{e}
Au Petit Riche 9^{e}
Perraudin 5^{e}
Chez Germaine 7^{e}

Cassoulet

(White Bean Casserole)

Auberge Pyrénées Cévennes (Chez Philippe) 6^{e}
À Sousceyrac 11^{e}
Auberge D'Chez Eux 7^{e}
Le Quincy 12^{e}
Joséphine (Chez Dumonet) 6^{e}
Baracane 4^{e}
Restaurant du Marché 15^{e}
Le Languedoc 5^{e}
La Fontaine de Mars 7^{e}
Le Fermette du Sud-Ouest 1er
La Gitane 15^{e}
Thoumieux 7^{e}
Aux Becs Fins 20^{e}
Le Petit Salé 17^{e}

Chou Farci

(Stuffed Cabbage)

Chez Pauline 1er
Restaurant Pierre au Palais Royal 1er
Le Quincy 12^{e}
Savy (Tuesdays) 8^{e}
Restaurant Bleu 14^{e}
La Gitane 15^{e}
La Tour de Monthléry (Chez Denise) 1er
Auberge Pyrénées Cévennes (Chez Philippe) 11^{e}
Aux Charpentiers (Saturdays) 6^{e}

Civet de Porc et Porcelet

(Pig Stew)

Au Gourmet de l'Isle 4e
La Rôtisserie d'en Face 6e
Chez Marcel (Antoine) 12e

Cochonnailles

(Assorted Pork Products)

La Régalade 14e
Auberge D'Chez Eux 7e
Chez Marcel (Antoine) 12e
Le Quincy 12e
L'Auberge Bressane 7e
Le Grizzli 4e
Cartet 11e
Le Petit Marguery 13e
La Fermette du Sud-Ouest 1er
La Fontaine de Mars 7e
Chez Maître Paul 6e
Allard 6e
Au Gigot Fin 10e
Chez Henri 5e
La Tour de Monthléry (Chez Denise) 1er
Chez René 5e
Le Caméléon 6e
Chez Georges 17e
Chez Fred 17e

Coq au Vin

(Chicken Stewed in Wine)

Marie-Louise 18e
L'Auberge Bressane 7e
Le Bourbonnais 14e
Auberge Pyrénées Cevénnes (Chez Philippe) 11e
L'Oeillade 7e
Chez René 5e
Chez Maître Paul 6e
À la Biche aux Bois 12e
Le Chardenoux 11e
La Maquis 18e
Chez l'Ami Jean 7e
Allard 6e

Côtes de Boeuf

(Ribs of Beef)

Les Fontaines 5^{e}
L'Ami Louis 3^{e}
Auberge D'Chez Eux 7^{e}
La Tour de Monthléry (Chez Denise) 1er
Chez Georges 17^{e}
Chez Pauline 1er
Au Moulin à Vent (Chez Henri) 5^{e}
Chez André 8^{e}
Le Petit Zinc 6^{e}
Les Gourmets des Ternes 17^{e}
Le Scheffer 16^{e}
Le Petit Salé 17^{e}
Thoumieux 7^{e}
Aux Charpentiers 6^{e}

Foie Gras

(Fattened Goose or Duck Liver)

L'Ami Louis 3^{e}
Joséphine (Chez Dumonet) 6^{e}
Auberge D'Chez Eux 7^{e}
Chez Toutoune 5^{e}
L'Auberge Bressane 7^{e}
L'Oeillade 7^{e}
À la Biche aux Bois 12^{e}
À Sousceyrac 11^{e}
L'Assiette 14^{e}
Restaurant du Marché 15^{e}
Anjou-Normandie 11^{e}
Le Bourbonnais 14^{e}
Aux Becs Fins 20^{e}
Le Brissemoret 2^{e}
Restaurant Pierre au Palais Royal 1er
Le Quincy 12^{e}
Le Petit Bourbon 1er
Le Villaret 11^{e}
Aristide 17^{e}
Le Petit Marguery 13^{e}
Le Chardenoux 11^{e}
La Fontaine de Mars 7^{e}
Baracane 4^{e}

Gateau de Riz (Riz au Lait)

(Rice Pudding)

L'Ebauchoir 12^{e}
Chez Pauline 1er
Chez René 5^{e}
Le Pouilly-Reuilly 19^{e}
Chez Germaine 7^{e}
Polidor 6^{e}

Chez La Vielle 1er
Le Brin de Zinc . . . et Madame 2e
Moissonnier 5e
Bistro de la Grille 6e

Gibelottes et Civets de Lapin/Lièvre

(Rabbit/Hare Stew)

Le Petit Marguery 13e
L'Oeillade 7e
Chez Marcel (Antoine) 12e
À l'Impasse (Chez Robert) 4e
Moissonnier 5e

Gigot d'Agneau

(Leg of Lamb)

Chez Georges 17e
Joséphine (Chez Dumonet) 6e
L'Ami Louis 3e
Au Gigot Fin 10e
Chez André 8e
Le Petit Zinc 6e
La Fontaine de Mars 7e
Le Languedoc 5e
Cartet 11e
Chez Georges 2e
Perraudin 5e

Gras-Double

(Inner Stomach of Ox)

Benoît 4e
Aux Becs Fins 20e
Moissonnier 5e
Le Petit Mâchon 15e
La Fermette du Sud-Ouest 1er
Allard 6e
Cartet 11e
Aux Lyonnais 2e

Hachis Parmentier

(*Meat-and-Potato Casserole*)

La Villaret 11e
La Régalade 14e
Chez La Vielle 1er
(must be ordered in advance)
L'Assiette 14e
Chez Georges 17e
Le Caméléon 6e
Restaurant des Beaux-Arts 6e

Haricot de Mouton

(*Lamb Stew with White Beans*)

Chez Georges 17e
La Tour de Monthléry (Chez Denise) 1er
Chez la Vielle 1er
Chez René (Tuesdays) 5e

Jambon

(*Regional Hams*)

Berrys 8e
Restaurant du Marché 15e
Le Grizzli 4e
Le Quincy 12e
Le Languedoc 5e
Chez Fred 17e
La Fermette du Sud-Ouest 1er
Joséphine (Chez Dumonet) 6e
Chez l'Ami Jean 7e

Jambon (Jambon Cuits)

(*Cooked Hams*)

Chez Maître Paul 6e
Auberge Pyrénées Cevénnes (Chez Philippe) 11e

Jambon Persillé

(Parslied Ham)

Chez Pauline 1er
Restaurant Pierre au Palais Royal 1er
Auberge Pyrénées Cevénnes (Chez Philippe) 11^{e}
Cartet 11^{e}
Chez Georges 2^{e}
Allard 6^{e}

Lapin à la Moutarde

(Rabbit in Mustard Sauce)

Astier 11^{e}
La Maquis 18^{e}
La Tour de Monthléry (Chez Denise) 1er
Polidor 6^{e}

Lièvre à la Royale

(A Complex Preparation of Hare; see "Les Plats")

À Sousceyrac 11^{e}
Restaurant du Marché 15^{e}
Le Petit Marguery 13^{e}
Chez Pauline 1er
Benoît 4^{e}
Restaurant Pierre au Palais Royal 1er

Rable de Lièvre/Lapin (Lapereau)

(Saddle of Hare/Rabbit)

Le Villaret 11^{e}
Les Fontaines 5^{e}
Le Grizzli 4^{e}
Chez Janou 3^{e}
Au Petit Riche 9^{e}
Marie et Fils 6^{e}

MAQUEREAU

(Mackerel)

Restaurant Pierre au Palais Royal 1er
À la Pomponnette 18^{e}
La Grille 10^{e}
Le Petit Marguery 13^{e}
Le Brissemoret 2^{e}
Cartet 11^{e}
Lescure 1er
Chez Marcel (Antoine) 12^{e}
Au Pied de Fouet 7^{e}

NAVARIN

(Lamb Stew)

Allard 6^{e}
Le Cochon d'Or des Halles (Chez Beñat) 1er
Le Scheffer 16^{e}
Chez Marie 6^{e}
Joséphine (Chez Dumonet) 6^{e}
Chez Edgard 8^{e}
Chez la Vielle 1er
Savy 8^{e}
Perraudin 5^{e}
Marie et Fils 6^{e}
Le Grizzli 4^{e}
Chez Germaine 7^{e}
Chez André 8^{e}
Restaurant des Beaux-Arts 6^{e}

PETIT SALÉ

(Lightly-Salted Pork Tenderloin)

Chez Georges 17^{e}
Allard 6^{e}
Moissonnier 5^{e}
La Maquis 18^{e}
L'Ebauchoir 12^{e}
Le Petit Salé 17^{e}
Auberge Pyrénées Cévennes (Chez Philippe) 11^{e}
Chez Fred (Tuesdays) 17^{e}
Perraudin 5^{e}
Aux Charpentiers (Wednesdays) 6^{e}
Polidor (Tuesdays) 6^{e}

Pieds de Porc

(Pigs' Feet)

À Sousceyrac 11^{e}
Chez Marcel (Antoine) 12^{e}
Moissonnier 5^{e}
La Tour de Monthléry (Chez Denise) 1er
Thoumieux 7^{e}
Le Petit Mâchon 15^{e}
Aux Charpentiers 6^{e}

Pot-au-Feu/Boeuf Gros Sel

(Beef with Vegetables and Coarse Salt)

Le Boeuf Gros Sel 20^{e}
Le Roi du Pot-au-Feu 9^{e}
Chez la Vielle 1er (order in advance)
La Poule au Pot 1er
Restaurant des Beaux-Arts 6^{e}
Chez Fred (Thursdays) 17^{e}
La Gitane 15^{e}
Bistro de la Grille 6^{e}
La Tour de Monthléry (Chez Denise) 1er
Chez Georges (Wednesdays) 17^{e}
Savy (Fridays) 8^{e}
Le Chardenoux 11^{e}
Chez Germaine 7^{e}

Poule-au-Pot

(Poached Stuffed Chicken)

La Poule au Pot 1er
Restaurant du Marché 15^{e}
Auberge D'Chez Eux 7^{e}
Polidor 6^{e}
Lescure 1er
Savy (Tuesdays) 8^{e}
Le Petit Zinc 6^{e}

Raie

(Skate)

Chez Pauline 1er
Le Petit Marguery 13^{e}

Le Cochon d'Or des Halles (Chez Beñat) 1er
Les Fontaines 5^{e}
Chez Marie 6^{e}
La Cagouille 14^{e}
Chez Fernand (Les Fernandises) 11^{e}
Restaurant Pierre au Palais Royal 1er
Le Pouilly-Reuilly 19^{e}
Aux Lyonnais 2^{e}

SAUCISSON CHAUD

(*Hot Garlic Sausage*)

Benoît 4^{e}
Le Grizzli 4^{e}
Le Vieux Bistrot 4^{e}
Marie-Louise 18^{e}
Chez Georges 17^{e}
Chez René 5^{e}
Restaurant Pierre au Palais Royal 1er
Le Petit Mâchon 15^{e}
Chez Maître Paul 6^{e}
À Sousceyrac 11^{e}
Chez Marcel (Antoine) 12^{e}
Cartet 6^{e}
Moissonnier 5^{e}
Bistro de la Grille 6^{e}

SAUTÉS/RAGOUTS D'AGNEAU

(*Lamb*)

Chez André 8^{e}
Chez la Vielle 1er
À la Biche aux Bois 12^{e}
Le Caméléon 6^{e}
Polidor 6^{e}
La Maquis 18^{e}
Chez Fred (Saturdays) 17^{e}

SAUTÉS/RAGOUTS D'PORC

(*Pig*)

Chez Edgard 8^{e}
Polidor 6^{e}
Cartet 11^{e}
La Fermette du Sud-Ouest 1er

Sautés/Ragouts de Lapin

(*Rabbit*)

Le Quincy 12^{e}

Chez Germaine 7^{e}

Tabliers de Sapeur

(*Lyonnais, Pan-Fried Version of Gras-Double*)

Moissonnier 5^{e}

Le Petit Mâchon 15^{e}

Tête de Veau

(*Calf's Head*)

Benoît 4^{e}
La Régalade 14^{e}
Chez Pauline 1er
Le Petit Bourbon 1er
À la Pomponnette 18^{e}
Les Fontaines 5^{e}
Au Becs Fins 20^{e}
Chez Georges 17^{e}
La Grille 10^{e}
Marie-Louise 18^{e}
L'Ebauchoir 12^{e}
Le Brin de Zinc . . . et Madame 2^{e}
La Fontaine de Mars 7^{e}
Bistro de la Grille 6^{e}

Tripe

Anjou-Normandie 11^{e}
Restaurant Pierre au Palais Royal 1er
Thoumieux 7^{e}
Le Quincy 12^{e}
Campagne et Provence 5^{e}
La Tour de Monthléry (Chez Denise) 1er
Chez Marcel (Antoine) 12^{e}
Chez Fernand (Fernandises) 11^{e}

Tripoux

(Auvergnat Preparation of Veal or Mutton Tripe)

Le Chardenoux 11^{e}
Restaurant Bleu 14^{e}
Le Petit Mâchon 15^{e}
Le Petit Zinc 6^{e}

Bistros Open On Sunday

(Listed by Arrondissement)

It is always advisable to call first as a particular restaurant may not be open for both lunch and dinner.

1er Arrondissement
La Poule au Pot

3^e^ Arrondissement
L'Ami Louis

4^e^ Arrondissement
Au Gourmet de L'Isle
Le Trumilou
Le Vieux Bistro

5e Arrondissement
Le Languedoc
Moissonnier (lunch only)
La Rôtisserie du Beaujolais

6e Arrondissement
Bistro de la Grille
Le Petit Zinc
Polidor
Restaurant des Beaux-Arts

7e Arrondissement
Thoumieux

8e Arrondissement
Chez André

9e Arrondissement
Au Petit Riche

14e Arrondissement
L'Assiette
Le Bistrot du Dôme
La Cagouille

15e Arrondissement
Le Petit Plat
Restaurant du Marché

16e Arrondissement
La Butte Chaillot
Le Relais du Parc

17e Arrondissement
Le Bistro D'À Côté
Chez Georges
Le Petit Salé

18e Arrondissement
À La Pomponnette (lunch only)

Other Reliable Paris Bistros

(Listed by Arrondissement)

Each seasoned traveler to Paris has cultivated a list of favorite restaurants and if you talk to any Parisian he may divulge a "special discovery." The list that follows is a selection of these bistros, some fairly well known but most completely obscure. They are all reliable and highly recommended.

1er Arrondissement

Au Petit Ramoneur
74, rue Saint-Denis
Paris, 75001
Tel: 42-36-39-24
Inexpensive

Le Bistro Saint-Honoré
10, rue Gomboust
Paris, 75001
Tel: 42-61-77-78
Moderate

Chez Clovis
33, rue Berger
Paris, 75001
Tel: 42-33-97-07
Moderate

Chez Elle
7, rue des Prouvaires
Paris, 75001

Batifol
14, rue Mondétour
Paris, 75001
Tel: 42-36-85-50
Moderate

Le Châtelet Gourmand
13, rue des Lavandières
Ste.-Opportune
Paris, 75001
Tel: 40-26-45-00
Fairly Expensive

Le Dauphin
167, rue Saint-Honoré
Paris, 75001
Tel: 42-60-40-11
Moderate

L'Émile
74, rue Jean-Jacques-
Rousseau

Tel: 45-08-04-10
Moderate

Paris, 75001
Tel: 42-36-58-58
Moderate

L'Épi d'Or
25, rue Jean-Jacques-Rousseau
Paris, 75001
Tel: 42-36-38-12
Moderate

L'Incroyable
26, rue de Richelieu
Paris, 75001
Tel: 42-96-24-64
Inexpensive

Louis XIV
1bis, place des Victoires
Paris, 75001
Tel: 40-26-20-81
Fairly Expensive

Paul
15, place Dauphine
Paris, 75001
Tel: 43-54-21-48
Moderate

Le Petit Mâchon
158, rue Saint-Honoré
Paris, 75001
Tel: 42-60-23-37
Moderate

La Providence
6, rue de la Sourdière
Paris, 75001
Tel: 42-60-46-13
Moderate

Le Relais du Sud-Ouest
154, rue Saint-Honoré
Paris, 75001
Tel: 42-60-62-01
Inexpensive

Le Souletin
6, rue de la Vrillière
(Place des Victoires)
Paris, 75001
Tel: 42-61-43-78
Moderate

Le Terminus de Châtelet
5, rue des Lavandières-Sainte-Opportune
Paris, 75001
Tel: 45-08-50-44
Moderate

La Vigne (Chez Sabine)
30, rue de L'Arbre-Sec
Paris, 75001
Tel: 42-60-13-55
Moderate

2e Arrondissement

Aux Crus de Bourgogne
3, rue Bachaumont
Paris, 75002

Bistrot du Louvre
48, rue d'Argout
Paris, 75002

Tel: 42-33-48-24
Fairly Expensive

Le Bougainville
5, rue de la Banque
Paris, 75002
Tel: 42-60-05-19
Inexpensive

Chez Pierrot
18, rue Étienne-Marcel
Paris, 75002
Tel: 45-08-17-64
Fairly Expensive

Tel: 45-08-47-46
Moderate

Le Canard d'Avril
5, rue Paul-Lelong
Paris, 75002
Tel: 42-36-26-08
Moderate

3e Arrondissement

L'Auberge de Nicolas Flamel
51, rue de Montmorency
Paris, 75003
Tel: 42-71-77-78
Moderate

Le Valet de Carreau
2, rue du Petit-Thouars
Paris, 75003
Tel: 42-72-72-60
Moderate

L'Imprimerie
101, rue Vieille-du-Temple
Paris, 75003
Tel: 42-77-93-80
Moderate

4e Arrondissement

Au Petit Fer à Chevel
30, rue Vielle-du-Temple
Paris, 75004
Tel: 42-72-47-47
Moderate

Le Bistrot du Dôme
2, rue de la Bastille
Paris, 75004
Tel: 48-04-88-44
Moderate

Au Pont Marie
7, quai de Bourbon
Paris, 75004
Tel: 43-54-79-62
Moderate

Le Colimaçon
44, rue Vieille-du-Temple
Paris, 75004
Tel: 48-87-12-01
Moderate

Les Fous d'en Face
3, rue du Bourg-Tibourg
Paris, 75004
Tel: 48-87-03-75
Moderate

Le Monde des Chimères
69, rue Saint-Louis-en-L'Île
Paris, 75004
Tel: 43-54-45-27
Fairly Expensive

Au Jambon de Bayonne
6, rue de la Tacherie
Paris, 75004
Tel: 42-78-45-45
Inexpensive

Le Temps des Cerises
31, rue de la Cerisaie
Paris, 75004
Tel: 42-72-08-63
Inexpensive

5e Arrondissement

Le Bistrot d'À Côté
"Saint-Germain"
16, blvd. Saint-Germain
Paris, 75005
Tel: 43-54-59-10
Moderate

L'Estrapade
15, rue de L'Estrapade
Paris, 75005
Tel: 43-25-72-58
Moderate

Chez Léna et Mimile
32, rue Tournefort
Paris, 75005
Tel: 47-07-72-47
Moderate

Chez Pento
9, rue Cujas
Paris, 75005
Tel: 43-26-81-54
Moderate

Le Buisson Ardent
25, rue de Jussieu
Paris, 75005
Tel: 43-54-93-02
Moderate

Le Grenache "Espace
Hérault"
8, rue de la Harpe
Paris, 75005
Tel: 47-07-31-06
Moderate

Mets Bistro-Quai
30, rue des Bernardins
Paris, 75005
Tel: 43-26-10-20
Moderate

Le Petit Navire
14, rue des Fossés-Saint-
Bernard
Paris, 75005
Tel: 43-54-22-52
Fairly Expensive

Le Petit Plat
3, rue des Grands-Degrés
Paris, 75005
Tel: 40-46-85-34
Moderate

Le Refuge du Passé
32, rue du Fer-À-Moulin
Paris, 75005
Tel: 47-07-29-91
Fairly Expensive

6e Arrondissement

Au Petit Lutetia
107, rue de Sèvres
Paris, 75006
Tel: 45-48-33-53
Moderate

Bistrot d'Alex
2, rue Clément
Paris, 75006
Tel: 43-54-09-53
Fairly Expensive

Les Bookinistes
53, Quai des Grands Augustins
Paris, 75006
Tel: 43-25-45-94
Moderate

La Cafetière
21, rue Mazarine
Paris, 75006
Tel: 46-33-76-90
Fairly Expensive

L'Écaille de PCB
5, rue Mabillon
Paris, 75006
Tel: 43-26-73-70
Fairly Expensive

La Hulotte
29, rue Dauphine
Paris, 75006
Tel: 43-33-75-92
Moderate

La Lozère
4, rue Hautefeuille
Paris, 75006
Tel: 43-54-26-64
Moderate

Le Mâchon d'Henri
8, rue Guisarde
Paris, 75006
Tel: 43-29-08-70
Inexpensive

Chez Marcel
7, rue Stanislas
Paris, 75006
Tel: 45-48-29-94
Moderate

Le Petit Saint-Benoît
4, rue Saint-Benoît
Paris, 75006
Tel: 42-60-27-92
Inexpensive

Restaurant du Luxembourg
44, rue d'Assas
Paris, 75006
Tel: 45-48-90-22

La Rôtisserie Chez Dumonet
117, rue du Cherche-Midi
Paris, 75006

Inexpensive

Tel: 42-22-81-19
Moderate

7e Arrondissement

Aux Fins Gourmets
213, blvd. Saint-Germain
Paris, 75007
Tel: 42-22-06-57
Moderate

Le Chevert (Auberge Comtoise)
34, rue Chevert
Paris, 75007
Tel: 47-05-51-09
Inexpensive

Lou Cantou
20, rue Bellechasse
Paris, 75007
Tel: 47-05-11-11
Moderate

Le Petit Niçois
10, rue Amélie
Paris, 75007
Tel: 45-51-83-65
Moderate

Le Roupeyrac
62, rue de Bellechasse
Paris, 75007
Tel: 45-51-33-42
Inexpensive

Le Bistrot de L'Université
40, rue de L'Université
Paris, 75007
Tel: 42-61-26-64
Moderate

La Cigale
11bis, rue Chomel
Paris, 75007
Tel: 45-48-87-87
Moderate

Nuit de Saint-Jean
29, rue Surcouf
Paris, 75007
Tel: 45-51-61-49
Moderate

La Poule au Pot
121, rue de L'Université
Paris, 75007
Tel: 47-05-16-36
Inexpensive

8e Arrondissement

Les Amis du Beaujolais
28, rue d'Artois
Paris, 75008
Tel: 45-63-12-64
Moderate

L'Assiette Lyonaise
21, rue Marboeuf
Paris, 75008
Tel: 47-20-94-80
Inexpensive

Le Bistrot de Chalosse
10, rue de la Trémoille
Paris, 75008
Tel: 47-23-53-53
Fairly Expensive

Chez Germain
19, rue Jean-Mermoz
Paris, 75008
Tel: 42-25-36-06
Moderate

La Gouluc (Chez Pom)
47, rue Laborde
Paris, 75008
Tel: 45-22-15-45
Inexpensive

Le Montalivet
15, rue Montalivet
Paris, 75008
Tel: 42-65-41-98
Inexpensive

9e Arrondissement

Le Bistro des Deux Théâtres
18, rue Blanche
Paris, 75009
Tel: 45-26-41-43
Moderate

L'Excuse
21, rue Joubert
Paris, 75009
Tel: 42-81-98-19
Moderate

Le Relais Beaujolais
3, rue Milton
Paris, 75009
Tel: 48-78-77-91
Moderate

Ty-Coz
35, rue Saint-Georges
Paris, 75009
Tel: 48-78-34-61
Fairly Expensive

10e Arrondissement

L'Anchotte
11, rue Chabrol
Paris, 75010
Tel: 48-00-05-25
Inexpensive

11e *Arrondissement*

Les Cinq Points Cardinaux
14, rue Jean-Macé
Paris, 75011
Tel: 43-71-47-22
Inexpensive

Chez Paul
13, rue de Charonne
Paris, 75011
Tel: 47-00-34-57
Inexpensive

Le Roudoulié
16, rue de la Vacquerie
Paris, 75011
Tel: 43-79-27-46
Fairly Expensive

Le Navarin
3, av. Philippe-Auguste
Paris, 75011
Tel: 43-67-17-49
Fairly Expensive

La Ravigote
41, rue de Montreuil
Paris, 75011
Tel: 43-72-96-22
Moderate

12e *Arrondissement*

Au Limonaire
88, rue de Charenton
Paris, 75012
Tel: 43-43-49-14
Inexpensive

Les Broches À l'Ancienne
21, rue Saint-Nicolas
Paris, 75012
Tel: 43-43-26-16
Inexpensive

Le Square Trousseau
1, rue Antoine-Vollon
Paris, 75012
Tel: 43-43-06-00
Fairly Expensive

Le Bouchon de Beaujolais
27ter, blvd. Diderot
Paris, 75012
Tel: 43-43-62-84
Moderate

Le Saint-Amarante
4, rue Biscornet
Paris, 75012
Tel: 43-43-00-08
Moderate

13e Arrondissement

Le Boeuf Bistrot
4, place des Alpes
Paris, 75013
Tel: 45-82-08-09
Moderate

À Côté
18, rue de la Providence
Paris, 75013
Tel: 45-81-18-02
Inexpensive

Chez Paul
22, rue de la Butte-aux-Cailles
Paris, 75013
Tel: 45-89-71-64
Moderate

La Touraine
39, rue Croulebarbe
Paris, 75013
Tel: 47-07-69-35
Moderate

À la Bouillabaisse (Chez Keryado)
32, rue Regnault
Paris, 75013
Tel: 45-83-87-58
Moderate

Chez Grand-Mère
92, rue Broca
Paris, 75013
Tel: 47-07-13-65
Moderate

Le Terroir
11, blvd. Arago
Paris, 75013
Tel: 47-07-36-99
Fairly Expensive

14e Arrondissement

Les Comestibles
10, rue de la Sablière
Paris, 75014
Tel: 45-45-47-12
Inexpensive

La Route du Château
36, rue Raymond-Losserand
Paris, 75014
Tel: 43-20-09-59
Moderate

L'Auberge du Petit Tonneau
51, rue Hallé
Paris, 75014
Tel: 43-27-55-85
Fairly Expensive

Au Rendez-Vous des Camionneurs
34, rue des Plantes
Paris, 75014
Tel: 45-43-43-38
Inexpensive

Les Petites Sorcières
12, rue Liancourt
Paris, 75014
Tel: 43-21-95-68
Moderate

L'Auberge du Centre
10, rue Delambre
Paris, 75014
Tel: 43-35-43-09
Fairly Expensive

15ᵉ Arrondissement

L'Oie Cendrée
51, rue Labrouste
Paris, 75015
Tel: 45-31-91-91
Moderate

Chez Quinson
5, place Étienne-Pernet
Paris, 75015
Tel: 45-32-48-54
Moderate

Le Gastroquet
10, rue Desnouettes
Paris, 75015
Tel: 48-28-60-91
Fairly Expensive

Chez Filoche
34, rue du Laos
Paris, 75015
Tel: 45-66-44-60
Fairly Expensive

Au Passé Retrouvé
13, rue Mademoiselle
Paris, 75015
Tel: 42-50-35-29
Moderate

Le Bistrot D'André
232, rue Saint-Charles
Paris, 75015
Tel: 45-57-89-14
Inexpensive

Le Boeuf Gros Sel
299, rue Lecourbe
Paris, 75015
Tel: 45-57-16-33
Moderate

Le Saint-Vincent
26, rue de la Croix-Nivert
Paris, 75015
Tel: 47-34-14-94
Moderate

L'Os à Moelle
3, rue Vasco-de-Gama
Paris, 75015
Tel: 45-57-27-27
Moderate

Chez Pierre
117, rue de Vaugirard
Paris, 75015
Tel: 47-34-96-12
Fairly Expensive

Chez Yvette
1, rue d'Alençon
Paris, 75015
Tel: 42-22-45-54
Moderate

16e Arrondissement

Le Bistrot de L'Étoile
"Lauriston"
19, rue Lauriston
Paris, 75016
Tel: 40-67-11-16
Moderate

Les Chauffeurs
8, chaussée de la Muette
Paris, 75016
Tel: 42-88-50-05
Inexpensive

Nahmias-Olympe-Bassano
17, rue Jean-Giraudoux
Paris, 75016
Tel: 47-23-66-55
Moderate

Le Petit Boileau
98, rue Boileau
Paris, 75016
Tel: 42-88-59-05
Moderate

Le Petit Rétro
5, rue Mesnil
Paris, 75016
Tel: 44-05-06-05
Moderate

17e Arrondissement

Le Bistrot D'À Côté "Villiers"
16, av. de Villiers
Paris, 75017
Tel: 47-63-25-61
Moderate

Le Bistrot de L'Étoile "Niel"
75, av. Niel
Paris, 75017
Tel: 42-27-88-44
Moderate

Le Bistrot de L'Étoile "Troyon"
13, rue Troyon
Paris, 75017
Tel: 42-67-25-95
Moderate

Chez Laudrin
154, blvd. Pereire
Paris, 75017
Tel: 43-80-87-40
Fairly Expensive

Chez Léon
32, rue Legendre
Paris, 75017
Tel: 42-27-06-82
Moderate

La Rôtisserie d'Armaille
6, rue d'Armaille
Paris, 75017
Tel: 42-27-19-20
Moderate

18e Arrondissement

L'Assommoir
12, rue Girardon
Paris, 75018
Tel: 42-64-55-01
Fairly Expensive

20e Arrondissement

Chez Roger
145, rue d'Avron
Paris, 75020
Tel: 43-73-55-47
Moderate

Books of Interest

For those interested in further reading, we recommend the following books:

Bond, Michael. *The Pleasures of Paris, A Gastronomic Companion.* New York: Clarkson M. Potter, Inc., 1987

Chadwick, Brian and Klaus Boehm, eds. *The Taste of France, A Dictionary of French Food and Wine.* Boston: Houghton Mifflin Co., 1982.

Dannenberg, Linda. *Paris Bistro Cooking.* New York: Clarkson Potter, 1991.

Escaig, Roland and Maurice Beaudon. *The French Way, An Insiders Guide to the Hotels and Restaurants of France.* New York: Warner Books Inc., 1988.

Gault/Millau. *The Best of Paris.* Los Angeles: André Gayot Publications, 1994.

George, Rosemary. *French Country Wines.* London: Faber & Faber, 1990.

Gloaguen, Philippe. *Le Guide du Routard 1994/1995 Restos & Bistrots de Paris.* Paris: Hachette, 1994.

Lagrandeur, Henri-Noël. *Guide des Bistrots à Vins, Paris et Banlieue.* Paris: Éditions Garancière, 1984.

Lazareff, Alexandre. *Le Guide Lazareff.* Paris: Éditions Julliard, 1994.

Lebey, Claude. *Le Guide Lebey des Restaurants de Paris, 1994,* 7th edition. Paris: Éditions Bourin/Julliard, 1993.

Lebey, Claude. *Le Petit Lebey 1994 des Bistrots et des Bars à Vins.* Paris: Éditions Julliard, 1994.

Lichine, Alexis. *Guide to the Wines and Vineyards of France.* New York: Knopf, 1979.

Siedeck, Wolfram. *Die Schönsten Bistros von Paris.* Munich: Wilhelm Heyne Verlag, 1993.

Spurrier, Steven. *Concise Guide to French Country Wines.* New York: Putnam, 1983.

Wells, Patricia. *The Food Lover's Guide to Paris,* 3rd Edition. New York: Workman Publishing, 1993.

Index of Bistros and Wine Bars

E

F

G

H

I

J

K

L

M

N

O

P

Q

R

S

T

V

W

Y

Z

About the Authors

Robert and Barbara Hamburger were born and raised in New York City. Robert received a bachelor of arts degree from Columbia University; Barbara was graduated from St. Lawrence University, also with a bachelor of arts degree. Following college, they were married and entered the family bridal gown manufacturing business together, with Robert as president and Barbara as designer of their company. For the past thirty years they have holidayed in France, admiring the countryside, the towns, and the French way of life, while developing a special interest in French food and wine. Though they remain active in the apparel business, Robert has become a private art dealer, and Barbara is the author of *Zooming In* (Harcourt Brace Jovanovich, 1974).